ART AND INDUSTRY

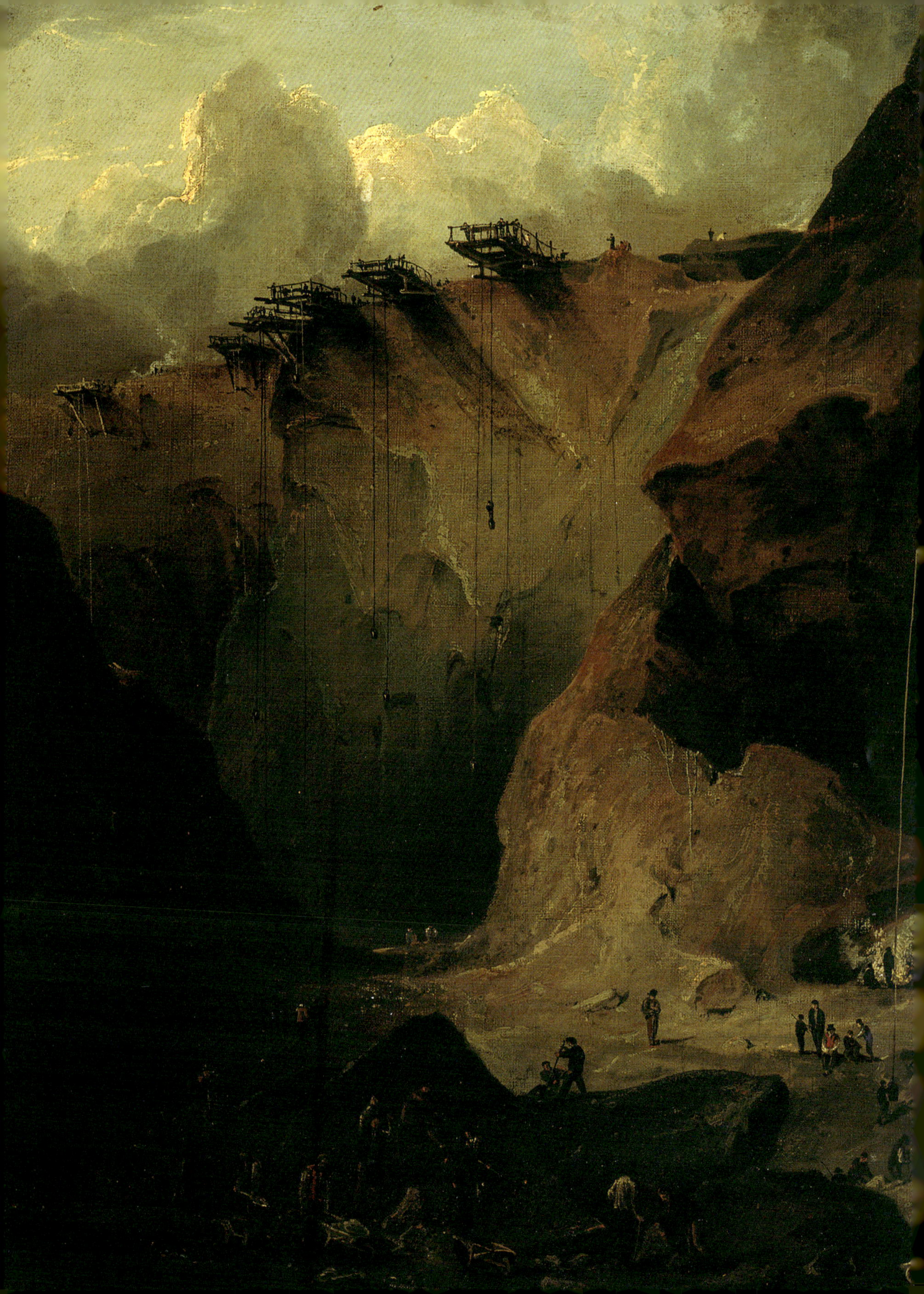

ART AND INDUSTRY

Seven Artists in Search of an Industrial Revolution in Britain

David Stacey

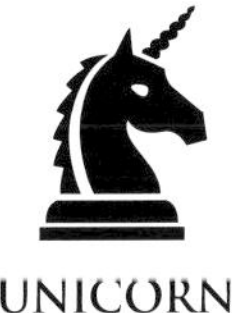

UNICORN

In memory of Esther and for Dan and Kate

Published in 2021 by
Unicorn, an imprint of Unicorn Publishing Group LLP
5 Newburgh Street
London
W1F 7RG
www.unicornpublishing.org

ISBN 978 1 913491 29 1

10 9 8 7 6 5 4 3 2 1

Designed by Nick Newton Design

Frontispiece
Detail of *Parys Mountain Copper Mine*, *c.*1803/4, by William Havell (see page 73).

Contents

Preface

The paintings discussed in this book come predominantly from the years between 1780 and 1830, a period of great change in Britain when land enclosure and investment in technological innovation triggered an industrial revolution. At that time some of my forebears could be found among the flax spinners of Montrose and the owners of coalmines in Northumberland. I mention this because, while writing about paintings of the industrial landscape, I have been constantly reminded that the responses of the artist to an industrial scene and of the viewer to their painting of it are unlikely to be the same. Moreover, the response of a flax spinner or a mine owner to such a painting 200 years ago, had they had the opportunity to see it, would have been very different to my response today or to that of any reader of the chapters that follow.

On my way to school in the early 1950s I used to walk along the canals and beside the old mills and factories in Manchester. In the 1960s I worked for a short time in a large industrial foundry in the Midlands. These experiences have no doubt affected my response to images of the industrial landscape and to the people working in it. But each of us, in addition to his or her own background and experience, brings their appreciation of the history of art to an understanding of a painting. Some will look at the form of the work or the technical detail; others will explore the impact of patronage, or the schools and aesthetic movements of the day, or compare a work with works of an artist's contemporaries. Other art history or cultural and psychological analyses may also be appropriate. These all have relevance here but I have tried to view the pictures discussed in this book in the context of a time which saw the advent of a capitalist system in British industry and the emergence of a new class structure within the country's population.

The paintings mostly illustrate scenes of industrial activity. Those populating the paintings include patrons of the works of art, owners of the industries portrayed, and the men, women and children employed by them. The paintings reveal to us today something of the lives they led but, despite the handicap of our ever-changing understanding and perception of social, technological, economic and environmental factors and their political context, I have tried to detect the elusive purpose of the artists when they created these rare paintings of early industrial Britain.

The research, writing and discussions I have had while preparing the book
have given me considerable enjoyment. I hope that your exploration of these
early images of the industrial scenes discussed in the text will give you as much.

D.B.S.
Herne Hill, London

Introduction

Between 1750 and 1830, Britain saw unprecedented changes to its landscape and to the lives of many of its inhabitants. In a period roughly twice the average lifespan of someone living in Britain at that time, the country underwent what was subsequently recognised as an industrial revolution.[1] The impact of the changes has been comprehensively described in the literature but artists who visited or encountered industrial sites have only provided a limited vision of industrial Britain.[2] Sketches and drawings of industrial sites have survived in gallery and museum archives and in private collections but less than a score of the paintings of the period are of the industrial landscape or speak of an industrial revolution. The few paintings that have emerged, however, have left us with a surprisingly coherent picture of the effect that rapid industrial growth was having in Britain.

Paintings from the 1780s to the 1830s by seven artists, some of whom were born or lived close to centres of industry and others who were inspired by the unfamiliar industrial landscapes that they encountered on their travels, provide the basis for this book. The seven essays in the succeeding chapters discuss works by Joseph Wright of Derby (1734–97), John Opie (1761–1807), Philippe-Jacques de Loutherbourg (1740–1812), Penry Williams (1802–85), William Havell (1782–1857), Joseph Mallord William Turner (1775–1851) and Henry Hawkins (1800–81).

Francis Klingender (1907–55), in *Art and the Industrial Revolution*, 1947, was the first to write a book on this neglected area of art history. The illustrations and paintings he discusses are taken from between 1750 and the late Victorian period. Through them, particularly in the later works, he alerts the viewer to the inequality and class divisions he sees as endemic in a capitalist society and as fundamental features of the Industrial Revolution. His book was edited and expanded in 1968 by Arthur Elton.[3] *Art and the Industrial Revolution* was first published over seventy years ago but since then notable additions to the discussion of the subject have come from James Hamilton in *Turner and the Scientists* and William Rodner in *J.M.W. Turner: Romantic Painter of the Industrial Revolution*, both of whom dwell on the works of the artist who responded the most consistently and extensively to the impact of new technology.[4] In the 1990s, Peter Lord in *The Visual Culture of Wales* brings together and discusses images of industrial society and in 2009 Celina Fox adds significantly to the discussion in her substantial and wide-ranging *The Arts of Industry in the Age of Enlightenment*.[5]

Few would claim that images of new technologies and the industrial landscape lie at the centre of the history of British Art but the works discussed in the following chapters have an important place in that history. They illustrate how, in the last quarter of the eighteenth century, '... subjects that had hitherto generally been confined to popular art and technical illustrations first entered the orbit of the fine arts'.[6] Images of industry found a toehold there in the early nineteenth century.

An industrial revolution can be said to take place when significant change arises through the introduction of new technologies and the intensive use of capital, and one which has an impact on social mobility and the rise of new social classes.[7] These conditions were to be found in Britain at the end of the eighteenth century. The impact was to be seen in the movement of labour from agricultural to industrial employment arising from investment in the development of mines and quarries and the iron and non-ferrous metal industries, in the establishment of new mills and factories, and in the associated spread of an urban and transportation infrastructure. These changes were underpinned by the country's access to an abundant energy source – coal – and the development of an increasingly efficient source of motive power – the steam engine. New industrial and urban landscapes emerged during the period which provided artists with new subject-matter to dwell upon.

Landscape painting in Britain came under several powerful influences during the second half of the eighteenth century. The works of the French and Italian artists, Claude Lorrain, Gaspard Dughet and Salvator Rosa, and in turn the seventeenth-century Flemish and Dutch landscapists informed much of the landscape painting of the period. These influences were met by a discourse which arose from a growing interest in the British landscape itself and a series of widely circulated critiques on aesthetic concepts. A demand for paintings and prints of the country's buildings and picturesque landscape contributed to a developing concept of British identity. The demand was later to feel the impact of the emerging 'romantic movement' in literature. This was the context in which artists would have to address the new and often brutal industrial landscape that began to spread across parts of Britain and face the conditions of those employed there. Artists would have to break convention to enter this field and seek new patrons for this type of subject-matter.

Apprenticeships, sketching tours and the formation of sketching groups led to an exchange of views between artists, students and their patrons. The Old Watercolour Society, The Society of Artists, The Royal Academy and other clubs and societies provided the opportunity for artists to discuss current trends, fashions and theories. Works such as Edmund Burke's *A Philosophical Enquiry into the Origin of our Ideas of the Sublime and the Beautiful* of 1757 aimed to develop and extend aesthetic theory. Burke sought to develop concepts linking both the natural landscape and landscape painting itself with the emotional responses evoked by them. 'The passion caused by the great and sublime in *nature*, when those causes operate most powerfully, is Astonishment … and astonishment is that state of the soul, in which all its motions are suspended, with some degree of horror.'[8] This did not entirely exclude the industrial landscape but Immanuel Kant's more profound observations nearly a decade later on the sublime describes the external world as the product of sensations conditioned by forms of consciousness.[9] And this external world certainly included the new and developing industrial landscape which could provoke a variety of responses in the artist or observer.

Sir Joshua Reynolds' fifteen *Discourses on painting and the fine arts*, delivered to students at The Royal Academy between 1769 and 1790 were influential.[10] The writings of Rev. William Gilpin (1724–1804), Uvedale Price (1747–1829) and Richard Payne Knight (1751–1824) present theories behind the realisation of the sublime and the picturesque in both the natural world and the landscaped prospect but industrialisation brought new motifs to the 'man-made' landscape which did not fit easily within either the natural ecology or Price's 'improved real landscape'.[11] The few artists who addressed industrial subject-matter were bound to re-consider current trends and contemporary aesthetic movements when encountering the new industrial infrastructure and confronting the conditions of those employed in the industrial workplace. In the following chapters we will see how our artists responded to these conditions.

With hindsight, the broad sweep of change that characterised the Industrial Revolution is clearly identifiable but the pace of industrial development during the period was subject to varying economic conditions and market forces, and was affected by random events and a myriad of changes and interventions arising from new and evolving technologies. It depended on entrepreneurs, the men and women who, with their financial resources, were prepared to take risks and support the introduction of these new technologies and means of production; it depended on the scientists, engineers and their assistants who were prepared to apply their minds to technical problems and find practical solutions; but it also depended significantly on the contributions of artisans and an expanding workforce of both child and adult labour.

Some of the entrepreneurs, adventurers and ironmasters of this period who invested in industrial development came from the aristocracy, some came from established families and some from those who borrowed money hoping to make their fortunes by investing in new technologies. In the chapters that follow, discussion of the works by our seven artists covers industrial developments which were financed or owned by Henry Paget, 1st Earl of Uxbridge (1740–1812), George Hay Dawkins-Pennant (1764–1840) who inherited property from Lady Penhryn, George O'Brien Wyndham, the 3rd Earl of Egremont (1761–1837), the Cornish mining adventurer Thomas Daniell of Truro (1715–93), the Quaker families of the Darbys and Reynolds, and two families who came from modest backgrounds and who achieved considerable financial success, Sir Richard Arkwright (1732–92) and William Crawshay II (1788–1867).

The period under discussion covers a time when the economic climate was at times uncertain, when the effect of the wars with France, Holland and the American colonies was being felt and when competition between individual producers within Britain and with mainland Europe was intensifying. It saw Britain prospering through commerce and colonial expansion, and for those like George Hay Dawkins-Pennant with plantations in Jamaica, benefiting from profits that depended on slavery. Success was by no means guaranteed for entrepreneurs investing in the industrial field. The impacts of technological change and fluctuating demand for their products had to be borne by employers and were reflected in the type, conditions and uncertainties of employment. At times strikes and riots erupted through the failure of employers like William Crawshay II to maintain the delicate balance of power between themselves and their employees.

The Industrial Revolution, which can so easily be characterised by a series of technological developments, saw profound changes in the relationships between the employer and the employed, and the new demography led to a re-definition of class in Britain.[12] Paintings of the British rural landscape in the mid-eighteenth century were rarely devoid of figures. These were often deployed by artists to animate a view but they were sometimes included to illustrate the relationship of the landowner or the agricultural worker to the land. An individual drawing or painting of this period or genre may not tell an authentic story of these relationships. A review of these scenes shows many artists satisfying their patrons by presenting a culture of contentment on the estate or in the rural landscape.[13] Artisans and labourers broadly knew their place in the traditional agrarian economy until the second half of the century but the enclosure movement fuelled the distress and discontent of the rural poor. Settled communities were disrupted by the migration of labour, particularly of the young, to the expanding industrial sector.

This sector saw the development of a new structure of relationships between artisans and labourers and the ironmasters, mill owners and managers, many of who themselves were in transitional class relationships. The former, who developed new skills and took up new jobs, were subject to demanding working conditions in new and rapidly expanding industries. This threw up unprecedented subject-matter for artists which did not fit simply into the principal *exempla* of paintings they were commissioned or encouraged to paint. The artists and the paintings discussed in this book reflect on the roles and relationships of those working in an industrial landscape and reveal the origin of some of the grim and unacceptable conditions that later established themselves in the Victorian period and which flowed in part from unrestrained capitalist-led industrialisation. These features were on view both to the artists who lived close to industrial developments and to those who came across them or sought them out on their sketching tours. Our seven artists from different backgrounds respond to them in different ways but reveal, in the works discussed, an awareness of the incipient problems arising during this period of change.

Joseph Wright of Derby's *Arkwright's Cotton Mills by Night* is discussed in Chapter 1.[14] Richard Arkwright built the first water-powered and mechanised cotton mill in Derbyshire's Derwent Valley at Cromford in 1771, extending it in 1775 and again in 1777. By 1780 more than 600 men, women and children were employed in the Cromford mills. At that time, artists were beginning to explore the picturesque scenery of Derbyshire and the few early sketches of the mills that exist come from the hands of local artists. Joseph Wright was the first to take the subject beyond a mere topographical view in *Arkwright's Cotton Mills by Night*. In his enigmatic painting he asks us to question not only what we see in this moonlit scene but also what we do not see. He encourages us to imagine the conditions inside the mill during the nightshift and the child labour employed. We are left to consider whether this is an image of the mills at the time of the September 'Wakes' (the annual holiday) and the 'Candle-lighting' (which floodlit the mill while the employees processed from the mills round the town of Cromford singing the praises of their 'bountiful Master'), or whether Wright, famous for his 'candlelights' and 'moonlights' was simply attracted by the subtle chiaroscuro of the scene. Wright did not go on in later life to explore the impact of industry on the lives of the new 'working class' in industrial Britain, but in *Arkwright's Cotton Mills by Night* is he signalling that the industry may be taking its toll on the adult and child labour employed?

Two of our seven artists painted scenes relating to the copper industry, John Opie in Cornwall and William Havell on the Isle of Anglesey. Their works are discussed in Chapters 2 and 5, respectively. Opie's double portrait *A Gentleman and a Miner* was exhibited at the Royal Academy in 1786.[15] His painting of a mining captain handing a specimen of copper ore to a major investor in the mines in West Cornwall not only indicates their working relationship but also suggests an underlying conflict relating to the status of the two men. There was no other artist of the period whose origins and experience would have led them to paint this scene at a critical time in the development of the mining industry in Cornwall. In the 1780s, the Birmingham partnership of Matthew Boulton and James Watt had begun to supply steam-engines and pumps to improve the drainage in Cornish mines. Chapter 2 draws on unpublished correspondence between Boulton and Watt and on the writings of Rev. Richard Polwhele and Opie's second wife Amelia for views on the development of the Cornish mines and the two figures in Opies's painting. Opie's image encourages us to muse on age, class, technology and the use of capital.[16]

In Chapter 5, William Havell in his *Parys Copper Mine* of 1803/04 takes us to the Isle of Anglesey.[17] The Parys and Mona mines employed about 1,200 men and women in the 1780s but by 1806 the number working there had shrunk to 200. When Havell visited the mines, it was becoming difficult to find profitable areas for open cast work and there was a dip in the demand for copper. The mines faced competition from those in Cornwall and young Havell's painting hints at the insecurity of employment while revealing the impact and grandeur of this immense man-made excavation. Industrialists, geologists and scientists, including Michael Faraday (1791–1867), visited the mines and the chapter draws on their journals to complement the painting and illustrate the effect that a visit to the mines had upon them.[18]

Havell was painting in a period when pre-Enlightenment concepts of heaven and hell were still alive. In *Parys Copper Mine* he portrays the miners in a place between heaven and a hell that man was exploring in the subterranean world below. Discussion of Havell's painting is complemented by the drawings of Julius Caesar Ibbetson (1759–1817) and others. Ibbetson has left us with distressing scenes of women at work at the Parys and Mona mines and employed in the copper industry at Swansea. His view is supported by the Royal Academician William Daniell (1769–1837) who describes the women there, '… without shoes or stockings, their clothes hanging about them, released, for the sake of ease, from pins and strings, and their faces as black as coals, except where channelled by the streams of perspiration that trickled down'.[19]

At the beginning of the eighteenth century the iron industry, even more than the non-ferrous metals industry, was already a significant feature of the country's economy in the Forest of Dean, the west Midlands and in the southeast and northeast of England. The manufacture of iron then relied on small blast furnaces and separate finery forges. The introduction of methods and materials for large-scale smelting and the processing of iron was to transform the industry and, by the late eighteenth century major ironworks were to be found in the Midlands at Coalbrookdale and in South Wales around Merthyr Tydfil.[20] These areas were close to the routes that artists took on their sketching tours as they sought the picturesque sites of historic interest and the places of natural beauty, the rivers, streams and waterfalls and the wilder mountain landscapes. Artists on their travels were unlikely to miss the sight of a new ironworks with its banks of furnaces and coke hearths ablaze, but very few chose to develop finished paintings of them. Of those few, the works of Philippe-Jacques de Loutherbourg who visited the developments at Coalbrookdale, and Penry Williams who was born near Merthyr Tydfil are discussed in Chapters 3 and 4, respectively.

Coalbrookdale by Night, perhaps the best known painting of the period of industrial development in Britain, comes from the hand of Philippe-Jacques de Loutherbourg, Diderot's *'phénomène étrange'*, an artist who was the youngest to be elected a member of *l'Académie royale de peinture et de sculpture de Paris*, who came to Britain in 1771.[21] Arriving in London, he was appointed chief scenographer at the Theatre Royal, Drury Lane by David Garrick where he worked for ten years to great acclaim. We find in de Loutherbourg, who was elected to the Royal Academy in 1781, a complex artist who demonstrates in his painting of the Bedlam furnaces near Coalbrookdale in the Severn Gorge the power of the grand picturesque and the impact of the sublime. He presents a scene of a subject that had been sketched by others but had not been committed to canvas before. He asks us to respond to the sight of the active labourers, figures working amidst the heat and smoke of the coke hearths and furnaces, and to be recognised as an integral part of an industrial drama. These are labourers driven by the imperatives of the industrial process and no longer subject to the seasonal changes that agricultural workers encountered.

The works of Penry Williams are discussed in Chapter 4. Williams was born and spent his early life near Merthyr Tydfil. As a teenager, he witnessed the discontent of the poorly paid colliers and ironworkers. One of his first known and a somewhat naïve painting is of the riots at Merthyr in 1816.[22] Between 1817 and 1820 he painted five oil paintings of the Cyfarthfa ironworks for the ironmaster William Crawshay II. These views, which record the impact of the developing iron industry near Merthyr Tydfil, are remarkable for having come from a largely untutored hand. At the age of about twenty-two, after three years at the Royal Academy Schools in London, on his return to Wales in 1825, he was commissioned by Crawshay to prepare two works, *Cyfarthfa Iron Works*, and *Cyfarthfa Iron Works at Night* to celebrate and expansion of the ironworks.[23] Penry Williams, now more confident in his artistry, serves his patron by realising the technical detail of the ironworks but the ironworkers he portrays tell another story. They have become anonymous figures in the industrial landscape. Williams appears to recognise the impact that this large established capitalist venture is having and the widening gap that is emerging between the ironmaster and the labour he employs.

The second half of the eighteenth century saw the beginning of the construction of a navigable canal system across Britain. The earliest canals in Britain were built to serve the requirements of individual entrepreneurs who wished to improve the import of raw materials and the export of finished goods to and from their factories. Of all the artists of the period, J.M.W. Turner responded most in his art to industrial development. His interest in the spread of the British canal system and his canal paintings are discussed in Chapter 6. The paintings include five areas of particular interest: the Lancaster Canal in the northwest of England; Kirkstall Lock on the Leeds and Liverpool Canal; the canal at More Park, near Watford; the ill-fated Chichester Canal sponsored by the 3rd Earl of Egremont, which was built between the River Arun and Chichester Harbour, in Sussex; and the canals at Dudley, Worcestershire in the heart of the Black Country.[24]

The new and expanding cities, conurbations and associated infrastructure required a wide range of construction materials. New mines and quarries were opened to meet these demands. Henry Hawkins visited the great slate quarry at Penrhyn, North Wales, and his painting, *Penrhyn Quarry* of 1832 is discussed in Chapter 7.[25] Hawkins is one of a large group of little-known British Victorian artists whose works are rarely seen and of whom little is known. He exhibited almost 150 works in oils and watercolour at the Society of British Artists' exhibitions and eight works at the Royal Academy. Despite his regular contributions to the Society's exhibitions, reviews of his works rarely appear. Where they are found they are mostly damning but in Hawkins we find a committed member of the Society of British Artists, a portrait painter who also turned his hand to landscapes and to mythological and religious subjects.

The Penrhyn open-cast slate quarry became a well-known landmark attracting tourists, scientists and artists from the late eighteenth century onwards. The quarry provided a substantial addition to the income accruing from the owner George Hay Dawkins-Pennant's Jamaican slave-based sugar plantations. Hawkins's painting reveals the vastness of the Penrhyn Quarry near Bangor, in which we see aristocratic visitors alongside site managers and labourers. In the early 1800s, 150 workers were wounded and seven or eight died each year in accidents at the quarry. Hawkins, who presents one of the most forthright images of the period, reveals the shocking conditions that quarry workers endured. He appears to recognise in the quarry a parallel with the image of Dante's Purgatory in Domenico di Michelino's 1465 fresco *La commedia illumina Firenze* and has the vision to present a scene which expresses the impact of the industry in the context of a nineteenth-century *Divine Comedy*.

The paintings discussed in the seven linked essays that follow include some of the few paintings that relate to and come from the period which is traditionally known as the Industrial Revolution in Britain. We do not find a complete picture of industrial development of the time but some common and developing themes emerge from the paintings which span the period of fifty years from Wright's *Arkwright's Mill* to Hawkins's *Penrhyn Quarry*. The seven artists, some perhaps only dimly aware of the Industrial Revolution they were witnessing and who went in search of industrial subject-matter, produced works which did not sit easily with the prevailing genres of the period. They responded, in the works discussed in the following essays, with a coherent message on the impact of new technology, the use of capital and on some of the distressing conditions that saw the emergence of new social classes in Britain.

Two appendices accompany the text. Appendix A contains a timeline for the period between 1750 and 1835, which relates the dates of technological inventions, industrial development and significant events to those of key industrial paintings and drawings of the period. Appendix B gives details and the whereabouts of sketches, drawings and paintings mentioned or discussed in the text and of other relevant images. Most of these can be accessed on websites but there is nothing better than to see the originals and I hope the reader will enjoy seeing them through visits to galleries and museums.

Notes

1 The expression 'die industrielle Revolution' was first used by Friedrich Engels, *Die Lage der arbeitenden Klasse in England*, in 1845. The first use of the term 'Industrial Revolution' is generally given to Arnold Toynbee, *Lectures on the Industrial Revolution in England*, published in 1884.
2 T.H. Ashton, 1948; Edward P. Thompson, 1968; M.A. Žmolek, 2013.
3 Francis D. Klingender, 1947, ed. and rev. by Arthur Elton, 1968. Klingender's original book arose from the 1945 exhibition sponsored by the Artists International Association (AIA) and was substantially revised in 1968 by Elton.
4 James Hamilton, 1998; William S. Rodner, 1997.
5 Peter Lord, 1998; Celina Fox, 2009.
6 Francis D. Klingender, 1947, p. 54.
7 T.H. Ashton, 1948, p. 114.
8 Edmund Burke, 1757, p. 36.
9 John T. Goldthwait, 1960, trans. from Immanuel Kant, 1766.
10 Sir Joshua Reynolds, 1825.
11 Rev. William Gilpin, 1782 and 1792; Uvedale Price, 1810; Richard Payne Knight, 1794 and 1805.
12 Edward P. Thompson, 1968.
13 John Barrell, 1980; David H. Solkin, 1982.
14 Joseph Wright of Derby, *Arkwright's Cotton Mills by Night*, *c*.1782–3.
15 John Opie, *A Gentleman and a Miner*, 1786.
16 Matthew Boulton and James Watt, 1777–1803, *Correspondence B&W Partners Papers, MS 3147*; Rev. R. Polwhele, 1831; John Opie, 1809, pp. 1–54.]

17 William Havell, *Parys Copper Mine*, 1803/04.

18 Dafydd Tomos, 1987; Captain Henry and Mrs Sara Hanmer, October 1819.

19 R. Ayton and William Daniell, 1814–25, vol. I, 1814, p. 64.

20 It was not until the early nineteenth century that Scotland and the northeast of England became important producers of iron and steel.

21 Philippe-Jacques de Loutherbourg, *Coalbrookdale by Night* (*A View of Colebrook Dale by Night*), 1801.

22 Penry Williams, *The Merthyr Riots*, 1816.

23 Penry Williams, *Cyfarthfa Iron Works*, 1825 and *Cyfarthfa Iron Works, Interior at Night*, 1825.

24 J.M.W. Turner, *Chichester Canal*, c.1828.

25 Henry Hawkins, *Penrhyn Slate Quarry*, 1832.

1 Joseph Wright of Derby and the cotton mills at Cromford

In his economic history of Britain, Eric Hobsbawm (1917–2012) writes:

> Whoever says Industrial Revolution says cotton! When we think of it we see, like the contemporary foreign visitors to England, the new and revolutionary city of Manchester, … where 'we observe hundreds of five- and six-storied factories, each with a towering chimney by its side, which exhales black coal vapour … .'[1]

However, it was at Cromford in the quiet craggy confines of Derbyshire's Derwent Valley that Richard Arkwright built the first water-powered cotton mill in 1771 and introduced the new cotton-spinning frame he had patented in 1769.[2] Arkwright, the son of a tailor, was born in Preston, Lancashire in 1732. He rose from barber and peruke-maker in Bolton to become one of the leading and best-known manufacturers of the day in the textile industry. His success was based primarily on the introduction of new cotton spinning machinery but it was also built on the new administrative and factory employment systems he introduced with their more efficient but demanding sequential processes.

The image of Sir Richard Arkwright of Cromford (Figure 1.1), in which this tough entrepreneur sits facing the viewer with legs apart, feet firmly planted on the floor with a model of the patented spinning frame on the table beside him, is arresting. The painting is one of which Arkwright is said to have been proud and of which those who knew him regarded as a good likeness. It was commissioned by Arkwright and comes from the hand of Joseph Wright of Derby (1734–97) who painted it in 1789–90, a few years after Arkwright had been knighted. Arkwright paid Wright 50 guineas for the painting.[3] In this chapter I will be discussing Richard Arkwright, Joseph Wright's paintings of him and the mills he built and operated at Cromford.

In Wright's image of Sir Richard, by then a rich and established figure in his late fifties, we find a solid, powerful and one might sense obdurate figure. Arkwright's right to the patents for the spinning frame was contested in the courts many years before Joseph Wright's portrait but, clearly aware of these disputes,

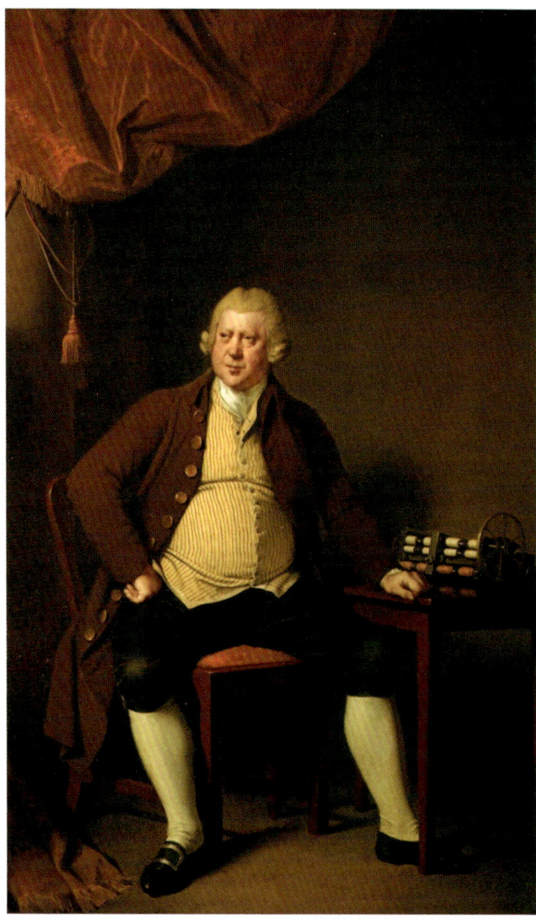

1.1 *Sir Richard Arkwright (1732–92) with spinning frame*, 1789–90, by Joseph Wright of Derby, oil on canvas, 241.3 x 152.4 cm. Derby Museums and Art Gallery.

Wright pictures Arkwright almost challenging the viewer and guarding the model of the rollers which formed the crucial part of the patents. For some, the painting has attained iconic status as an image that represents the nature of the entrepreneurs who advanced the Industrial Revolution in Britain. Joseph Wright was not renowned for flattering his sitters and it is useful to compare the three-quarter-length portrait painted a few months later for Arkwright's London house at 6 Adam Street, London by the American Mather Brown (1761–1831) in Figure 1.2.

Brown confirms the view of Arkwright as a resolute figure but he gives him a dynamic quality and energy which Wright's defensive figure does not attract. Brown's Arkwright, with a rolled-up document or plan in his hand, sitting on a comfortable armchair rather than the rather insubstantial seat that Wright gives him, appears as solid and as powerful but as a more positive and intelligent man, one who looks as if he is prepared to negotiate. Joseph Wright painted an earlier half-length portrait of Arkwright, recently found, but the

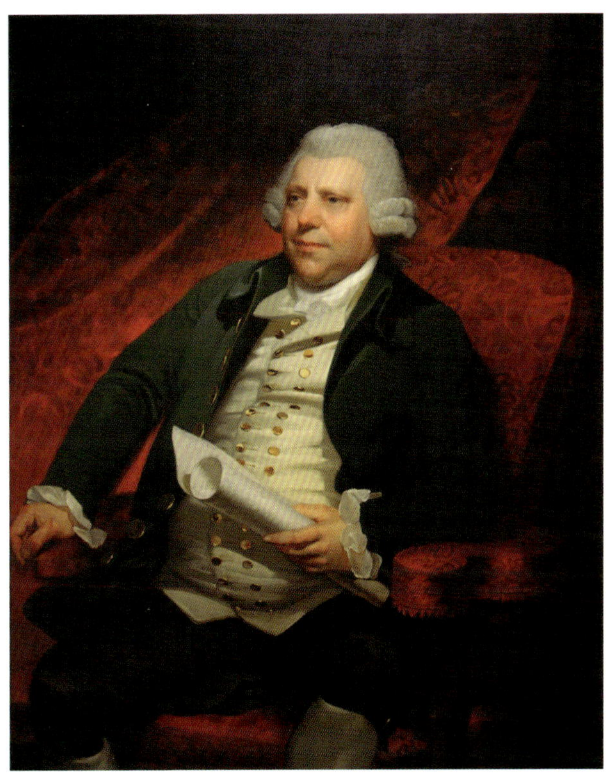

image in Figure 1.1 may point, as we shall see, to Wright's attitude to this financially successful self-made man and his industrial empire.[4]

Richard Arkwright was greatly respected by his peers in Derbyshire for the successful introduction of water-powered machinery to his cotton mills at Cromford but the technology was already to be found nearby. The silk mill built by the Lombe brothers in 1721 in Derby, some 15 miles from Cromford and to be seen as a prominent feature in a topographical view painting *A Prospect of Derby (Derby and the Silk Mill)*, *c.*1725, employed water-powered silk spinning and throwing machinery based on Italian designs.[5] The five-storey building there served as a prototype on which Richard Arkwright's first cotton mill at Cromford was to draw.[6] The River Derwent and its tributaries provided them both with a convenient source of power. Following the success of his first water-powered cotton mill at Cromford, Arkwright went on to develop the site, extending the mill in 1775 and adding a new seven-storey mill two years later. He then established mills at Bakewell in 1778, Wirksworth in 1780 and at Cressbrook and Masson near Matlock Bath in 1783. In Derbyshire, Arkwright led the field.[7] Elsewhere in Lancashire, Yorkshire and Lanarkshire, he and other manufacturers were soon building significant cotton-spinning enterprises.

Arkwright's mills in Derbyshire, an early feature of Britain's Industrial Revolution, were hardly likely to attract artists at a time when views of the picturesque and sublime scenery of the surrounding countryside were becoming fashionable and it is worth a short diversion here to consider this competition. From the mid-seventeenth century visitors had travelled to see Derbyshire's 'Seven Wonders of the Peak', first brought to their attention by Thomas Hobbes (1588–1679) in his poem *De Mirabilibus Pecci* of 1636. He writes of '*Aedes, mons, barathrum, binus fons, atraque bina*' or, in a later translation, 'two fonts, two caves, one palace, mount and pit'. These were the Ebbing and Flowing Well at Tideswell, St Anne's Well at Buxton, the Peak Cavern (or Devil's Arse), Poole's Cavern, Chatsworth House, Mam Tor and Eldon Hole, all natural phenomena apart from Chatsworth.[8]

Sir James Thornhill (1635/6–1734) has left us sketches of several of these wonders.[9] Thomas Smith of Derby (1720–67) called upon some of the country's leading engravers for *Eight of the Most Extraordinary Prospects in the Mountainous Parts of Derbyshire and Staffordshire Commonly Called the Peak and the Moorlands*, published in 1743.[10] Philippe-Jacques de Loutherbourg, chief scene designer at the Theatre Royal, Drury Lane in London, visited Derbyshire in 1778 to collect material for *The Wonders of Derbyshire*, a show which was developed with Richard Brinsley Sheridan and performed at Drury Lane between 1779 and 1781.[11] Thomas Hearne (1744–1817) and Paul Sandby (*c*.1730–1809) came to sketch the limestone crags and rocky bluffs of Dovedale in the 1770s, and John Webber (1751–93) and William Day (1764–1807) in the late 1780s.[12] None of these visiting artists thought the new mills at nearby Cromford worthy of even a sketch, never mind a painting. This was left to local artists, some of whom were commissioned by their patrons with commercial interests. One of the first views of Arkwright's mills at Cromford by an unknown artist comes from about 1775, to be followed a few years later by a watercolour of *Cromford's Second Mill from the East, c*.1779, by Zachariah Boreman (1738–1810). Boreman's view was later adapted for use by the Derby Porcelain Manufactory as a decorative roundel for plates and saucers.[13]

These early drawings provide valuable historical records of the mills but are little more than topographical views of the buildings. They do nothing to suggest the substantial impact that the new cotton mills had on the region. In Arkwright's first mill, 200 labourers – mainly women and children – worked twelve-hour shifts and, apart from one hour at night reserved for maintenance of the machinery, the mills were in operation during the remaining twenty-three hours of the day and night. We must turn to Joseph Wright of Derby for a more considered response. Wright has left us two views of the mills,

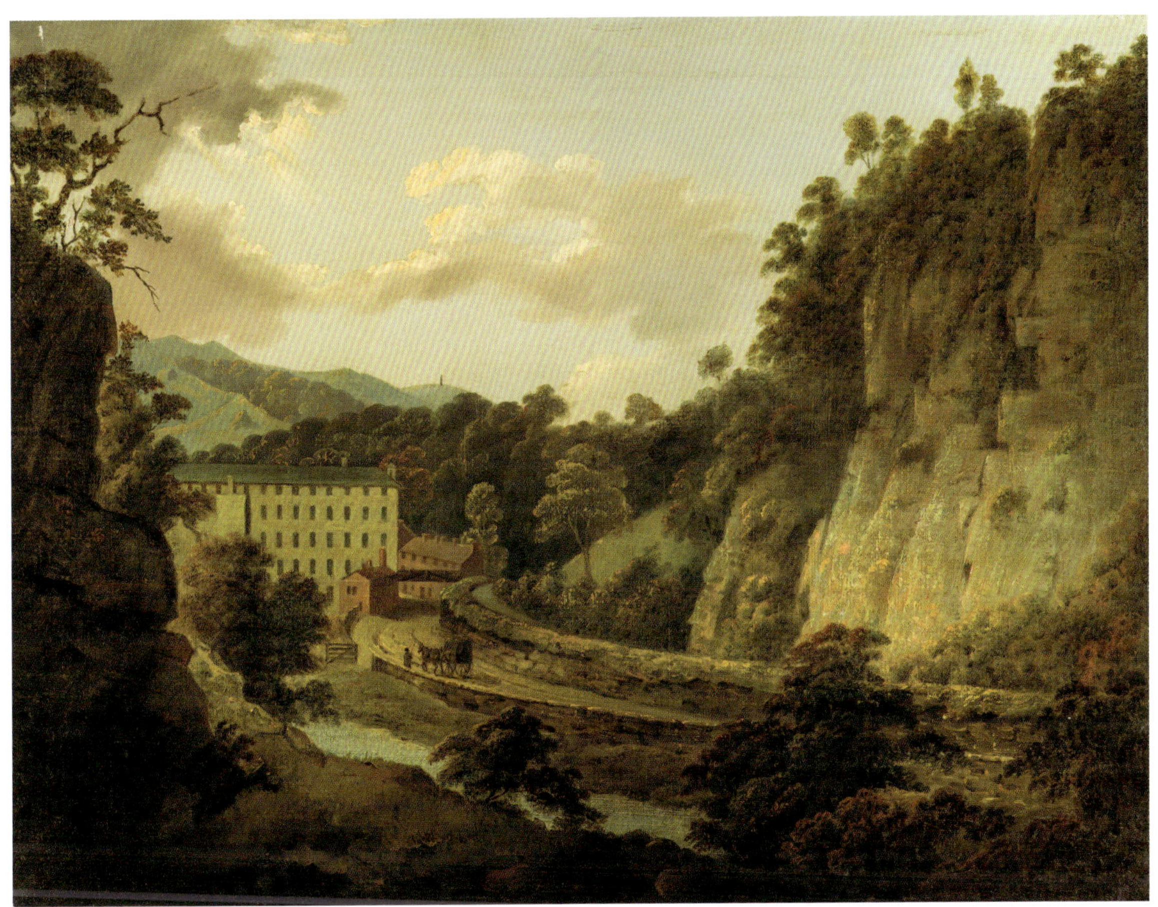

Arkwright's Mills [by day], *c.*1795–6 (Figure 1.3), and *Arkwright's Cotton Mills by Night*, of which two versions exist, the first from *c.*1782/3 and the second from *c.*1794/5.

In the smaller of the mill paintings *Arkwright's Mills* [by day], we find the mills viewed from the northwest, tucked neatly and comfortably into the natural landscape. In this work we see Joseph Wright with his gentle use of colour showing his love of the Derbyshire landscape and establishing a view in which the contemporary buildings are embraced by the surrounding hills. Wright makes no effort in this quiet and peaceful scene to comment on the lives of the adults and children employed in the mills. Details in the painting suggest that it was painted a few years after Arkwright's death.[14] By then development of the extensive mill complex was substantially complete and the first mill, twenty-five-years-old, had become an established and almost unremarkable feature of the valley. A companion piece to this painting, *A View of Cromford Bridge*, includes a view of Richard Arkwright's other addition to the Cromford landscape, Willersley Castle, construction of which was completed after his death.[15] An entry in Joseph Wright's *Account Book* states that he sold the pair of paintings 'A View of Cromford Bridge [and] Its Companion of Arkwright's Mills' to Daniel Parker Coke (1745–1825) for 50 guineas.[16] Coke, a barrister and independent Member of Parliament for Nottingham and previously for Derby, probably commissioned them from Wright. As a collector of works of art, Wright was well known to him and the first version of *Arkwright's Cotton Mills by Night* had previously been acquired by the Coke family.

The enigmatic view of *Arkwright's Cotton Mills by Night, c.*1782/3, is one of the earliest mill paintings of the period. Two almost similar versions of the painting are known to exist. Both were immediately taken into private hands and passed on by descent for nearly 200 years. The version of *c.*1782/3, now in poor condition, began its journey in the hands of Daniel Parker Coke's family, where the image of Arkwright's mills with the dark clouds overhead, the night shift at work and the lone carter in the foreground would have given the Member of Parliament for Nottingham something to think about. Would he, as we might with hindsight, have questioned the effect that this industry might be having on the lives of the men, women and children apparently working in the mill at night? A second version, a near copy of the *Arkwright's Cotton Mills by Night* by Joseph Wright, was painted in the early 1790s, and is thought to have been given by Wright to Thomas Haden (1761–1840), a Derby physician and his friend and neighbour. It was later passed to his daughter Sarah Oakes and then by descent through the family.[17] The two paintings may well have been seen by the Cokes and the Oakes' friends familiar with the Derbyshire landscape as emblematic of the country's industrial progress but apart from their descendants and their friends few others saw these two paintings which are now mostly known through illustrations.[18] Neither was exhibited publicly until the second half of the twentieth century.

In *Arkwright's Cotton Mills by Night* (Figure 1.4), Joseph Wright takes a view from the top of Mill Lane.[19] The painting shows the first mill which was built in 1771, its later extension and, behind these buildings and at an angle to the first mill, the top floor of the seven-storey second mill. Wright would have noticed the establishment and development of the mills during the 1770s and 1780s. Although he spent a total of about twenty-five months living and working in Liverpool between October 1768 and September 1771, he would have seen the first mill being built at Cromford as he passed by on his way between Liverpool and Derby.[20] Between October 1773 and September 1775, he and Hannah, his newly married wife, lived in Italy. Then after a brief visit to Derby in November 1775 they moved to Bath before returning to Derby in

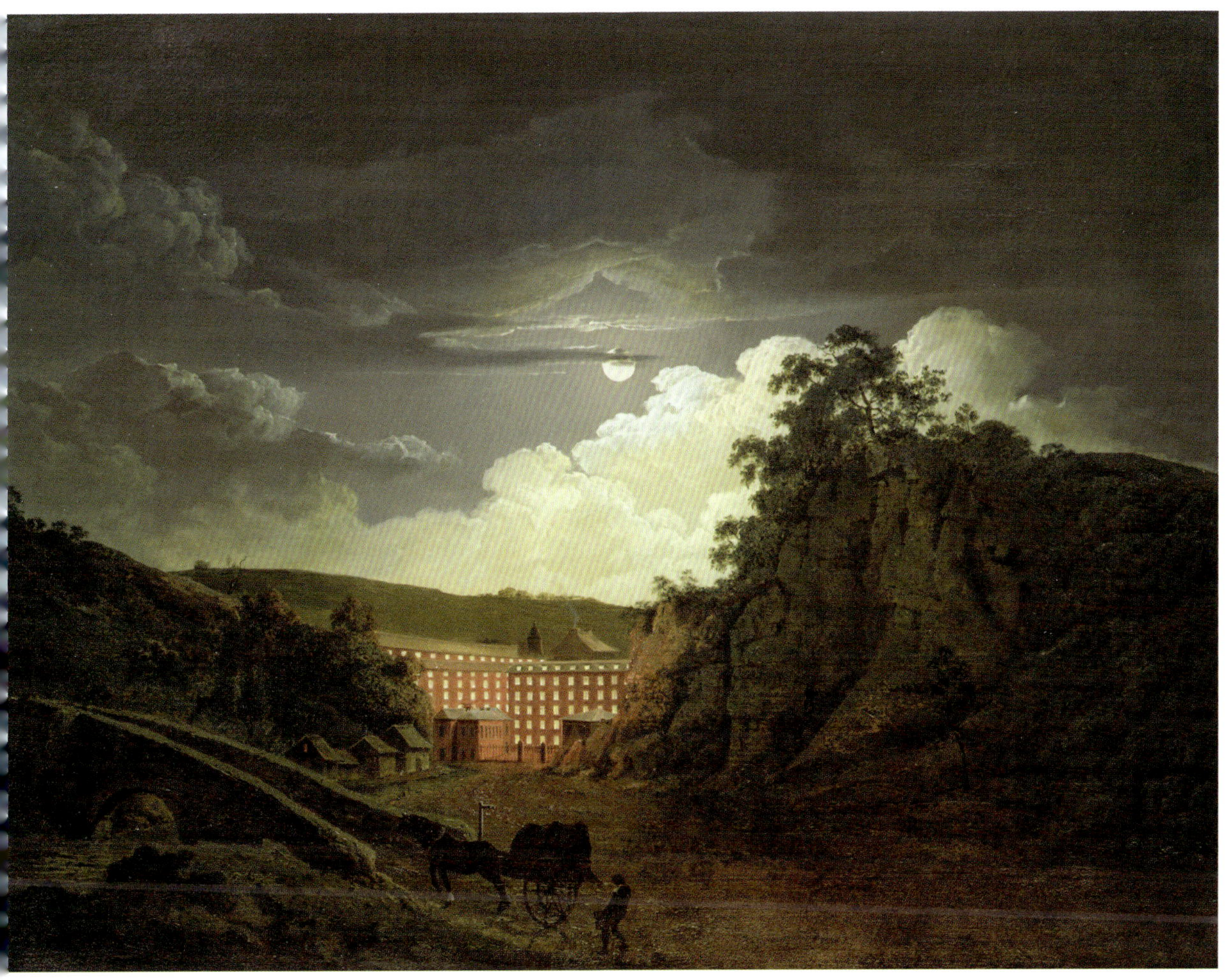

June 1777. After settling back in Derby, Wright would have seen the continuing development of the mill complex as he explored the Derbyshire countryside and on the trips he took when preparing sketches for the several paintings he was to make of the imposing Matlock Tor.[21] What would Wright have seen, heard and thought of Arkwright and this new and expanding industrial development set in a previously peaceful part of the Derwent Valley?

By 1780 Arkwright's mills at Cromford employed more than 600 men, women and children. Of the children, some 25 per cent would have started work at the age of eight and more than half by the age of ten.[22] The diarist John Byng, 5th Viscount Torrington, visiting Derbyshire records details of his visit to Arkwright's mills on an evening stroll and writes that he

> … wou'd have enter'd it, but entrance was denied, for this (no doubt right) reason, however odd, 'That I shou'd disturb the girls'![23]

He then continues,

> … saw the workers issue forth at 7 o'clock [in the evening], a wonderful croud [sic] of young people, made as familiar as eternal intercourse can make them; a new set then goes in for the night, for the mills never leave off working … .[24]

We do not know whether Byng or Wright ever managed to see inside the mills. Both leave us to speculate on the conditions that Arkwright's workforce were having to endure in an interior lit by tallow candles, the atmosphere filled with cotton dust, and the building resonating to the continuous and often deafening buzz and chatter of the dozens of spinning machines.

For those employed in the mills day after day or night after night there would have been little respite from the arduous tasks of cleaning, carding and processing the yarn, as well as answering the spinning machinery's continual demand for attention. An entry in the local *Derby Mercury*, however, recounts one event that may have provided some relief – the celebration during the Wakes that became an annual affair for those employed at the mills by Arkwright. Five years after the construction of the first mill, on 13 September 1776, the *Mercury's* correspondent writes:

> … on Monday last (being the Wakes there, as well as the Candle-lighting at the Cotton Mills of Messrs. Arkwright and Co.) a grand Procession was made from the Mills round the Town, by the Workmen, Children, &c. in Number about 500 … .[25]

They were led by a band and returned to the mills to be '… plentifully supplied with Buns and Ale, Nuts, Fruit, &c.' and an evening which '… concluded with Music and Dancing'. Two years later, a column in the same journal reports that the employees '… walked in Procession, in their different Uniforms, with White Staves, &c. … amongst Thousands of Spectators from Matlock Bath, and the neighbouring Towns … .'[26]

As this annual celebration became established, verses composed by one of the workmen for the event at Cromford, praising and giving thanks to Richard Arkwright, the 'bountiful Master', were sung to the tune of the *Roast Beef of Old England*, an English patriotic ballad written by Henry Fielding for his play *The Grub-Street Opera*.[27] The rousing final verse promised health and wealth to all:

> Ye Hungry and naked, all hither repair, No longer in Want don't remain in Despair, You'll meet with Employment, and each gets a Share, &c.

Ye Crafts and Mechanics, if ye will draw nigh, No longer you need
to lack an Employ, To our noble Master, a Bumper then fill, the
matchless Inventor of this Cotton-Mill. &c … Huzza.[28]

Arkwright, recognising the importance of retaining his employees, provided basic housing for some of them to rent and gave annual prizes to the local shopkeepers who provided good service to his employees, which, in John Byng's words '… bespeaks of Sr Rd's prudence and cunning for without ready provisions, his colony cou'd not prosper'.[29] Later Arkwright was to introduce a Sunday school for the children he employed. Many of those originally working in the mill were recruited from families working in the local lead mines and Arkwright must have enticed them with higher wages and better conditions. However, as the enterprise grew, at the time he was fitting out the second mill in the winter of 1777, he was obliged to advertise:

WANTED at Cromford joiners, carpenters, wood-turners, foargers [sic], filers, and frame-smiths and Likewise wanted at the same Place, a Number of Children, seven Years or upwards … .[30]

The early mill owners do not appear to have seen or envisaged any adverse effects of employing children as young as seven years of age. Until the end of the eighteenth century, their employment in the mills was not regarded as particularly detrimental to their development and, importantly, at Arkwright's mills their small size proved to be a valuable asset, enabling them to gain access to the underside of the spinning machinery to fix the yarn. By the early part of the nineteenth century, however, the impact of industrialisation on the population in the manufacturing towns of Britain was palpable. Children as young as six were being employed. The Welsh textile manufacturer and social reformer Robert Owen (1771–1858) observed that the manufacturing systems had effected '… an essential change in the general character of the mass of the people …', and of children '… passing on from childhood to youth, they become gradually initiated, the young men particularly, but often young females also, in the seductive pleasures of the pot-house and inebriation: for which their daily hard labour, want of better habits, and the general vacuity of their minds, tend to prepare them'.[31] Owen demanded improved conditions but ones which would still be unacceptable today; a maximum twelve-hour working day, including a one-and-a-half-hour break for meals in the mill towns, a minimum age of ten for children working in the mills and then not more than six hours' work per day until they were twelve years old, and no admission to a mill until a child could read, write and understand the first four arithmetic rules and until girls 'were competent in sewing'! However, the employment of child labour had another significant effect by adding to the problem of adult unemployment which arose from the increased mechanisation of cotton processing.

During the 1770s Arkwright built several mills outside Derbyshire, including one at Birkacre near Chorley, not far from his birthplace in Lancashire. The mill was capable of carrying out a complete sequence of cotton processing operations. It was operational in October 1779 when, in the period of economic depression which followed the American War of Independence, between 4,000 and 5,000 broke into the mill, destroying the machinery and setting the buildings alight. A dozen or more smaller factories in the area suffered a similar fate. Subsequently, threats were made to destroy a number of Arkwright's other mills, including those at Cromford, but he made preparations to stave off any attack should it arise.[32] Arkwright appears to have taken extensive precautions to defend the Cromford mills. In a copy of a letter in the *Derby Mercury* from Cromford to a gentleman in Manchester, the author responds to an earlier letter:

> In your last you expressed some Fear of the Mob coming to destroy the Works at Cromford, but they are well prepared to receive them should they come there. All the Gentlemen in this Neighbourhood being determined to support Mr Arkwright, in the Defence of his Works, which have been of such Utility to this Country, Fifteen hundred Stand of Small Arms are already collected from Derby and the neighbouring Towns, and a Battery of cannon raised of 9 and 12 Pounders, with Plenty of Powder and Grape Shot, besides which, upwards of 500 Spears are fixt in Poles of between 2 and 3 Yards long. The Spears and Battery are always to be kept in Repair for the Defence of the Works and Protection of the Village, and 5 or 6,000 Men, Miners, &c. can at any Time be assembled in less than an Hour, by Signals agreed upon, who are determined to defend to the very last Extremity, the Works, by which many Hundreds of their Wives and Children get a decent and comfortable Livelihood.[33]

This correspondence in the *Derby Mercury* appeared a couple of years before *Arkwright's Cotton Mills by Night* was painted. Joseph Wright would have been aware of these moments of industrial unrest and no doubt had a significant understanding of the issues arising from the region's industrial development through his contacts with several leading figures of the period. He would have been aware of the thinking of those whose portraits he had painted, among them the polymath and doctor of medicine Erasmus Darwin (1731–1802) and the scientist and geologist John Whitehurst FRS (1713–88), both members of the Lunar Society of Birmingham, and Francis Hurt (1722–83), owner of

Derbyshire lead mines and smelting works.[34] Before his visit to Italy, his reputation was principally based on his portrait and subject paintings. After his return from Italy he began to devote more time to landscape painting.

Wright's views of Virgil's tomb near Naples and several grotto and moonlit scenes emerge at this time and we see him, in his views of Matlock Tor and Dovedale, recognising in the rocks and crags of Derbyshire a resemblance to the Roman Campagna. When Wright revisited the Derbyshire dales and the Peak District, he could not have been insensitive to the parallels. His recollection of Tivoli seen in the classical *Italian Landscape – A View near Tivoli*, *c.*1783–6, and painted about ten years after he returned from Rome, unmistakeably echoes the Derbyshire landscape.[35] At Matlock and Cromford, the massive cliffs and the meandering valley bottom exhibit these similarities but, at night at Cromford, Wright finds the distant view cut short by Arkwright's mills. John Byng records that they, '… when lighted up, on a dark night, look most luminously beautiful' but they also reminded him of 'a first rate man of war', an image in itself enough perhaps to deter any 'Mob coming to destroy the works'.[36] Although Joseph Wright would have been familiar with the lighted windows of Lombe's silk mills in his home town of Derby, the cotton mills at Cromford, forming a barrier across the valley, presented an imposing and awe-inspiring sight.

In the context of Joseph Wright's association with the region and the local clerisy, the painting of *Arkwright's Cotton Mills by Night* attracts a variety of interpretations. His response compels us to consider several contrasting features and raises several questions. Clearly, we are encouraged to compare the qualities of moonlight and candlelight, and to observe the contrasting features of the rugged natural limestone crags of the valley and the orderly impressive man-made and 'luminously beautiful' cotton-mills. However, is Wright, through the presence of the lone figure crossing the bridge with his cart, the only explicit sign of human activity in the painting, alerting us to the unseen figures employed behind the lighted windows? Are we being asked to consider the rigours of the nightshift and the child labour employed? Or, if we were to recognise this as the season of the September Wakes and the Candle-lighting, we might see the painting as a celebration of Arkwright and his industrial enterprise. Or was Joseph Wright, famous for his 'Candlelights' and his 'Moonlights', simply attracted by the subtle chiaroscuro? He finds it in the moonlight and the candlelit mill confined within the dark masses of the valley sides and succeeds in revealing the magical glow which arises from a blend of naturally reflected moonlight and Arkwright's powerful candlelit display. In *Arkwright's Cotton Mills at Night*, we see Wright responding triumphantly to the complex illumination of the mills and cliffs at Cromford but seeming to ask, as he does in so many of his subject pictures, whether there is a more serious issue to which we should respond.

We shall never know precisely what was in Joseph Wright's mind when he was painting this night scene in the 1780s but we do know that the 1770s had been a period of change in his life. Wright, the son and grandson of attorneys at law and from the established middle class was already a successful artist when he returned to Derby from Liverpool and married Ann (also known as Hannah) Swift in 1773. While Wright was in Liverpool he had painted more than two dozen portraits of local merchants and dignitaries, many of whose businesses were supported through profits from slavery and the slave trade. These portraits include the elderly Richard Gildart, 1768, ship-owner and merchant dependent on sugar plantations in the West Indies, Thomas Staniforth, 1769, who took over and expanded the family ship-owning business engaged in the African slave trade, and Mrs John Ashton, *c.*1769, wife of John Ashton, a merchant with dealings in the salt industry and the slave trade.[37]

Joseph Wright also appears to have had issues of slavery in his mind when he composed *A Conversation of Girls*, *c.*1770, a painting which raises issues of race and colonial power. In the painting a handsome black servant girl on bended knee holds up a basket of flowers and jewels to two white girls, one of whom engages and looks down on her while the other takes items freely from her basket.[38] Sarah Parsons has pointed out that 'The kneeling pose [of the girl] in which the figure gazes up was only codified by the visual culture of abolition over a decade after Wright's painting was exhibited. The image of the kneeling slave beneath the phrase "Am I not a Man and Brother" first entered circulation as a stamp for the Society for the Abolition of the Slave Trade in the mid-1780s.' It was soon made popular as a decorative medallion produced by Josiah Wedgwood but here in *A Conversation of Girls*, as perhaps in *Arkwright's Cotton Mills by Night*, Wright gives us on the surface a 'luminously beautiful' painting with an underlying message. John Bicknell (1746–87) and Thomas Day (1748–89), a member of the Lunar Society whose portrait Wright also painted at this time, published their essay on the abolition of slavery *The Dying Negro: a Poem* in 1773.[39] We see Joseph Wright close to those involved in issues of the exploitation of human beings in the detestable institutions of slavery and the slave trade.

Wright was also at odds with his close family in the early 1770s. His parents has passed away by then but Wright had met his future wife Ann Swift, the twenty-four-year-old daughter of a lead miner, described by his brother's daughter Hannah Wright as 'a person in an inferior situation of life'.[40] They were married in July 1773 and soon set off for Italy. Wright kept the marriage secret from his family for three months. The relationship clearly caused distress and in a letter to his brother Richard, written just as Ann and he were about to sail for Italy, he breaks the news and writes:

> … give me leave to send the joint love of me & my Dear Wife to you and Sister – And if I have done anything that wore the face of slight and Disaffection, say not, love was banished, but Fear stood foremost and prevented my actions.[41]

Is it possible that Wright's marriage to a miner's daughter, the rupture with his close family and the dealings with the Liverpool merchants connected with the slave trade significantly affected his attitude to the prosperous classes and turned his thoughts to the virtues of the artisan, the labourer and the servant classes. For this period coincides with him expressing, in his *Blacksmith's Shop* and the *Iron Forge* paintings, 1771–3, an evolving sympathy for persons he, the son of an attorney, might have seen as 'in an inferior situation of life'. Jane Wallis writes of these works, 'Could his [Wright's] growing attachment to Hannah [Swift] account for his portrayal of working men with such dignity, and their families with such tenderness, in this series of paintings?'[42] And did this affect Wright in both his later portrait of Sir Richard Arkwright, the 'bountiful Master', and in his painting of *Arkwright's Cotton Mills by Night* at Cromford?

A German writer in the early part of the nineteenth century, responding to nothing more but Joseph Wright's portrait of Arkwright (Figure 1.1), writes:

> Richard Arkwright, it would seem, was not a beautiful man; no romance-hero with haughty eyes, Apollo lip, and gesture like the herald Mercury; a plain almost gross, bag-cheeked, pot-bellied Lancashire man, with an air of painful reflection, yet also of free digestion … .[43]

It is important not to forget Mather Brown's painting of Arkwright (Figure 1.2), which gives a more sympathetic reading.[44] However, Wright appears to have been close to the thinking of the members of the Lunar Society who had a somewhat ambivalent attitude towards Arkwright, which may have influenced his portrayal of Arkwright and his view of the Cromford cotton mills. Members of the Lunar Society were impressed by Arkwright's ambition and his cotton-spinning machinery, which Erasmus Darwin describes lovingly in *The Botanic Garden*, but less by his imperious attitude and the fact that he had patented a stolen technology.[45] They were themselves committed to the pursuit of knowledge and its practical application to commerce and industrial development, and each to a greater or lesser extent to building a distinct reputation and personal fortune, but they were mostly Non-conformists, humanists and free thinkers.

We have seen Wright's sympathetic humanist approach appear in the 1770s and this can also be found in some of his works of the 1780s and 1790s. During that period he was supported by influential patrons working in a milieu which gave him ample opportunity to observe and reflect on the social hierarchies and injustices of the day. We do not find him in later life exploring the impact of industry on the lives of the new 'working class' in Britain but it is almost impossible today not to discern Wright signalling, in *Arkwright's Cotton Mills by Night*, both his reservations on the effect that industrial cap-italism was having on the lives of the mill workers and, an admirer of the Derbyshire landscape, picturing the consequences of industrial development on the Derwent Valley.

Joseph Wright's paintings of Arkwright's water-powered cotton mills at Cromford in the latter part of the eighteenth century bear silent witness to the incursion of the developing textile industry into the Derbyshire countryside and the initial impact of an Industrial Revolution. As John Byng, in sympathy with Wright, and aware of Britain's developing industrial sector goes on to observe in his travel journal of 1790, after his visit to Cromford:

> I dare not, perhaps I shou'd not repine at the increase of our trade, and (partial) population; yet speaking as a tourist, these vales have lost all their beauties, the rural cot has given place to the lofty red mill, and grand houses of overseers; the stream perverted from its course by sluices, and aqueducts, will no longer ripple and cascade. Every rural sound is sunk in the clamours of cotton works … .[46]

Within the next fifty years the introduction of the steam engine would trans-form the cotton industry and there would emerge, as contemporary foreign visitors to England noted, 'hundreds of five- and six-storied factories, each with a towering chimney by its side, which exhales black coal vapour'.

It is to the steam engine and those engaged in the tin and copper mines of Cornwall pictured in John Opie's *A Gentleman and a Miner*, to which we turn in the next chapter. The earliest machines used were the bulky fixed fire engines designed by Thomas Savery (1650–1715) and Thomas Newcomen (1663–1729).[47] John Smeaton FRS (1724–94) and James Watt FRS (1736–1819) were then instrumental in improving the efficiency of the steam engine. Watt's early designs were introduced to Cornwall in 1778 where Matthew Boulton and he set up their partnership to supply steam engines and pumps for drainage of the mines. It was in the tin mining area of Cornwall, near St Agnes, that John Opie was born.

Notes

1 Eric Hobsbawm, 1968, p. 56.

2 Arkwright's spinning machine or 'water frame' enabled cotton to be spun through rollers to produce a high-quality strong thread. Arkwright may have drawn on the inventions of James Hargreaves – whose Spinning Jenny was invented (but not patented) some six years before Arkwright patented his machine in 1769 – and of Daniel Bourn who had experimented with rollers in the manufacture of woollen yarn.

3 *Wright's Account Book*, *c.*1755–97, 60r [JJ,58], in Elizabeth E. Barker (ed.), 2009, p. 39.

4 *Wright's Account Book*, *c.*1755–97, 65v [Y], in Elizabeth E. Barker (ed.), 2009, p. 41.

5 *A Prospect of Derby (Derby and the Silk Mill)*, 1725, by an unknown artist.

6 By the 1770s more than two dozen water-powered silk factories, modelled on the Lombe brothers' factory, could be found in Derbyshire and Cheshire employing a labour force of more than 4,000. Richard Arkwright, without the experience and financial resources required to exploit his invention, turned to Jedediah Strutt and Samuel Need, successful Belper and Nottingham hosiers, respectively, to finance the first mill at Cromford.

7 A. Menuge, 2001, p. 39. Arkwright introduced steam power to pump water to the waterwheel at Haarlem Mill, Wirksworth, *c.*1780, possibly its earliest application in the textile industry.

8 Thomas Hobbes, 1678.

9 Sir James Thornhill, *Sketchbook 1699–1716*, No. 1884.0726.40.16a, British Museum.

10 Eight Plates, each 39.0 × 54.5 cm. Maps K. Top. XI/19 (b to i), part of King George III's Topographical Collection, British Library, London. Also see David Stacey, 'Thomas Smith of Derby (1720–67)', pp. 4–12, *British Art Journal*, vol. XVI, No. 3, 2016.

11 Anon., 1779.

12 Trevor Brighton, 2004.

13 *Arkwright's First Mill at Cromford*, *c.*1775, by an unknown artist. *The Second Mill at Cromford*, 20 cm diameter ceramic plate decoration, *c.*1780, from *Cromford's Second Mill from the East*, *c.*1779, by Zachariah Boreman.

14 The distant tower at Crich in *Arkwright's Mills* [by day] was built by the Hurt family of Wirksworth and Alderwasley, Derbyshire in 1788, the year after the death of Richard Arkwright.

15 This neo-Gothic mansion was built just north of the mill complex but was not completed until a few years after Sir Richard Arkwright's death. *Arkwright's Mills* [by day], *c.*1795–6, and *A View of Cromford Bridge* by Joseph Wright of Derby, *c.*1795–6, were sold at Christie's, New York on 13 April 2016 as *Arkwright's Cotton Mill, Cromford*, and *Willersley Castle, Cromford*, and bought by the Derby Museum and Art Gallery, Derby.

16 '*A View of Cromford bridge Its Companion of Arkwright's Mills – Sold to D:P:Coke 52 10 x*'
Wright's Account Book, *c.*1755–97, 12r [19, 12], Elizabeth E. Barker (ed.), 2009, p. 15.

17 *Arkwright's Cotton Mills by Night* by Joseph Wright of Derby

Version 1	Version 2
Mrs Sacheverell Coke, Brookhill Hall, Notts	Thomas Haden
By descent Coke family, Brookhill Hall, Notts	His daughter, Sarah Oakes
	Oakes Collection, Riddings House, Derbyshire
Mr Booth, *c.*1967	By descent
By descent	Sotheby's sale, 24 November 2005, lot 13
	Restoration by Philip Mould & Co and to present owner.

18 Francis Klingender (1st edn, 1947), p. 177; Arthur Elton (rev.), 1968, Plate 28; Benedict Nicholson, vol. I, 1968; Judy Egerton, 1990, p. 198, cat. 127; Stephen Daniels, 1998, p. 59; Celina Fox, 2009, p. 434. Version 2 exhibited *Joseph Wright of Derby*, Derby Art Gallery, 1883, in *Art and the Industrial Revolution*, 1968 (72), Manchester City Art Gallery, 31 May–14 July 1968.

19 Version 2, restored by Philip Mould & Co. (see note 17) is illustrated in Figure 1.4. See also http://www.historicalportraits.com/Gallery.asp?Page=Item&ItemID=2397&Desc=Cotton-Mills-|-Joseph-Wright-of-Derby-ARA (accessed 23 July 2020).

20 Elizabeth E. Barker and Alex Kidson, 2007, pp. 44–5.

21 *Matlock Tor, Moonlight* by Joseph Wright of Derby, *c.*1777–80; *Matlock Tor by Daylight*, by Joseph Wright of Derby, *c.*1778.

22 Jane Humphries, 2010, p. 177.

23 John Byng, C. Bruyn Andrews (ed.), 1934, vol. 2, 18 June 1790, pp. 190–91.

24 John Byng, C. Bruyn Andrews (ed.), 1934, vol. 2, 18 June 1790, p. 195.

25 *Derby Mercury*, Friday 13 September 1776, p. 4.

26 *Derby Mercury*, Friday 25 September 1778, p. 4.

27 The lyrics are given in the *Derby Mercury*, 25 September 1778. *The Grub-Street Opera* was first performed in 1731.

28 *Derby Mercury*, 25 September 1778.

29 John Byng, C. Bruyn Andrews (ed.), 1934, vol. 2, p. 196.

30 *Derby Mercury*, 21 November 1777, p. 1. The *Derby Mercury*, 12 May 1785 reports that forty or fifty unemployed Scots came from Perth and were found work by Arkwright and '… provided with good Quarters'.

31 Robert Owen, 1817, pp. 5–10.

32 M.A. Žmolek, 2013, p. 434.

33 *Derby Mercury*, 9 October 1779.

34 *Erasmus Darwin*, *c.*1770–76; Francis Hurt, *c.*1780; John Whitehurst FRS, 1782–3; and a family portrait which shows Rev. D'Ewes Coke, his wife Hannah and Daniel Parker Coke MP, *c.*1782. All by Joseph Wright of Derby.

35 *Italian Landscape – A View near Tivoli*, *c.*1783–6, by Joseph Wright of Derby.

36 John Byng, C. Bruyn Andrews (ed.), 1934, vol. 2, pp. 190–91.

37 Sarah Parsons, pp. 104–20, in Elizabeth E. Barker and Alex Kidson, 2007, pp. 116–8.

38 *A Conversation of Girls*, *c.*1770, by Joseph Wright of Derby. Sarah Parsons, pp. 104–20, in Elizabeth E. Barker and Alex Kidson, 2007, pp. 105–07.

39 *Thomas Day*, *c.*1770, by Joseph Wright of Derby. See John Bicknell and Thomas Day, 1775.

40 *Hannah Wright's Memoir, 1850*, MS 11172, Derby Local Studies Library in 'Joseph Wright of Derby', pp. 1–216, in Elizabeth E. Barker (ed.), 2009, p. 162.

41 Joseph Wright, 'Letter to "Nancy" Wright, Winter 1771–72', from *Hannah Wright's Memoir, 1850*, in Elizabeth E. Barker (ed.), 2009, p. 74. Wright's sister, Ann Elizabeth, was known as Nancy.

42 Jane Wallis, 1997, p. 13.

43 Anon., 'Geschichte de Teutschen Sippschaft' pp. 69–88, in Thomas Carlyle, *Chartism*, 1940, p. 84.

44 Or Joseph Wright's less severe three-quarter-length portrait *Richard Arkwright*, *c.*1783–5.

45 Erasmus Darwin, 1791, Part II. pp. 65–6. Robert S. Fitton, 1989, p. 98.

46 John Byng, C. Bruyn Andrews (ed.), 1938, vol. 2, 19 June 1790, p. 197.

47 'Fire Engine' – the term for an 'engine to raise water by fire' used by Captain Thomas Savery in his pamphlet on *The Miner's Friend*, *c.*1698, for which a patent was granted in 1699. *Trans. Royal Society*, vol. xxi, No. 253.

2 John Opie's Cornish *Gentleman and a Miner*

In the second of his *Lectures on Painting* delivered at the Royal Academy of Arts in 1807, John Opie (1761–1807) had no reservation in reprimanding the throngs visiting the Academy exhibitions:

> … one's very soul is rent with hearing crowd after crowd sweeping round, and instead of discussing the merits of the different works on view (as to conception, composition, and execution), all re-iterating the same dull and tasteless questions, 'who is that?' and 'is it like?'[1]

This chapter focuses on one of John Opie's paintings, the double portrait of *A Gentleman and a Miner* (Figure 2.1), which he exhibited at the Royal Academy Exhibition in 1786.[2] It would be ungracious in discussing this painting not to respond to Opie's frustration and to disregard the 'conception, composition and execution' of the painting but now, after more than 200 years, the work has climbed the ranks in the eighteenth-century hierarchy of subject-matter from 'portrait' to 'history painting' and I feel free to discuss 'who is that?' and 'is it like?'

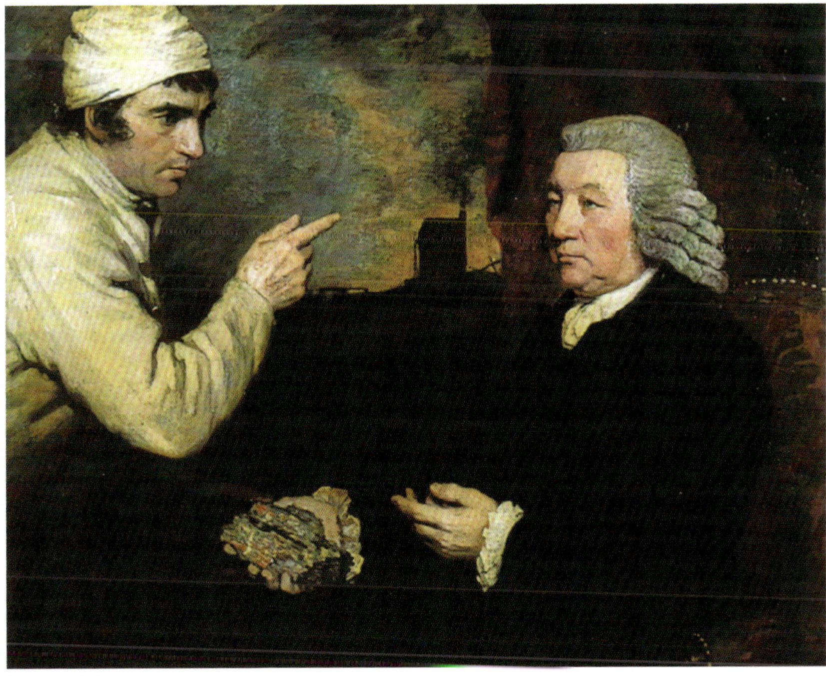

2.1 *A gentleman and a miner*, 1786, by John Opie, oil on canvas, 99.5 x 112 cm. The Royal Institution of Cornwall, Royal Cornwall Museum, Truro.

The subject of the painting is unique for Opie and highly unusual for the time. It is one of the earliest paintings exhibited in Britain which pictures not only one of the most significant and potent symbols of the Industrial Revolution – the steam engine – but also those involved in the application of this developing technology. In the painting we see the miner Captain Joseph Morcom (1744–1827) on the left, handing a specimen of copper ore to a major investor in the mines of west Cornwall, the mining adventurer Thomas Daniell of Truro. Captain Morcom appears to be indicating that the extraction of copper ore had been made possible by the installation of a new steam engine housed in the building shown on the horizon but the image also appears to indicate an underlying tension and an uneasy relationship between the two men.

The dislocation of the figures, with Daniell sitting indoors on a chair and Morcom standing in the open air, suggests that the young Opie painted the figure of the elderly Thomas Daniell at his studio in London and developed the other half of the painting during a visit to his birthplace and his parents' home at St Agnes, Cornwall. There, he appears to have collected the details which allowed him to add the distant engine house and the lively forty-one-year-old Captain Joseph Morcom and integrate the two disparate halves of the painting.[3]

The portrayal of skilled workers such as Joseph Morcom and of labourers and their families cannot be fully understood without recognising the constraints that determined how they should or should not be represented in paintings in the late eighteenth century. Paintings which include them are generally presented in a form in which the concerns of the artist's patron, which here appears to have been Thomas Daniell, are uppermost.[4] As John Barrell has pointed out in *The dark side of the landscape; the rural poor in English paintings, 1730–1840*, artists were mostly subject to both social and aesthetic constraints in their works and the resulting images were mainly constructed to indicate a stable and contented society.[5] Or as the art historian David Solkin puts it: 'The task of the poet or painter [in late eighteenth century Britain] lay not in revealing conflict but in denying its very existence.'[6]

In Opie's painting, however, we see the artist giving Morcom the upper hand, challenging this very idea and questioning the established hierarchy in the industrial setting. There were no other artists of the period whose origins and experience would have led them to this subject or would have considered exhibiting it publicly.[7] The young Opie had moved to London in 1781 and was achieving success as a society portrait painter by the time he painted *A Gentleman and a Miner* four or five years later. We might ask whether the experience of meeting the upper echelons of society at the start of his professional career in London acted as a catalyst and alerted Opie, with his relatively humble origins in Cornwall, to the inequities of the industrial hierarchy in the mining areas of Cornwall.

Commentaries on John Opie's works and anecdotes of his life are readily found in nineteenth- and twentieth-century literature, and for indications of his character we can draw on a number of authors. These are principally his contemporaries and include the writer, artist and Secretary for Foreign Correspondence at the Royal Academy, Prince Hoare (1755–1834), Opie's second wife, the novelist and poet, Amelia Opie (1769–1853), the Scottish author and poet, Allan Cunningham (1784–1842), and the historian of Cornwall and Devon and poet, the Rev. Richard Polwhele (1760–1838). Opie's later biographers include the author and Conservative MP for Helston, Cornwall, John Jope Rogers (1816–80), and the author of the most comprehensive biography of John Opie, Ada Earland (1863–1927).[8] A synthesis of these sources, which are for the most part consistent, provide us with sufficient detail to summarise Opie's early life and career.

John Opie was born in May 1761 in the tin mining area of West Cornwall, in the village of Mithian 2 miles east of St Agnes. His father was a house carpenter and wheelwright; his grandfather was a carpenter.[9] Both would have been employed in work close to, or associated with, the mining industry. The Rev. Richard Polwhele, who knew John Opie and sat to him *c*.1778, describes Opie's father and grandfather as having the 'skill and ingenuity above their brother-artificiers'.[10] He regards the family of Opie's mother, Mary (née Tonkin) as one of 'the *little* gentry of Cornwall'.[11] A number of tales are told of the young Opie's dogged perseverance, his skill at mathematics and his talent as an artist. His knowledge of writing and arithmetic led him at the age of twelve to set up an evening school to teach the poor children of St Agnes.[12] As a young teenager he was apprenticed first to his father and later to a sawyer but his early enjoyment in sketching in chalks and charcoal and his attempts at portraiture of local people brought him to the attention of Dr John Wolcot of Truro (1738–1819). The story goes that Wolcot, after visiting a patient where he saw some of Opie's drawings, sought him out to find him working in a saw pit, '… an uncouth country lad, girt with the leather apron of his trade'.[13]

Dr John Wolcot, also known as the satirist Peter Pindar, a well-connected practising doctor and a sometime artist, recognised Opie's raw talent and invited him to join him in his house next to the Britannia Inn at the end of Prince's Street in Truro. Wolcot, to be followed later by the county historian and poet, Rev. Richard Polwhele, was a tenant of our Thomas Daniell at this address. Daniell was no doubt aware of the talented young Opie at this time and Opie of Thomas Daniell, who lived in the centre of Truro.[14] Wolcot taught and supported Opie, encouraging him to find work in Cornwall. There, Opie painted portraits of both the poor and the local gentry before Wolcot took the opportunity of taking Opie to London, acting as his agent and sharing the profits from the sale of his paintings. When they moved to London in 1781 Wolcot proved effective in finding the fashionable and the prosperous to sit for Opie. Writing in 1783 as the satirical poet Pindar and recognising the qualities that the talented but unsophisticated prodigy from distant Cornwall presented, Wolcot did not hesitate to promote him in his *Odes to the Royal Academicians* as 'The Cornish boy, in tin mines bred.'[15]

Sir Joshua Reynolds (1723–92), then President of the Royal Academy, thought highly of Opie, who at the age of twenty-one successfully exhibited five works at the Academy in 1782 of Cornish country folk, including *Boy and Dog*, *An Old Woman* and *A Beggar*.[16] The same year he was introduced to King George III (1738–1820) and Queen Charlotte (1744–1818). The king kept two of Opie's paintings of subjects, one from each end of the social order, *A Beggar and his Dog* and the other, which had been painted at the king's request, a *Portrait of a Lady*.[17]

Opie began to meet a wide range of people in London society and in December 1782 he married his first wife Mary Bunn at St Martin-in-the-Fields.[18] The marriage did not turn out well and was dissolved by an Act of Parliament in December 1796. The early years in London could have overwhelmed the young Opie but, in demand from the aristocracy, the well-off and the well-placed, he took commissions for nearly five dozen portraits and exhibited thirty-one paintings at the Academy between 1782 and 1786. John Opie was elected an Associate of the Royal Academy in 1786, the year he exhibited *A Gentleman and a Miner*, and a Royal Academician the following year. The exceptionally rapid rise in interest in John Opie's paintings, the high praise he received for the works painted in distant Cornwall and the acclaim which he attracted during his early years in London rested not only on the unusual quality of his early paintings but also on the encouragement he gained from Sir Joshua Reynolds and the entrée John Wolcot was able to provide to influential patrons.

The need to promote British artists and reject applications from foreigners became the subject of intense debate at the Royal Academy during the 1780s. When founded in 1768, Reynolds had made a significant effort to support the election of a substantial foreign presence among the Academicians. More than a quarter of the elected members were foreigners and Reynolds was accused of a lack of patriotism, but by supporting them he also stressed the need to stimulate a British art scene which was at the time short of indigenous talent. John Opie, bringing his natural talent from Cornwall, was a welcome addition, helping to sustain this enterprise. No foreigner was elected to the Academy from the date of Opie's election in 1786 to the time of his death. By then the concept of an English School of painting was beginning to be discussed.[19]

Opie was painting at a time when artists were admired for showing their love of nature's variety and for demonstrating their talent by raising their subject to a higher level of perfection or, as Reynolds puts it to his students in his *Third Discourse at the Royal Academy*, '… the perfection of this art does not consist in mere imitation, … all the arts receive their perfection from an ideal beauty, superior to what is to be found in individual nature.'[20] Opie's portraits in Cornwall certainly show his ability to capture nature's variety and contrasts, but he was criticised for his unwillingness to flatter or to raise his portrait-ure, other than in his 'fancy pictures', beyond straight representation. When in Cornwall, Wolcot had counselled the young Opie: 'Stare folks in the face. Mark their features, air, manner, gesture, attitude.'[21] However, in London in a letter of 1782 to Mr Colborn, a bookseller, he recognises that Opie may need something more if he is to gain a lasting reputation:

> I have again called on Reynolds with a pair of John Opie's pictures
> … on which he expressed surprise at the performance by a boy in
> a country village containing excellence that would not disgrace the
> pencil of Caravaggio. … It strikes me that Reynolds expects Opie to
> be as perfect in the delineation of the graces as in the hands of vulgar
> nature, and in consequence become a formidable rival. But here I am
> sorry to say he will be fortunately mistaken; Opie, I fear, is too fond
> of imitating coarse expression. …To him at present elegance appears
> affectation.[22]

Wolcot's conclusion was later echoed by others but in Opie's early years in London the directness he brought to the subjects he exhibited was admired.

We would not have *A Gentleman and a Miner*, a rare image of this period relating to Britain's industrial past, without Opie's early life experience rooted among the artisans of Cornwall, his acquaintance with the mining hierarchy, his lack of affectation and his refusal to flatter. In her *Memoir*, Amelia Opie writes of her husband that he '… possessed the art of representing strongly the ridiculous in men and things, which he instantly and sensibly felt … .'[23] Amelia had not known Opie in his youth but her description adds fruitfully to our appreciation of the double portrait of Thomas Daniell and Captain Joseph Morcom. However, what else do we know about these two men?

Thomas Daniell was a financially successful merchant and mining adventurer whose forbears included William Daniell, the Member of Parliament for Truro between 1600 and 1603 and former mayors of Truro.[24] In the early years of his career Thomas Daniell was chief clerk to the adventurer and mine merchant, William Lemon (1696–1760), before being taken into partnership to develop new quays for shipping on the Hayle Estuary near St Ives.[25] The Rev. Richard Polwhele writes of Lemon and Daniell, 'Both "made" (as the Cornish say) "by good luck" but not without ingenuity and perseverance, and a bold adventurous spirit in mining and merchandize.'[26] And these qualities served Thomas Daniell well. He married Elizabeth Elliot, the niece of Ralph Allen of Prior Park, and in 1759, using Bath stone which had been a gift from Allen, built the fine house now known as the Mansion House in Prince's Street, Truro, a house which the Rev. Polwhele describes as unquestionably the best in the town.[27]

In Opie's *A Gentleman and a Miner*, however, we see Thomas Daniell a quarter of a century later appearing as an elderly established figure wearing the formal morning dress of the period. Perhaps, conscious of the image he would like Opie to present, he wears a wig in the latest fashion of the day, a style that was introduced in or about the date of the painting; the hair is swept back covering the ears and the wig has four 'buckles' or rigid hollow rolled curls. We might read into Opie's portrait signs of an assured but uncompromising or even stubborn figure, and we might infer, from the gesture of his left hand that he is a man accustomed to command and get his way.

Thomas Daniell played a prominent role in the development of the tin and copper mines in the region between Truro and Redruth in West Cornwall. During the latter part of the eighteenth century he and other Cornish adventurers were looking to increase profits by reducing the cost of mine drainage so that the overall cost of extracting copper ores from the deeper strata could compete with that of ores being mined in the Parys and Mona mines on the Isle of Anglesey. It is here that the manufacturer Matthew Boulton (1728–1809) and the engineer and inventor James Watt, based in Birmingham, come into the picture. In 1778 they established the Boulton & Watt Steam-engine Partnership in Cornwall. The aim of their business was to introduce their more efficient steam engines to replace the Newcomen engines then in use in the Cornish mines. These would reduce operating costs by making valuable savings in coal consumption. The Boulton & Watt Papers, held in the Archives of Soho in the Birmingham Reference Library, comprise a rich and extensive correspondence covering the period of their business in Cornwall. They include a string of references to Thomas Daniell and Joseph Morcom which illuminate Opie's painting and add valuable insights into their character and our understanding of the 'gentleman' and the 'miner'.[28]

Some years after the painting had left the possession of the Daniell family, John Jope Rogers, in his biography of Opie, identifies the 'gentleman' and 'the miner' in Opie's painting. He believed the 'gentleman' to be the young Ralph Allen Daniell (1762–1823), only twenty-four when the portrait was painted, rather than his father the seventy-year-old Thomas Daniell, so it is worth confirming that the 'miner' we have in view is Captain Joseph Morcom.[29] Practical operations at the Cornish mines were controlled by a number of captains or agents who supervised the work of the tributers (miners paid a percentage of the value of the ore they raised) and tutmen (miners paid at a fixed rate) working underground or in dressing the ore at ground level. Captains were invariably chosen from among the miners themselves for their shrewdness, management ability and knowledge of mining. A captain, who generally wore a white drill coat, held an important and influential position in-between the management and the miners, and was responsible for seeing good returns from the mine at the minimum of expense.[30]

The correspondence between Matthew Boulton and James Watt, who were resident in Cornwall at various times, mentions several mining captains associated with Thomas Daniell, so we should clear up any possible confusion. At the time of Opie's painting Captain William Paul and Captain Joseph Morcom (Boulton sometimes refers to him as Captain Jo Malcomb) are the two most prominently associated with Daniell. On 23 September 1785 Boulton writes from Chasewater to Watt in Birmingham (Figure 2.2):

> I attended the ♀ [Copper] Committee yesterday at Truro & afterwards dined with the adventurers of ye Consolodated Mines at ye Kings head [Truro] which was held for the purpose of takeing into Consideration the precarious State of W^l [Wheal] Virgin Mine … . The business was opend by D^l. & Mor^m [Thomas Daniell and Joseph Morcom] who first wanted to know how much we would give them towards sinking 2 Engine Shafts …

and later he continues:

> I observd that although I understood most of the circumstances of the Mine yet I should not presume to offer any plan, as their own Captains had had more experience & were certainly more competent than I was (Cap^tn Jo Malcomb was present, but not Cap Paul who sent word he had the Gout …).[31]

At the time, Joseph Morcom was forty-two and William Paul in his late fifties, so there is little doubt that the mining captain in the white drill coat in Opie's painting (as John Jope Rogers believed) is Captain Joseph Morcom.[32] With

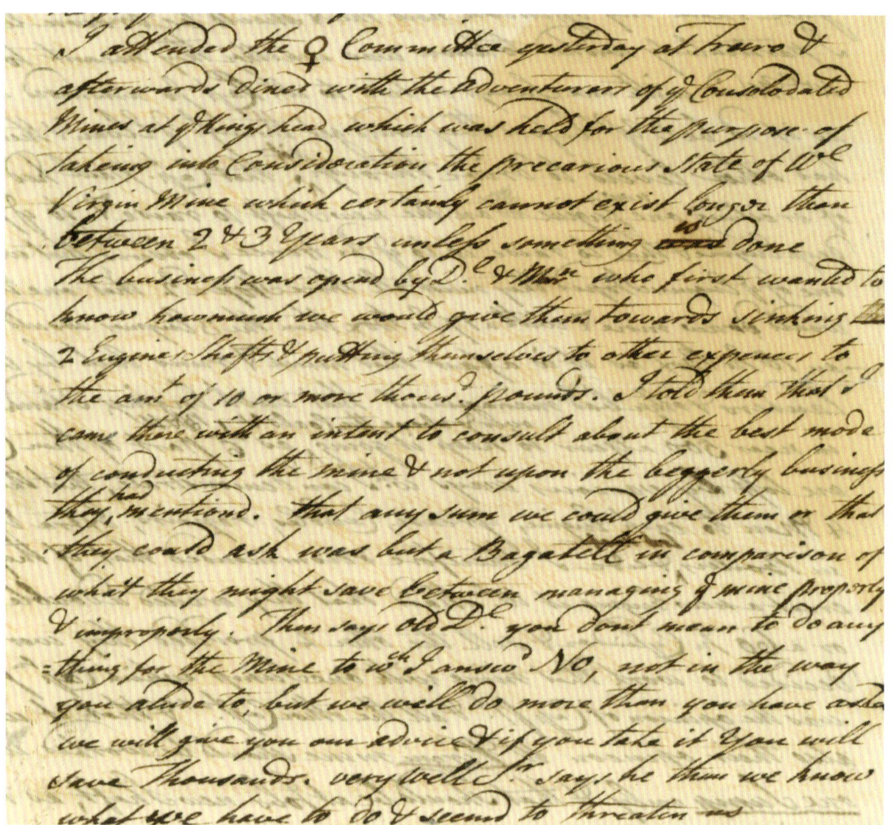

Opie's 'who is that?' if not his 'is it like?' out of the way, we will see what other insights can be gleaned from observations in the Boulton & Watt Partnership correspondence and how they bear on Opie's painting.

The regular exchanges between these two men, while one was living in Cornwall and the other working at the Soho Works in Birmingham, are particularly revealing. In Boulton's letters to Watt there is a clear sense of their business relationship with Thomas Daniell and of how all three were careful to protect their own interests. They tell us of the lengthy process of finalising an agreement between Daniell and his fellow adventurers and the Bolton & Watt Partnership for the supply of the steam engines for the Wheal Virgin mine, and we learn something of Daniell's character and of the financial ups and downs of the Cornish tin and copper mining industry as it competed with the Welsh mines in the 1780s.

The first reference to Thomas Daniell comes in the record of a Resolution agreed by a group of adventurers and sent by Daniell to Boulton and Watt on 26 October 1779, requesting the partnership to supply five steam engines to improve drainage for the Wheal Virgin mine.[33] Nearly a year later, on 18

September 1780, Boulton went to the Wheal Virgin mine to meet Thomas Daniell to discuss the agreement but he writes, '… the gout imprisoned him [Daniell]'.[34] Clearly frustrated by the lack of progress, he writes to Watt that very little was done other than eating beef with Captain Paul and the other captains, and failing to finalise the technical details of any agreement and a date when work should begin. A fortnight later Boulton, now somewhat distrustful of the Cornish adventurers, writes to say that he hears that Daniell had chaired a meeting of the adventurers who discussed alternative plans for managing Wheal Virgin mine and that he had met Captains Paul and Morcom who had expressed doubt about the ability of the Boulton & Watt steam engines to pump effectively from the deep shafts.

Recognising that negotiations were not going well and the importance of developing good relations with the influential Thomas Daniell, he wrote to Watt, 'I beg you to cause Mr Walker to enquire if any market can be found at Birmingham for Imree Stone from Turkey.[35] Mr Daniel has 20 ton from Turkey and wants to sell it & I wish to oblige him.'[36] And in early October, at a meeting of the adventurers with Thomas Daniell in the chair, there was still disagreement about how they should calculate the payments to be made to the Boulton & Watt partnership.[37] A few days later Boulton reports on Daniell's use of the time-honoured basis of smoothing the way in a business relationship:

> On Fryday [sic] last [6 October] I dined at Mr Daniels [sic] of Truro
> with Sr. Francis & Lady Bassett, Mr Beauchamp his sister & others.
> Sr. Francis was very civil to me & promised to bring Lady Bassett
> (who is a Beautifull [sic] young Lady & a little stately) to Plengwarry
> on Monday morng. next from where we go to the United Mines to
> see the Engines … .[38]

At the end of December 1780, the agreement was finally signed for the provision of five steam engines and pumps for Wheal Virgin, more than a year after the proposition was first mooted.

Matthew Boulton and James Watt spent several lengthy periods in Cornwall negotiating contracts, refining designs and advising on installation and operation. Boulton's mistrust of Cornishmen is evident in a number of letters to Watt but he seems to have had some respect for Thomas Daniell. He often refers to 'Old Daniel', a term he sometimes uses to distinguish him from his son, Ralph Allen Daniell who took over his business in the late 1780s.[39] In one letter, written at about the date of Opie's painting, he says that Old Daniel had shown him greater civility than any man in Cornwall, other than Mr Vivian, the Lawyer, and that Daniell had often asked him to dinner.[40] And perhaps he enjoyed some of Old Daniell's celebrated punch. The Rev. Richard Polwhele, recalling the attention Thomas Daniell gave to preparing it for his guests in Truro writes, in one of his letters to the Rev J. Cotton, somewhat tongue in cheek, that Daniell's punch is said to be better than anything ever tasted in old England or Caledonia and reflects great credit on him for its 'unrivalled composition'. He writes of the

> … ludicrous solemnity of countenance with which the old merchant squeezed the lemons, flung in the sugar and the water, and regularly gratified his company with a smack of sherbet and discussed its qualities, and the delicacy attainable by few in mixing those ingredients, before the rum was poured in – proportionate in quantity; and in reconciling the discordant elements, and rendering sour, and sweet, and weak, and strong, delicious in their blending.[41]

Disputes between the adventurers and the partnership continued during the construction of the steam engines and pumps, although these were usually resolved satisfactorily.[42] Boulton describes the resolution of one such:

> It all ended in good humour. On Tuesday I p'd my respect to our Truro friends. I engaged my Wife in a Quadrille party at the Daniel's and I attended the Ticketing of United Mines ores & and a Sale of 3/62 of Poldice Mine … .[43]

And Boulton himself entertains the Boulton & Watt agents and the mining captains, including Captain Jo Morcom, at the local pub, which if not in quite the same style as a party at Thomas Daniell's, appears to have been appreciated:

> I thought it but respectful to give our own Folks a dinner at a publick [sic] house near W^{l} Virgin today … for the Engines are all now finished, and they (our own Folks) have all behaved well and are attached to us![44]

Opie's *A Gentleman and a Miner* includes the image of equipment that was an important feature of the mining scene and in widespread use at mines and quarries – a whim (or gin). It can be seen to the left of the engine house below Captain Morcom's hand and would have been used for lifting materials, equipment and ore from the mineshaft. It comprised a large horizontal winding drum connected to lifting tackle, and usually driven round by horses in harness.[45] In 1784 the Boulton & Watt partnership developed a whim driven by a steam engine for the Consolidated Mines adventurers at the Wheal Maid and Wheal Virgin mines. Boulton records that over 1,000 people came to see the first one operating.[46] There were many teething troubles and Boulton, writing a couple of months later, reveals something of the tetchiness of Thomas Daniell:

> … the balance rope broken almost every day, … Mister Martin
> making great complaint & old D[l]. [Daniel] in a passion – ore not
> being drawn – have some reason to complain on that acc[t] but there
> is a friendly & an unfriendly way of doing it – a genteel one & an
> ungenteel one.[47]

In late 1785, just after Opie had painted the double portrait of Morcom and
Daniell, the challenge from the Anglesey mines, where the ore was more easily
accessible, began to take effect. Daniell, financially stretched, asked Boulton
for help. He was told, quite bluntly, that he was in Cornwall to advise on the
best way of managing the mine and that they would save more by taking his
advice rather than begging for money from him.

> Then says old D[l]. you dont mean to do anything for the Mine to w[ch]
> I answ[d] NO, not in the way you allude to, but we will do more than
> you have asked, we will give you our advice & if you take it you will
> save Thousands. Very well S[r]. says he then we know what we have to
> do & seem[d] to threaten us.[48]

The economics of mining deeper ores depended significantly on the cost of
labour and the cost of installing and operating more efficient steam engines
and pumping equipment. On a number of occasions when mines were closed
down as the extraction of ores became uneconomic, the miners' discontent
erupted and their employers were threatened with violence. We find Thomas
Daniell writing on behalf of the adventurers at Wheal Virgin asking for an
abatement of the contracted payments to Boulton & Watt with a request to
them to lower their charges.[49] By April 1787 Daniell was writing on behalf
of Consolidated Mines that the cost of operating the Wheal Maid engine
was uneconomic in meeting the current low price of ore. He – and later his
son Ralph Allen Daniell – pressed Boulton & Watt repeatedly for abatement
of payment during 1787 and 1788.[50] Several of the mines were temporarily
closed down and miners were out of work. In October 1787, Boulton wrote:
'There are 400 Miners already assembled & are calling all they can together
and are going to pull down Vivian's House.'[51] And later he wrote from Soho,
Birmingham, to Watt in London to say that he had heard from Mr Wilson,
their agent in Cornwall, who stated that he was in a very unpleasant situation,
as the miners had formed a plot to kill him, as they believed it was he who
stopped the operations at the North Down mine.[52]

Overall, the Boulton & Watt correspondence tells us as much about Matthew
Boulton as it does about Thomas Daniell or Joseph Morcom but it helps us
understand Opie's portrayal and provide a response, in Opie's words, to the '…
dull and tasteless questions, "who is that?" and "is it like?"' However, more than

this we find that Opie's unusual double portrait, painted about the middle of 1785, shows Daniell and Morcom just before the Cornish mines felt the impact of the slump in demand and the severe competition from the Welsh mines.

Thomas Daniell was prospering or, as Boulton puts it, 'Mr Daniel has become a great Man since Wheal Virgin hath appeared profitable …'. Opie was experiencing life in London meeting the well-born, rich and fashionable after his youthful experience in the mining areas of Cornwall. King George III had chosen two of his paintings. On his visit home in 1785, the contrast between the clientele visiting his studio in London and those living in the mining areas of West Cornwall would have been stark, and in the painting Opie's sympathies appear to lie with the competent and lively mining Captain Joseph Morcom rather than the elderly and established adventurer Thomas Daniell.

Opie does not hesitate to give Captain Morcom the upper hand both metaphorically and in the image itself. Maybe Morcom had come to tell Daniell of the success of the steam-driven pumping engine draining the mine, allowing the miners to extract the copper ore, but the carefully constructed composition with which Opie brings the disparate halves of the painting together, seen in the detail of Figure 2.3, is instructive. Opie appears to reflect on age (the younger Morcom and the elderly Daniell), class (Morcom the practical

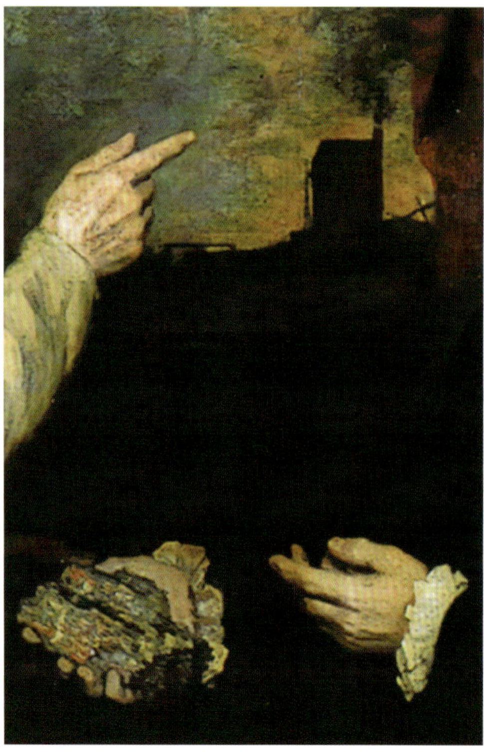

2.3 *A gentleman and a miner by John Opie*, 1786 (detail from Figure 3.1).

hands-on miner working for the established adventurer who has time to sit for Opie in his London studio), technology (the impact of the steam engine) and the use of capital (the adventurer's investment in new technology to extract the valuable copper ore). These are issues which probably struck the twenty-four-year-old John Opie anew on a return visit from London to his birthplace and to which he responded in his painting.

Opie had grown up living among the tin mines of Cornwall and his career as an artist exposed him to men and women who inhabited a wide band of the social spectrum. The late eighteenth century began to witness significant changes in its composition as new towns and cities began to grow around new industries and as labour previously employed in agriculture migrated from the country. The county of Shropshire saw the establishment and growth of the iron-industry around Coalbrookdale during the eighteenth century and it is there we turn in the next chapter to discuss the work of our next artist, Philippe-Jacques de Loutherbourg. De Loutherbourg, a Frenchman and an émigré, a very successful scenographer at David Garrick's Theatre Royal, Drury Lane in London, a sometime faith healer and a prominent landscape artist at that time, had exceptional talent. He takes a view of the Bedlam furnaces near Coalbrookdale, 'the cradle of the Industrial Revolution'.

Notes

1 Delivered on 23 February 1807. John Opie, 1809, pp. 76–7.

2 Also see David Stacey, 'A Gentleman and a Miner, by John Opie', pp. 7–14, in the *Journal of the Royal Institution of Cornwall*, 2011.

3 Opie's move to Great Queen Street, Lincoln's Inn Fields, took place in 1783. He had previously moved into lodgings with John Wolcot at Orange Court, Castle Street, Leicester Fields in the autumn of 1781. Rev. R. Polwhele, 1831, vol. II, p. 114. Opie's portrait of the writer and philanthropist *Hannah More (1745–1833)*, 1786, Girton College, Cambridge, shows her sitting in the same (studio) chair as Thomas Daniell. Daniell probably visited London regularly on business. A visit to London in June 1785 is recorded in a letter from Matthew Boulton in London to James Watt in Birmingham, 'Old Daniel is in Town', 5 June 1785. Boulton & Watt Papers, MS 3147/3/9.

4 *A Gentleman and a Miner* by John Opie – Provenance: With Thomas Daniell's family; purchased at Bath, 1825 by a member of the Pendarves family and then by descent to Mrs Warwick Pendarves, lent to the Royal Institution of Cornwall, Truro by Mrs Pendarves from 1953. Note: 'And old Mr Daniell's admirable picture by Opie was sold to Mr Pendarves, June 1825. Mr Pendarves is a man of taste. We lament its alienation from the family: but it could not have fallen into better hands.'

Rev. R Polwhele, *Biographical Sketches in Cornwall*, 3 vols, 1831, vol. II, p. 115.

5 John Barrell, 1980, pp. 1–5.

6 David H. Solkin, 1982, p. 25.

7 Thomas Rowlandson (1756–1829), Opie's contemporary, drew extensively in Devon and Cornwall. Despite the affectionate and satirical views he took of rural industry there, he did not touch on this aspect of the industrial scene. See Catherine Lorigan, 2002, pp. 32–49.

8 Prince Hoare, Saturday 25 April 1807; John Opie, 1809; Allan Cunningham, 1830; Rev. R. Polwhele, 1831; John Jope Rogers, 1878; Ada Earland, 1911.

9 Mary Peters, 1962, p. 4, says Opie's father was a 'mine carpenter' but I can find no early reference to this.

10 *The Reverend Richard Polwhele, c.1778,* by John Opie.

11 Rev. R. Polwhele, 1831, vol. II, pp. 113–14.

12 Allan Cunningham, 1830, p. 180.

13 Ada Earland, 1911, p. 7.

14 Rev. R. Polwhele, 1836, vol. II, p. 144.

15 Peter Pindar, 1783.

16 Exhibits nos 224, 371 and 384.

17 Ada Earland, p. 33.

18 Mary was the daughter of Benjamin Bunn, a solicitor and moneylender. Ada Earland, 1911, p. 44.

19 Anne Puetz, 'Foreign Exhibitors and the British School at the Royal Academy, 1768–1823', in David H. Solkin (ed.), 2001, pp. 229–41 and Table 4, p. 254; and Kay Dian Kriz, 1997, p. 106.

20 Joshua Reynolds, 1819, vol. I, *Third Discourse, 14 December 1770*, p. 53.

21 Rev. R. Polwhele, 1831, vol. II, p. 114.

22 Quoted in John Jope Rogers, 1878, pp. 19–20.

23 Amelia Opie in John Opie, 1809, pp. 1–54.

24 R. Thorne (ed.), 1986.

25 Letter from Rev. R. Polwhele to Rev. J. Cotton, Truro, September 1784. Rev. R. Polwhele, 1836, vol. II, p. 140. Charlotte MacKenzie, 2007, p. 49.

26 Rev. R. Polwhele, 1836, vol. II, p. 140. William Lemon was one of the first to work mines on a large scale with the help of Newcomen 'fire engines'. He traded at Hayle and later at Truro. His influential paper on the benefits of a policy of removing duty from coal was sent to Robert Walpole. Rev. R. Polwhele, 1831, vol. I, pp. 7–8.

27 Rev. R. Polwhele, 1836, vol. II, p. 140. The Daniells called their son Ralph Allen Daniell.

28 Boulton & Watt Papers, *Archives of Soho*, Birmingham Archives & Heritage, Birmingham Reference Library: (MS 3147).

29 John Jope Rogers, 1878.

30 John Vivian, 1970, p. 28.

31 *Correspondence B&W Partners*, MS 3147/3/9, 23 September 1785, MB, Chasewater to JW, Birmingham.

32 Captain Joseph Morcom lived in Whitehall, a small village between Redruth and Chasewater, from before 1780 to after 1813. Matthew Boulton and James Watt stayed at their agent Mr Wilson's house at Whitehall from time to time. www.morcom.one-name.net/GentlemanandMiner.html (accessed 4 January 2019).

33 *Boulton & Watt Papers*, Series Part 14, MS 3147/3/458, Microfilm A.20068, Reel 269.

34 *Correspondence B&W Partners*, MS 3147/4, 18 September 1780, MB, Redruth to JW, Birmingham.

35 Probably fine grained Limra white limestone from Antalya, Turkey.

36 *Correspondence B&W Partners*, MS 3147/3/4, 1 October 1780, MB, Redruth to JW, Birmingham.

37 *Correspondence B&W Partners*, MS 3147/3/4, 7 October 1780, MB, Redruth to JW, Birmingham.

38 *Correspondence B&W Partners*, MS 3147/3/4, 11 October 1780, MB, Redruth to JW, Birmingham. Sir Francis Basset (1757–1835) became 1st Baron de Dunstanville and Basset and a Fellow of the Royal Society. He married 'the beautiful … and a little stately' Frances Susanna Hippesley-Coxe in May 1780, a few months before Boulton met her at Daniell's house. Rev R. Polwhele writes, possibly ironically of him, 'A large portion of his income accrued from the mines [particularly Dolcoath] and his gratitude directed one conspicuous current of his benefactions to the relief of the poor miners who had laboured and suffered in support of his establishment.' Rev. R. Polwhele, 1831, vol. II, p. 27. He was pallbearer at John Opie's funeral in April 1807.

39 Rev. R. Polwhele, who was a childhood friend of Ralph Allen Daniell, says that 'From Seal-Hole mine he [R.A. Daniell] had an inundation of riches, at a rate of more than a guinea a minute.' Rev. R. Polwhele, 1836, vol. II, p. 142–3. I am grateful to Margaret Morgan, Documentation Officer, Royal Institution of Cornwall, Royal Cornwall Museum, Truro for references to: (i) a letter in the History File of the Courtney Library written by the late Senior Curator, Roger Penhallurick which indicates that Ralph Allen Daniell acquired the nickname 'guinea-a-minute' and (ii) Viv Acton, 1997, pp. 106–10. Matthew Boulton consistently gives Thomas Daniell's surname as Daniel or Dl. This spelling has been used where it comes from Boulton's correspondence.

40 *Correspondence B&W Partners*, MS 3147/3/9, 22 August 1785, MB, Chasewater to JW, Birmingham.

41 Letter from Rev. R. Polwhele to the Rev. J. Cotton (n.d.). Rev. R. Polwhele, 1836, vol. II, pp. 141–2.

42 Dispute over the employment of Jethro [Hornblower] by Boulton & Watt: *Correspondence B&W Partners*, MS 3147/3/5, 25 September 1781, MB, Soho to JW, Cornwall, replying to Watt's letter MS 3147/3/5 of 20 September from Cornwall. *Correspondence B&W Partners*, MS 3147/3/5, 13 October 1781, MB, London to JW, Cornwall, writes 'Don't get over vexed' with Thomas Daniell and the adventurers.

43 *Correspondence B&W Partners*, MS 3147/3/5, December 1781, MB, Truro, to JW, Soho, Birmingham.

44 *Correspondence B&W Partners*, MS 3147/3/6, 7 December 1782, MB, Cosgarne to JW, Birmingham.

45 Oil paintings at Coalbrookdale by George Robertson, *c*.1748–88, which were subsequently published by John and Josiah Boydell, London, as a series of engravings, February 1788, include *View of Mouth of Coalpit near Broseley*, an early illustration of a horse whim.

46 *Correspondence B&W Partners*, MS 3147/3/8, 15 July 1784, MB, Cosgarne, to JW, Birmingham.

47 *Correspondence B&W Partners*, MS 3147/3/8, 25 September 1784, MB, Cosgarne, to JW, Birmingham.

48 *Correspondence B&W Partners*, MS 3147/3/9, 23 September 1785, MB, Chasewater, to JW, Birmingham.

49 *Boulton & Watt Papers*, Series Part 14, MS 3147/3/458 Microfilm A.20068, Reel 269, 10 June 1785, Thomas Daniell, Truro, to Boulton & Watt, Birmingham.

50 *Boulton & Watt Papers*, Series Part 14, MS 3147/3. Microfilm A.20068, Reel 269, April 1787, TD, Truro, to B&W, Birmingham; 16 June 1787, TD, Truro to B&W, Birmingham; 15 July 1788, TD, Truro, to B&W, Birmingham; and 1 August 1788, RAD, Truro to B&W, Birmingham.

51 *B&W Partners Correspondence*, MS 3147/3/11, 6 October 1787, MB to JW, Birmingham.

52 *B&W Partners Correspondence*, MS 3147/3/13, 26 March 1789, MB, Soho to JW, London.

3 Philippe-Jacques de Loutherbourg and Coalbrookdale

The focus of this chapter is on images of Coalbrookdale, Shropshire, on *Coalbrookdale by Night* (Figure 3.1), and its creator Philippe-Jacques de Loutherbourg (1740–1812). De Loutherbourg was the youngest artist to be elected a member of *l'Académie royale de peinture et de sculpture de Paris* and his work was highly regarded in France in the 1760s. Denis Diderot admired his works at the Paris salon of 1763 and writes of him as this *'Phénomène étrange!'* but, following a domestic and financial scandal, de Loutherbourg fled France and arrived in Britain in 1771.[1] The painting of Coalbrookdale at night was not exhibited at the Royal Academy of Arts in London until thirty years later, so it is worth a brief review of de Loutherbourg's career in Britain first to provide background and context for the work.

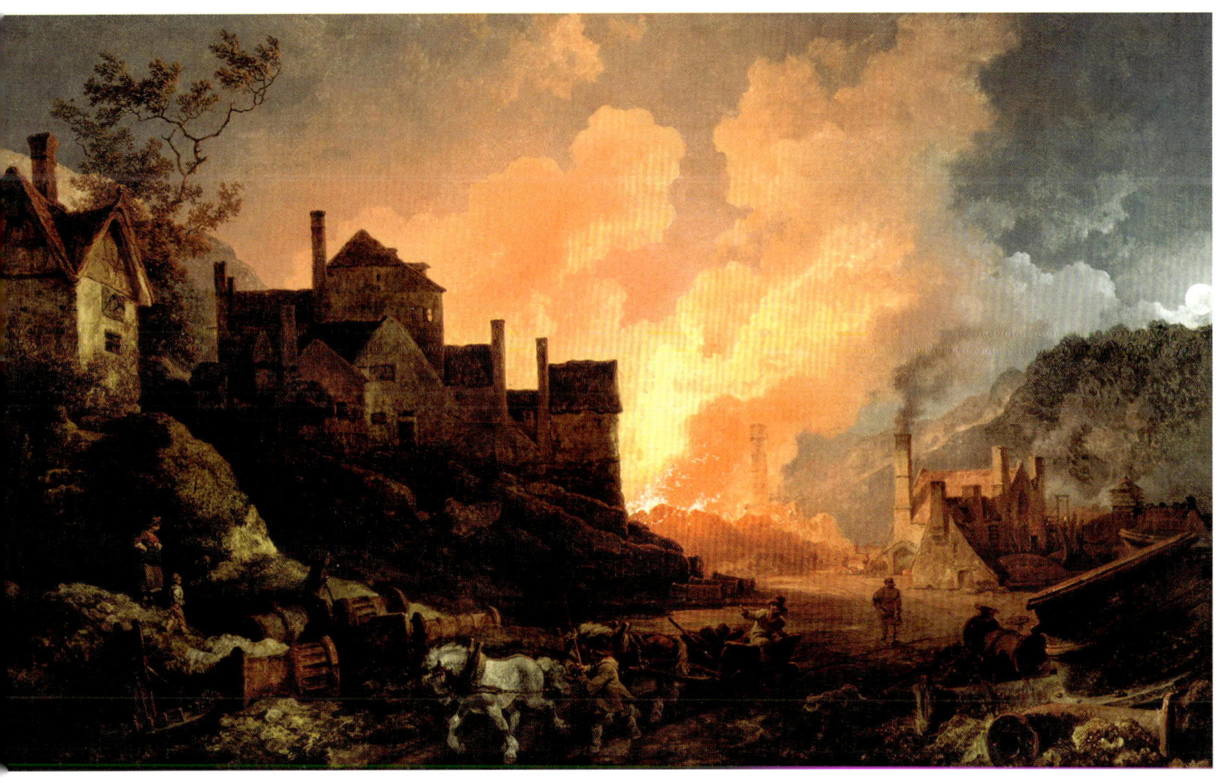

3.1 *Colebrook Dale [Coalbrookdale] by Night*, 1801, by P.J. de Loutherbourg, oil on canvas, 68 x 106.7 cm. The Science Museum, London.

Soon after arriving in London at the age of thirty-one, de Loutherbourg was appointed chief scenographer at the Theatre Royal, Drury Lane, which was then under the management of David Garrick. He worked there for ten years, where his set designs were highly praised. He left to create his successful miniature theatre or *Eidophusikon* in London where over a period of about three years he staged a variety of shows.[2] During this period de Loutherbourg continued easel painting and was elected a member of the Royal Academy of Arts in 1781. In the late 1780s de Loutherbourg's output as an artist was affected first by his encounter with the charlatan Count Cagliostro, and then by his spell as a faith healer, but he re-established his career as an artist in the 1790s and was elected to the Council of the Royal Academy in 1803. From 1783, de Loutherbourg and his wife Lucy, a young English widow whom he had married in 1774, lived in Hammersmith until his death in 1812.

The latter part of the eighteenth and the early nineteenth century saw substantial changes in perceptions of the national identities of France and Britain. These were influenced in Britain by the impact of colonial expansion, the early stages of an industrial revolution and the wars with France. De Loutherbourg can be found playing a part in promoting a version of Britain's new identity at the turn of the century. In the 1790s, when the wars following the French Revolution and battles under Bonaparte's command were gathering momentum, de Loutherbourg was commissioned by Valentin Green and the print dealer Christian von Mechel to paint some large canvases of contemporary conflicts.[3] These included scenes of two great battles: the attack on Valenciennes in 1793,[4] where the British army fighting with the Austrians defeated the French, and the victory of Lord Howe in 1794, one of the first naval battles between the French revolutionary forces and Britain.[5] These canvases were followed by commissions for paintings of Admiral Duncan's victory over a Dutch fleet at Camperdown in 1799[6] and Nelson's victory over the French at Aboukir in 1800.[7] These were all subjects that the Frenchman de Loutherbourg appears to have been happy to paint and which fed readily into a genre of painting which reinforced patriotic feeling and generated a contemporary sense of Britishness.

Perception of the country's developing industrial base also contributed to this sense of national identity. De Loutherbourg was one of the few artists who, during trips to the Midlands, the north of England and Wales, took an interest in the expanding quarrying and metal industries, bringing scenes of them to the theatre and to works he exhibited at the Royal Academy. His interest first appears during a visit to Derbyshire in 1778. There he began collecting material for *The Wonders of Derbyshire*, a pantomime entertainment devised with

Richard Brinsley Sheridan and first performed at the Theatre Royal, Drury Lane in January 1779. An abbreviated account of the production describes the variety of scenes and musical interludes included in the show. These begin with a 'View of Matlock at Sun-set', A 'View of Dove-Dale by Moonlight', followed by 'Lead Mines and a Landscape of the adjacent country'. The account explains that these three, 'Matlock, Dove-Dale, and the Lead-Mines, although not ranked among the Wonders of Derbyshire, are places so remarkable for beauty and public resort that it would have been arraigning the taste of Mr. de Loutherbourg had he not conducted the *Dramatis Personae* through such delightful scenes.'[8] Four years later, de Loutherbourg, on a more extensive tour of the north of England, passed through the Peak District again. During this visit he recorded a number of views of the mines and quarries and, in the next three years, exhibited four works on this subject-matter at the Royal Academy.[9] The following year de Loutherbourg visited Wales. At Swansea he made a number of small ink sketches of the White Rock copperworks and John Morris's Fforest Copper Works at Clasemont before making his first visit to the Severn Gorge and Coalbrookdale, Shropshire.[10] It is there that de Loutherbourg returned some fourteen years later to create *Coalbrookdale by Night*, his painting of the Bedlam furnaces, a significant feature of the iron industry there.

The development and success of the iron industry at Coalbrookdale and in the Severn Gorge relied principally on two important factors. First, the raw materials required for iron smelting (iron ore, coal and limestone) were close at hand, and secondly, two Quaker families, the Darbys and the Reynolds had the drive and ambition to exploit them and build a centre for the iron industry at Coalbrookdale, later to be dubbed 'the cradle of the Industrial Revolution'.[11] Abraham Darby I settled there in 1709. He had served his industrial apprenticeship in Birmingham in the 1690s before moving to Bristol where he worked with fellow Quakers and managed an iron foundry and brass mills.[12] In his foundry at Coalbrookdale he began by manufacturing simple domestic items such as pots, kettles and other hollowware but later he produced more complex castings: '... grates, smoothing irons, door-frames, weights, baking-plates, cart-bushes, iron pestles and mortars ... .'[13] Abraham Darby I (1678–1717) significantly improved the quality and finish of iron products by using coke rather than coal in the smelting process and introducing the use of sand moulds for castings.[14]

After Abraham I's death, the management of the works passed to his son-in-law, Richard Ford, as Abraham Darby II (1711–63) was only six years old when his father died. During Ford's time, the company began to manufacture and supply products to Britain's expanding mining industry. These included the first iron wheels for use on primitive railways and cast-iron cylinders for the Newcomen steam engines which were then principally being employed to pump water from mines, particularly in Cornwall and northwest England. In 1738 Abraham Darby II became a partner of the Coalbrookdale Company and the managing director in 1745. The enterprise expanded under his leadership. He built new furnaces, introducing steam-driven pumping engines to provide water supplies to the works, and he acquired land so that the company had control over the coal, ironstone and limestone reserves required at the ironworks.

In the second half of the eighteenth century, Coalbrookdale and the Severn Gorge were high on the list of picturesque industrial sites in Britain that tourists, encouraged by a number of published guides and journals, began to visit.[15] Several artists were commissioned to produce drawings and paintings of the new and developing industrial scene. The earliest views of the area are the engravings by the Huguenot artist Francis Vivares (1709–80) who had come to England at the age of eight. His two engravings of Coalbrookdale were based on drawings by George Perry (1719–71) and Thomas Smith of Derby and were published to accompany *A Description of Coalbrookdale in the County of Salop*, in 1758, a prospectus commissioned by Abraham Darby II.[16]

Plate I, *A View of the Upper Works at Coalbrookdale* (Figure 3.2), shows the blast furnaces where Abraham Darby I made a breakthrough by first smelting iron using coke. The smoking coke hearths adjacent to the Upper Furnace Pool appear in the foreground and a large diameter cylinder, part of a Newcomen engine, can be seen being transported along the Wellington Road.[17] The accompanying Plate II, *The South-West Prospect of Coalbrookdale*, looks towards the Church Stretton Hills and shows the furnaces seen through the wooded landscape of the upper dale, smoke billowing out from the coke hearths, with Abraham Darby II's home, Dale House, in the distance. The two views, as the prospectus makes clear, were chosen to show the happy co-existence of the iron industry and Darby's estates within the natural landscape, and are the earliest images of subjects which would later be recognised as significant features of the Industrial Revolution.

Comparison of the engravings with the prospectus, however, reveals something of a mismatch. Whereas the text evokes both the picturesque of the wooded valley and the sublime of the industrial complex, the views, chosen for publicity purposes, are rooted in the topographical tradition and neither the sublime nor the picturesque qualities are realised. Perry and Smith, in the prospectus, no doubt encouraged by Abraham Darby II, appear to have been keen to impress on the public the happiness of those living in the valley.

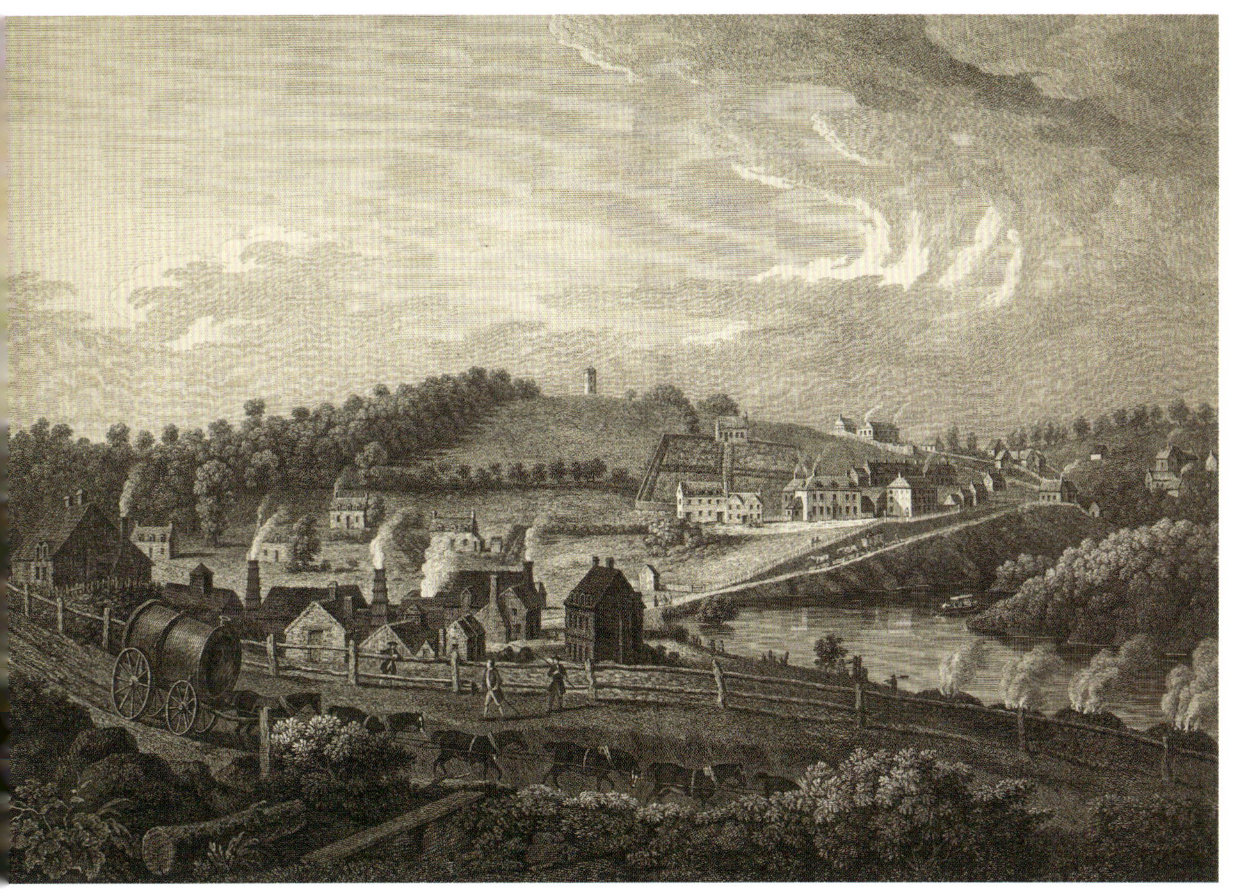

> … the lower class of people, who are very numerous here, are enabled to live comfortably; their cottages which almost cover some of the neighbouring hills, are thronged with healthy children, who soon are able to find employment, and perhaps cheerfulness and contentment are not more visible in any other place.

And they continue:

> Upon the whole … there are few places where rural prospects, and scenes of hurry and business are so happily united as at Coalbrookdale.

News of this happy valley, the expanding industry and the technological improvements adopted at Coalbrookdale soon spread widely and both Britons and foreigners began to visit the area in the 1760s and 1770s. Arthur Young (1741–1820), the author of treatises on the science of agriculture, describes the valley in his *Annals of Agriculture and Other Useful Arts* which was published after his visit to Shropshire in 1776:

> These iron works are in a very flourishing situation, rising rather
> than the contrary. Coalbrook Dale itself is a very romantic spot; it is
> a winding glen between two immense hills which break into various
> forms, and all thickly covered with wood, forming both the most
> beautiful sheets of hanging wood. Indeed too beautiful to be much in
> union with that variety of horrors art has spread at the bottom: the
> noise of the forges, mills &c. with all their vast machinery, the flames
> bursting from the furnaces with the burning of coal and the smoak of
> the lime kilns, are altogether sublime … .[18]

Young's description is borne out by two somewhat genteel images, each over a metre square, by William Williams (1727–91) of morning and afternoon views of Coalbrookdale, paintings that were exhibited at the Royal Academy in 1778.[19] Williams's morning view is taken from the upper part of Coalbrookdale (from Jigger's Bank) and looks southeast down the dale on a still morning, showing black oily smoke rising from an engine house in the distance. A team of horses in the left foreground is being managed by a single wagoner to bring coal by truck from the Coalbrookdale side of the river to the forges and furnaces further down the valley. The painting complements Young's eloquent description of the region.

In the afternoon piece, Williams takes a higher viewpoint on Lincoln Hill, looking to the west across the Upper and Lower Furnace pools at Coalbrookdale to the Church Stretton Hills beyond. The ironworks are almost hidden in the valley below, while above a gentleman in hunting pink speaks to his gardener as two well-dressed women converse by his side. Williams's paintings go beyond Perry and Smith's topographic drawings and are aimed at a different clientele, the landowners and ironmasters of the dale. The choice of viewpoints and compositions of both paintings owe something to Richard Wilson (1713/14–82) but Williams takes the opportunity to contrast nature with art, the romantic winding and thickly wooded glen with the sublimity of the ironworks in the valley below but, taking care for the sake of his potential clients, to keep art's 'horrors' at a safe distance.

At the time Arthur Young was writing, Abraham Darby III (1750–89) had succeeded his father as manager of the Coalbrookdale Company.[20] He built a new ironworks at Donnington Wood, enlarged the Coalbrookdale furnaces and built new forges at Horsehay and Ketley. However, he is perhaps best remembered for building the Iron Bridge. This was completed in 1781 and is now among the most notable iron structures of the period. Sixty-five years after Abraham Darby I had settled in Coalbrookdale and was producing between 5 and 10 tons of iron per week from his furnaces to be cast into domestic articles, his grandson was to build the Iron Bridge across the River Severn, which required 378 tons of structural cast iron in its construction.

After visiting Coalbrookdale in 1796 and staying at the Tontine Inn, which stands opposite the end of the bridge, the chemist Charles Hatchett FRS (1765–1847) writes: 'I was informed by the old Quaker who shewed us the works that in the district belonging to these two families [the Darbys and the Reynolds] between 30 and 40,000 souls are supported either by working in the Founderies or in the Iron and Coal Mines.'[21] The two families had become closely associated when Richard Reynolds (1735–1816) married Hannah Darby in 1757. Richard was born in Bristol and had come to Coalbrookdale as manager of the Horsehay Ironworks in 1756 but he soon joined the management of the Coalbrookdale Company. He was an influential member of the community who lobbied the government against the tax upon coal and its impact on the iron trade and, not far from the Bedlam furnaces which we see in de Loutherbourg's painting (see Figure 3.1), he laid out woodland walks where he encouraged workmen and their families to stroll on a Sunday afternoon. His son William Reynolds (1758–1803), the most versatile and talented of all the Shropshire ironmasters and later a partner in the Coalbrookdale Company, took over the Bedlam Furnaces when the Darby-Reynolds partnership was dissolved in 1796.[22]

De Loutherbourg first visited Coalbrookdale on his way to Wales in 1786. His small ink sketch, (Figure 3.3) which shows the Boulton and Watt 'Resolution' steam engine installed at Coalbrookdale in 1781 probably comes from this visit. It was perhaps a memory of this trip that brought him back there,

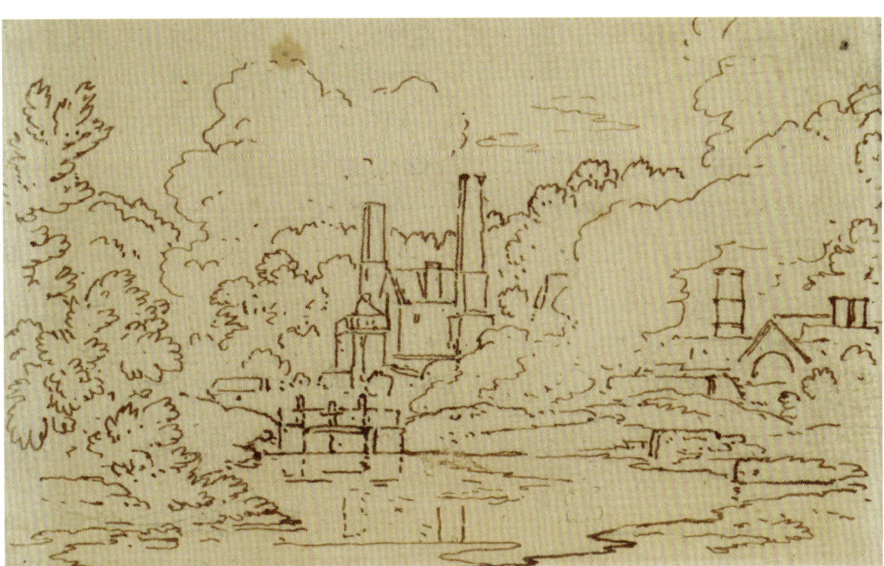

3.3 *The Resolution Steam-Engine, Coalbrookdale, Seen from the New Pool*, 1786 or 1800, by P.J. de Loutherbourg, pen and ink on card, 7.3 x 9.5 cm. Tate, London.

at the turn of the century, to prepare for his *Coalbrookdale by Night*, a painting to mark the occasion with a subject that spoke of Britain's industrial strength. William Reynolds was the senior partner of the Coalbrookdale Company which operated the ironworks at that time but the painting does not appear to have been commissioned by him. It seems to have been a speculative work which de Loutherbourg hoped – perhaps aware of the signal it gave at a time of war with France – would attract attention at the Royal Academy.

Coalbrookdale and the Severn Gorge had acquired a significant reputation not only for its picturesque features but also for its awe-inspiring industrial landscape. Henry Skrine (1755–1803), although recognising the picturesque nature of the dale with its high wooded hills, writes in 1798 of numerous fires, the clangour of the forges and scenes which transport the observer '… to the workshop of Vulcan or an epitome of infernal regions'.[23] And Henry Wigstead (d. 1800), describing the trip he made to Coalbrookdale with Thomas Rowlandson (1757–1827) a year earlier, writes:

> Our general pursuit, however, was nature, not art; we have found so
> many beauties demanding our attention that we knew not where to
> select; … We literally wandered in search of the *ne plus ultra*, till the
> evening's hasty approach had nearly prevented us making a slight
> sketch. … The face of the country is here in parts an entire blaze
> of red fire; the heat in passing these Aetnas in miniature is intense;
> indeed, scarcely bearable; and the thick black smoke emitted from
> the smelting houses almost suspends respiration. … The roads are
> entirely surfaced with clinkers, cinders and dross from the iron ore.[24]

These descriptions, 'in parts an entire blaze of red fire', the 'thick black smoke' and the roads 'surfaced with clinkers, cinders and dross from the iron ore', resonate closely with de Loutherbourg's *Coalbrookdale by Night* which, coming forty years after Perry and Smith's Coalbrookdale prospectus, delivers a fiery evocation of the coke hearths and furnaces at Bedlam. De Loutherbourg makes no attempt to show any happy co-existence of the iron industry with the Darby and Reynolds' estates within the valley.

De Loutherbourg, transferring the scene to canvas, draws on a composition that he had employed before. He contrasts the solid dark silhouetted mass of the buildings in the foreground with the intense concentration of light from the ironworks beyond, isolating the buildings from the rest of the scene and introducing a diagonal sweep across the canvas which leads the eye to the industrial complex. This formal synthesis can be found in several of de Loutherbourg's earlier works where he appears to draw on some of the Neapolitan coast scenes of Claude-Joseph Vernet (1714–89) and Claude Lorrain

(1600–82).[25] A similar form can be found in de Loutherbourg's paintings of the same period, *Conway Castle* of 1800 and *Harlech Castle* of 1801. In *Coalbrookdale by Night* the buildings on the left stand firm in the new industrial landscape, essentially replacing Edward I's thirteenth-century castles.[26] De Loutherbourg finds at Coalbrookdale a subject which suited his sense of theatre. With the coke hearths ablaze in the distance and the moon casting a cool light on the hills beyond, he presents a vivid and not wholly unbelievable scene of the Bedlam furnaces, a grandly picturesque and sublime scene of a subject that had not been committed to canvas before.[27]

The painting received a generally positive reception when it was exhibited. The *St James's Chronicle*, 7–9 May 1801, found the 'contrast of the dark buildings with the strong light of the fire, has an excellent effect' and the *Oracle and Daily Advertiser* of 14 May noted '… a scene of nocturnal grandeur worthy of the genius of Loutherbourg', while the reviewer for the *London Packet* of 29 April–1 May wrote, 'Mr. de Loutherbourg is generally happy in exhibiting the effects of fire, and in the picture before us he has been particularly successful. The light of the moon, contrasted with that of the blazing furnaces (the effect of which are truly volcanic), adds much to the sublimity of the scene.' The reviewer in the *Porcupine*, however, was not over-impressed:

> There is too much of a gaudy glare in his Works, though, indeed, they may also be considered as strong proof of genius, but genius not regulated by sound taste. In the Picture before us the artist has attempted too much.[28] He has given a vivid representation of the artificial light resulting from the foundery [sic], but not contented with what should have been the great object, he has attempted also, to shew *Moonlight* and the *Break of the day*.[29] The genuine aspect of this Picture is like the *nocturnal transparencies* which excites so much vulgar imagination in the *Print shops*.[30]

De Loutherbourg's style is often recognisably derivative and his apprenticeship to François Giuseppe Casanova (1727–1802) was no doubt influential. Many of his early paintings in France draw on Dutch and Flemish works by artists such as Nicolaes Berchem (1620–83) and Philips Wouwerman (1619–68). There are, however, some more general trends in mid-eighteenth-century French painting to take into account. Works exhibited by French painters in the biennial Paris salons had begun to reveal a change in content and style. There was a reaction against the perceived frivolity of Rococo taste. Strands of the anti-Rococo movement in France drew on principles adopted by sixteenth- and seventeenth-century painters that works should adopt fundamentally serious ideas. A sense of absorption or of significant human action presented within a unified formality began to be sought in works of the period.[31] The idea of dramatic action expressed at a single and significant moment appealed not only to history painters but also to the expressive powers of landscape painters like Claude-Joseph Vernet and later de Loutherbourg. Dramatic scenes of extreme storms on land and at sea where heroic figures are found at the limits of endurance and presented at a moment of change in the light or the atmosphere provided perfect vehicles for this. De Loutherbourg brought these ideas to Britain, reinforcing the concepts of both the 'grand picturesque' and the 'sublime' moment, concepts which he had tried to capture in his *Eidophusikon* and which are evident in *Coalbrookdale by Night*.[32] This was not the way of Richard Wilson, whose impact on English landscape painting was a more subtle blend of styles arising from his six years in Italy, nor was it Gainsborough's ordered formality and uniform tonality.[33]

During the wars with France, French art was seen as gaudy and devoid of taste, and de Loutherbourg's works were being regarded unjustly as supporting an outpost of the French School. Some held the view that he could not paint English nature because he lacked an English sensibility.[34] Few held the view that English artists could not paint Italian nature because they lacked an Italian sensibility. As an artist schooled in France, with his experience as a scenographer and wishing to satisfy a diverse market in Britain, de Loutherbourg brought a variety of styles to his work and *Coalbrookdale by Night* can be seen as an example of this.

In the previous chapter I referred to John Barrell's *The dark side of the landscape: the rural poor in English paintings, 1730–1840*, in which he discusses artists' portrayal of the poor (labourers and their families) in *rural* Britain in the late eighteenth and early nineteenth centuries.[35] Barrell argues that images of rural life can only be understood by recognising the moral and social constraints on how the poor could or could not be represented. He suggests illusory images are presented which can be identified with the interests of artists' patrons and not of those they portray, and that these images of workaday English rural life mainly speak of a stable and unified society.[36] David Solkin expresses the view that the prescribed (if unspoken) aim of the poet or painter in the eighteenth century was to present the *status quo* as an unimpeachable ideal, and to establish as broad a consensus of belief as possible in the values of the landed élite and in a '… patrician myth of the "happy rural life"',[37] but do we see this stratagem being employed in de Loutherbourg's painting of 'industrial life'?

Coalbrookdale by Night is one of the few oil paintings of industrial activity exhibited in a public gallery during the early years of the Industrial Revolution in Britain. Those encountering this scene at the Royal Academy exhibition in London in 1801 might have, after first reacting to what to most of them would have been the shock of the unfamiliar fiery industrial landscape, begun to see the figures hidden in the shadows in the foreground and the distant foundry men almost consumed by the light emanating from the coke hearths. None of those reviewing the painting when it was exhibited commented on the shire horses and the active and attentive wagoners who drive on past the woman and child waiting on the hillside, nor on the weary labourer who follows behind, or the distant labourers, committed figures working amidst the heat, smoke and steam of the coke hearths and furnaces. De Loutherbourg treats them as an integral part of an industrial drama. For those commenting on the work at the time it was first exhibited, the labourers and their families were ignored, appearing to be nothing more than the nominal 'staffage' of the scene. It was the awesome industrial scene that commanded their attention. However, this is not a rural landscape, this was not a commissioned painting and the labourers do not present an image of a 'happy industrial life'. In the iron industry at Coalbrookdale, labourers were not subject to the diurnal and seasonal changes which benefitted agricultural workers but were driven by the imperatives of the industrial process and here, in the words of E.P. Thompson, we begin to see 'the making of the English working class'.[38]

Adverse comments on works de Loutherbourg exhibited in London generally echo the two main criticisms that Denis Diderot had levelled at those he had shown at the Paris salons in the 1760s: first, his use of bright and unnatural colours and, secondly, his failure to observe nature's variety. Diderot had advised de Loutherbourg to get out of the *atelier* and look closely at nature herself. This advice sat well with contemporary views on landscape painting in Britain and Sir Joshua Reynolds, in his *Thirteenth Discourse* of 1786 may have had de Loutherbourg in mind when he writes that certain exaggerations and deviations from nature are acceptable in the theatre but 'no Art can be grafted with success on another art'.[39]

Critics in Britain, although often acknowledging de Loutherbourg's genius, continued to raise these issues, criticisms he never managed to shake off. An anti-French subtext sometimes emerged in reactions to his works. Joseph Pott, for example, wrote in 1782, 'His pictures are visionary, without a trait of nature, and are painted with all that French pomposity so unlike the truth of the Flemish, or the chaste elegance of the Italian manner.'[40] And later Edward Dayes (1763–1804), in his commentary on de Loutherbourg, wrote '… parts of his pictures are wonderfully fine; but they are often spotty, and destitute of repose, a defect which, in all probability, arose from his early connection with the French school'.[41] Dayes himself visited Coalbrookdale in about 1780 and

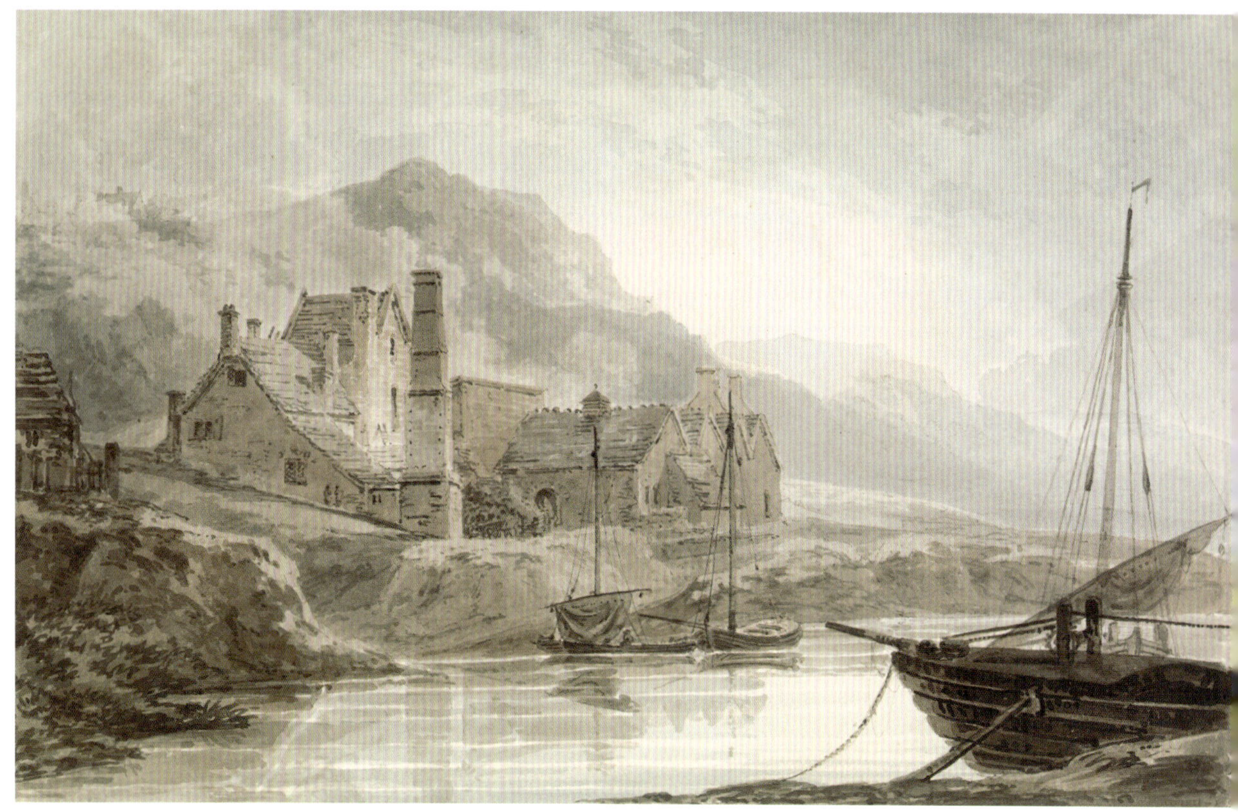

3.4 *Bedlam Furnace*, *c.*1780, by Edward Dayes, gouache, graphite and watercolour on paper, 31.6 x 44.0 cm. Tate, London.

his wash drawing of *Bedlam Furnace* (Figure 3.4) is of the relatively lifeless – although probably more accurate – representative complex of buildings and casting halls found in de Loutherbourg's painting.[42]

Dayes was often quick to find fault with his fellow artists and was not complimentary about de Loutherbourg's methods. Writing in 1803 on 'modern artists', he says of de Loutherbourg:

> This artist never condescends to draw from Nature; all he does is to make a few crude lines, where he thinks he may be able to recollect the scene, on card, and then corrects it at night; but he oftener works entirely from memory.[43]

It was, however, this process that allowed de Loutherbourg to raise many of his finished works from the mundane to the sublime. The sketches on card mentioned by Dayes, sometimes with shadows washed in, are presented with directness, simplicity and a clear sense of structure which, without losing sensitivity, leave us in no doubt of the features of the subject-matter. Some of his sketches are prepared as panoramic views, which are formed by linking two or three cards together.[44] The sketches are nearly all devoid of figures, unlike his finished landscape works in which he usually includes lively but often vulnerable groups of people. Figure 3.5, on a single card measuring 7.3 × 9.5 cm, gives an idea of the type of sketch de Loutherbourg may have used to build up his Coalbookdale painting.

When de Loutherbourg's belongings were auctioned after his death in 1812, the auctioneer Peter Coxe promoted his work in his Introduction to the catalogue with the words:

> De Loutherbourg … selected his views with judgment and collected all his natural material upon the spot. His facility of drawing enabled him to copy buildings, rocks and trees, with all their varieties, and every pictorial expletive necessary for his purpose, with rapidity and truth: hence his views in outline bore the strongest resemblance to the scenes.[45]

Another scene at Coalbrookdale by de Loutherbourg, an *Ironworks in Coalbrook Dale*, is included as a plate in *The romantic and picturesque scenery of England and Wales from drawings made expressly for the undertaking by P.J. de Loutherbourg*, published in 1805.[46] The plate, engraved by William Picknett from de Loutherbourg's drawing and coloured by John Clark, shows the smelters of the ironworks tucked away into the banks of the gently winding river, the chimneys emitting a grey-white smoke which softens the outline of the valley side. The engraving, tinted in soft greens, pinks and ochres, presents a scene which is picturesque if not romantic, in deep contrast to *Coalbrookdale by Night*. The engraving is described in the text as to '… exhibit the middle

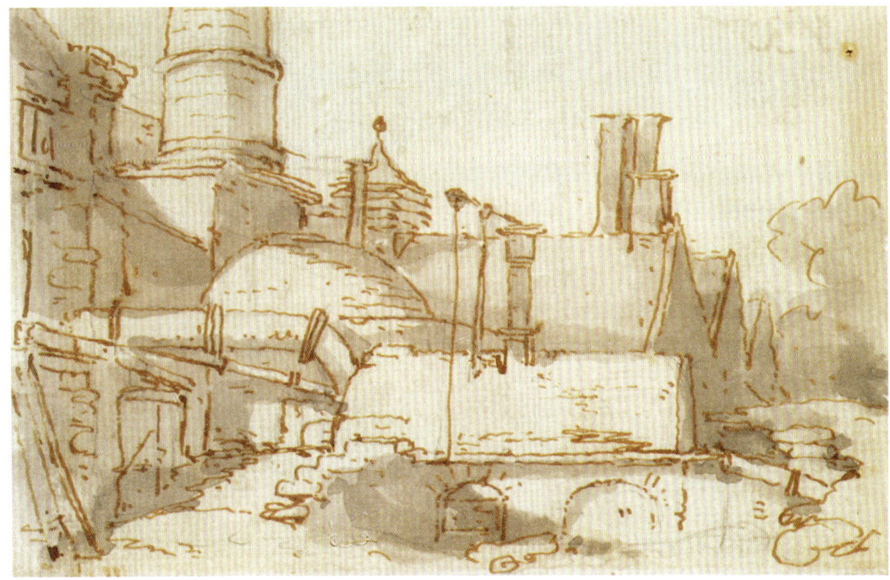

3.5 *Boiler, Engine House and Casting Halls, Coalbrookdale*, 1786 or 1800, by P.J. de Loutherbourg, pen and ink, graphite and watercolour on card, 7.3 x 9.5 cm. Tate, London.

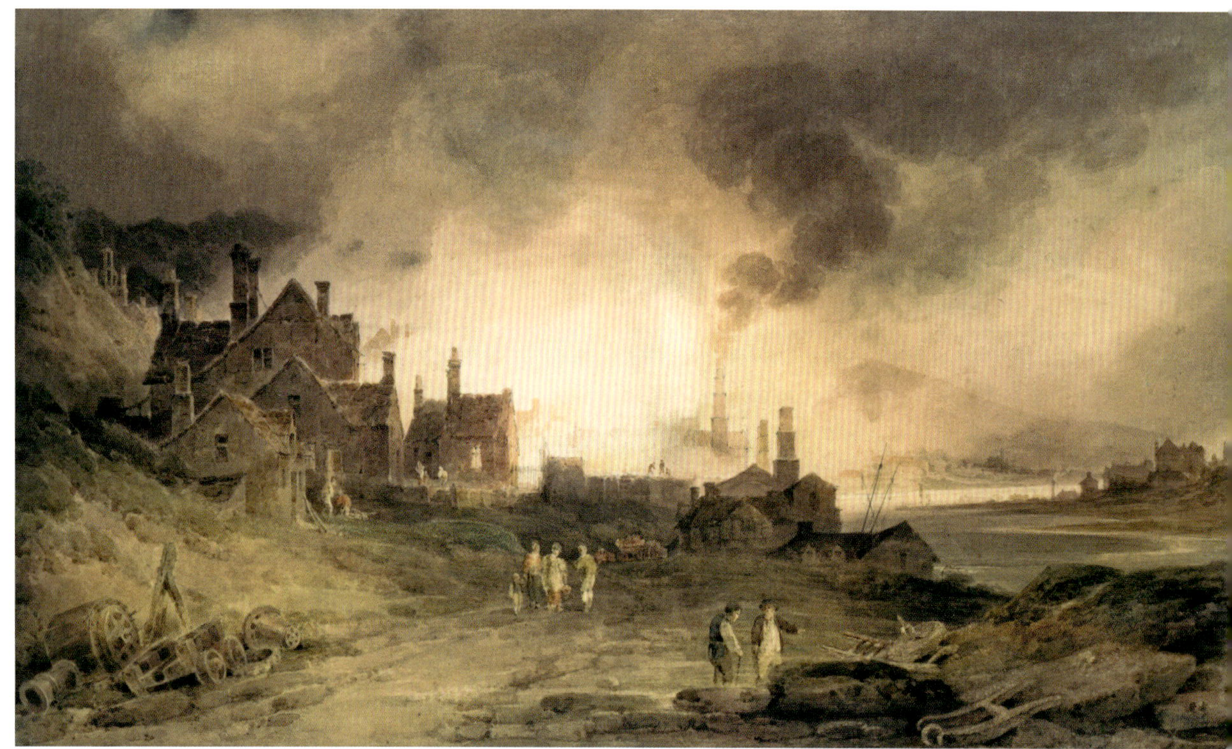

steam-engine in the Dale, with surrounding scenery', which suggests that the drawing was based on detailed observation.

It is instructive to compare de Loutherbourg's image of the Bedlam furnaces with the watercolour drawing of 1803 by Paul Sandby Munn (1773–1845), a view that was probably inspired by de Loutherbourg's painting of 1801 and which arises from Munn's trip to Coalbrookdale with John Sell Cotman in 1802. In this watercolour (Figure 3.6), Munn extends the view to include the River Severn and put the ironworks in a wider landscape. Munn also creates a vision of the daytime gloom that would have pervaded the areas surrounding the ironworks.[47] On a still day the sun would have been obscured by the haze of smoke and steam that filled the sky. This is an atmosphere with which those in Europe are mostly unfamiliar today, but it is one which became widespread in industrial Britain through the nineteenth and first half of the twentieth centuries, where distinct shadows are replaced by a flatness of light and where the air around seems to be almost tangible. Munn exhibited his watercolour drawing of Bedlam Furnace at the Royal Academy in 1803 and although it has lost some of its original colour and is only a quarter of the size of de Loutherbourg's oil painting exhibited two years earlier, it provides this important insight. We also see Munn, retreating from the realities of the industrial scene, staffing it with passive and apparently contented family groups and labourers, and introducing the concept of the 'happy industrial life'. De Loutherbourg, schooled in France in the 1760s, does not fall for this trap and, looking for a single and significant moment of action at the iron foundries of Coalbrookdale at night, points to conditions that foundry men and labourers were to endure as industrial life began to dominate the economy of Britain.

By the time de Loutherbourg's painting of the Bedlam furnaces was exhibited at the Royal Academy, Britain was clearly undergoing a period of unprecedented change. The country was witnessing the application of new technologies to its industries. At Coalbrookdale William Reynolds, deeply involved in the spread of the canal network, manufactured the world's first cast-iron canal aqueduct to cross the River Tern at Longdon-on-Tern and consulted with William Jessop and Thomas Telford on the construction of the innovative iron-lined aqueducts at Chirk and Pontcysyllte on the Ellesmere Canal. The demand for iron was increasing both for the country's infrastructure and for armaments. The Reynolds and the Darbys at Coalbrookdale were Quakers which ruled them out from manufacturing armaments but other ironmasters in the Severn Valley and those in South Wales near Merthyr Tydfil were there to provide both. The iron industry in South Wales was a scene with which the young Penry Williams was familiar. His response to the development there is discussed in the next chapter.

Notes

1 Denis Diderot, *Essais sur la peinture, 1765*, Gita May (ed.), *et Salons de 1759, 1761, 1763*, Jacques Chouillet (ed.), 1984, Paris: Hermann, p. 223. Olivier Lefeuvre in his *catalogue raisonné* discusses the affairs and financial improprieties that arose in France from de Loutherbourg's liaison and marriage to Barbe Burlat in 1764 and her relationship with Antoine de Meyrac. Olivier Lefeuvre, 2012, pp. 24–9.

2 De Loutherbourg's theatre presented simulations of natural scenes enhanced by changing lighting effects and moving scenery. *Eidophusikon*: from *eidoion* (image), *phusis* (nature) and *eikon* (likeness).

3 These scenes were then engraved by William Bromley and James Fittler.

4 *The Attack on Valenciennes, 1793*, 1794, by Philippe-Jacques de Loutherbourg.

5 *The Victory of Lord Howe, 1st June 1794*, 1795, by Philippe-Jacques de Loutherbourg.

6 *The Battle of Camperdown, 1799*, 1800, by Philippe-Jacques de Loutherbourg.

7 *The Battle of Aboukir, 1800*, 1800, by Philippe-Jacques de Loutherbourg.

8 Anon., 1779, p. 11.

9 Exhibited at the Royal Academy as *An Engine to Draw the Water out of a Lead Mine near Matlock Bath, Derbyshire*, 1785, by Philippe-Jacques de Loutherbourg. See Olivier Lefeuvre, 2012, p. 260.

10 Sir John Morris, 1st Baronet of Clasemont and Sketty, colliery proprietor, copper manufacturer and ship-owner, died in 1819. His sister Margaret (1731–1813) married Noel Joseph Desenfans (1745–1807) in 1778 and was instrumental in the establishment of the first public art gallery in Britain at Dulwich in South London.

11 John Whitehurst, 1778, Appendix, Plate V, gives a cross-section through Lincoln Hill, Coalbrookdale, Shropshire, showing the limestone and coal strata, details of considerable significance in the support of the iron industry there.

12 Abraham Darby I was backed by the influential Bristol merchant Thomas Goldney II (1664–1731) in establishing the iron foundry at Coalbrookdale.

13 Samuel Smiles, 1863, p. 82.

14 Patent No. 380 for casting iron pots using sand moulds was granted to Abraham Darby I in 1707.

15 See, for example: C.K. Hyde, vol. 6, 1973; R.R. Angerstein, 1755, trans. T. & P. Berg, 2001; Arthur Young, 1776, vol. IV.

16 George Perry and Thomas Smith, 1758.

17 Celina Fox, 2009, p. 410, suggests that the large diameter cylinder was sent to Cornwall and supplied to Jonathan Hornblower.

18 Arthur Young, 1776, vol. IV, p. 152.

19 *Morning View of Coalbrookdale*, 1777, and *Afternoon View of Coalbrookdale*, 1777, by William Williams.

20 Abraham Darby III married Rebecca Smith in 1776 but left her a widow in 1789 when he died of scarlet fever.

21 C. Hatchett, 1796, A. Raistrick (ed.), 1967, pp. 57–8.

22 Barrie S. Trinder, 2000, pp. 36–7, 43–4, 116–17 and 138–9.

23 Henry Skrine, in John Pinkerton, 1808, p. 618.

24 *ne plus ultra* – the perfect example, the ultimate. Henry Wigstead, 1800, pp. 9–10. Twenty-two aquatints by Rowlandson can be found in Wigstead, 1800. The drawings by Rowlandson of the iron industry are confined to *Meadow Wharf, Coalbrookdale*, c.1797, a rather sleepy scene downstream of the Iron Bridge, which shows a heap of castings of domestic and industrial items ready for loading at the wharf.

25 Olivier Lefeuvre draws attention to de Loutherbourg's debt to Claude Lorrain: Olivier Lefeuvre, 2012, p. 83.

26 *A View of Conway Castle*, 1800, and *A View of Harlech Castle*, 1801, by Philippe-Jacques de Loutherbourg. See Olivier Lefeuvre, 2012, pp. 305–06. Some contemporary artists, among them Sir Joshua Reynolds, accused de Loutherbourg of adopting a repetitive and Mannerist style at various periods of his life. Olivier Lefeuvre, 2012, pp. 92–6.

27 The coke hearths were constructed above the furnaces and supplied the coke, to which the limestone and iron ore were added in the furnace. Some remnants of the Bedlam furnaces are still to be found today on the north side of Waterloo Street. The group of buildings shown on the left of the painting were demolished to build the Ironbridge gas works in the 1830s. See Stuart Smith, 1979, p. 46.

28 Stephen Daniels makes a connection between *Coalbrookdale at Night* and Joseph Wright's *Arkwright's Cotton Mills at Night* with their illusionistic stagecraft, and finds *Coalbrookdale at Night* a '… patriotic and explicitly martial scene' and '… also a Masonic one deploying the alchemical imagery and theatrical effects Loutherbourg used in his painted scenes to accompany the Egyptian Rite of Freemasonry'. Stephen Daniels, 1998, p. 60.

29 The combination of 'moonlight' and 'artificial light' is a feature of Joseph Wright of Derby's painting of *Arkwright's Cotton Mills by Night* referred to in Chapter 1.

30 *The Porcupine*, undated 1801, Royal Academy Library and Archives.

31 Michael Fried, 1998, p. 75.

32 Joseph Burke in T.R.S. Boase, 1976, p. 376.

33 Robin Simon, *Richard Wilson, Rome, and the transformation of European landscape painting*, pp. 1–33, in Martin Postle and Robin Simon, eds, 2014, p. 11.

34 Kay Dian Kriz, 1997, p. 107.

35 John Barrell, 1980.

36 John Barrell, 1980, p. 5.

37 David H. Solkin, 1982, p. 25.

38 E.P. Thompson, 1986.

39 Joshua Reynolds, 1819, vol. 2, pp. 133–6.

40 Anon. (Joseph Pott), 1782, p. 77.

41 Edward Dayes, E.W. Brayley (ed.), 1805, pp. 335 and 338. The concept of a 'French School' of paintings had hardly been established when de Loutherbourg was in France in the 1760s.

42 *Bedlam Furnace*, c.1780, by Edward Dayes. De Loutherbourg may have seen this drawing by Edward Dayes as it and some of his own sketches at Coalbrookdale were found in J.M.W. Turner's collection of drawings and now form part of the Turner Bequest at Tate Britain. Among his pen and ink sketches on card (each about 8 × 12 cm) there are several of Coalbrookdale.

43 Edward Dayes, E.W. Brayley (ed.), 1805, p. 336.

44 See, for example, his panoramas in South Wales at Swansea and of *Aberdulais Mill*, a view which provides an interesting comparison with Turner's watercolour of 1796–7, Turner Bequest, Tate, London.

45 Peter Coxe, 1812, p. 3, quoted in Olivier Lefeuvre, 2012, p. 88 and pp. 354–8.

46 Robert Bowyer, 1805.

47 *Bedlam Furnaces, Madeley Dale, Shropshire*, 1803, by Paul Sandby Munn.

4 Penry Williams at Merthyr Tydfil

In 1819 Michael Faraday (1791–1867) was invited by the ironmaster J.J. Guest to visit the Dowlais Ironworks near Merthyr Tydfil, South Wales, to advise on the chemistry of iron processing. While staying at the Lamb and Flag Inn at Glynneath, Faraday was so impressed by some oil paintings he saw there that he immediately commissioned works from the artist and wrote to Guest asking for help with transport so that the paintings could be sent to his home in London.

> The Master of the Inn [Jenkin Price] where we now are has some oil paintings which though rough convey an excellent Idea of the place they represent, i.e. the falls of the vale. They were painted by a person of Merthyr, a Mr Williams, who I understand will do me a set if I can get them conveyed to London … . I will write to Mr Williams to place them in your hands immediately … . They will be eight or ten in number and four shillings each.[1]

'Mr Williams' or Penry Williams (1802–85), the son of a stonemason and house painter, was born at 3 Bridgefield Terrace, Merthyr Tydfil and then spent the early years of his life at Ynysfach near Merthyr. He showed a gift for drawing and between 1817 and 1820 painted half a dozen oil paintings of the Cyfarthfa ironworks at Merthyr for the ironmaster William Crawshay II (1788–1867). Some of the smaller paintings provided details which were later developed to form the basis of the engraved designs for the £1, £5 and £10 denomination banknotes of the Cyfarthfa and Hirwain Ironworks Bank.[2] These several views, which record the development of the iron industry near Merthyr Tydfil, although drawn with a somewhat erratic perspective, are remarkable for having come from a largely untutored hand. The paintings show Penry Williams's close observation and keen attention to detail and an approach which largely lacks the influences of contemporary aesthetic convention. In them Williams furnishes valuable representative images of the buildings and structures of the Crawshays' Cyfarthfa ironworks at Merthyr Tydfil. It was around Merthyr that the iron industry had begun to congregate in South Wales in the late eighteenth century. The Cyfarthfa ironworks were the largest of a group which included those at Dowlais, Pennydarren, Tredegar and Aberdare, all close to or within a few miles of the town.[3]

The iron industry was a competitive business. Wages, employment and profits were subject to fluctuations in the demand for iron products and were dependent on an ironmaster's management skills and his relationship with his employees. Coalminers and ironworkers often found themselves under threat of a pay cut or being laid off for a period. Strikes and riots at Merthyr Tydfil were widely reported in regional and national newspapers. In October 1800, 4,000 coalminers and ironworkers rioted and looted shops in Merthyr as they found themselves unable to afford basic food for themselves and their families. The riot quietened down after the arrival of cavalry from Cardiff barracks.[4]

In October 1816, several thousand miners and ironworkers assembled to protest against the reduction of 1*s* per day in their wages (equivalent to about £4 per day in 2020). The strike started at Tredegar ironworks from where groups of men, supported by others who joined them on their way, marched towards Merthyr, closing down the furnaces at all the ironworks in the area. The strikers went on to take over the ironworks in which they worked and overpowered the special constables who had been sworn in to control them.[5] William Crawshay II at Cyfarthfa was instrumental in calling in the military to quell the riot which lasted several days.

On the second day:

> About half an hour before the mob arrived, the Bristol soldiers (part of the 55th regiment) came in; they had scarcely had time to have a sup of Beer and a little bread in their hands at the Castle Inn (head quarter) before the mob came in thousands [some reports say 10,000]. Mr. Hill, the Sheriff for Glamorgan, Mr. Crawshay, and all the Gentlemen, mounted their horses with the cavalry. The Riot Act was read by Mr. Hill, the Sheriff. After great bustle and noise the mob were all dispersed … after they dispersed, near 40 of the ringleaders were made prisoners … .[6]

The ironworkers did not go back to work for several days; the colliers for several weeks.

The earliest known painting by Penry Williams records the 1816 Merthyr Riots (Figure 4.1). Williams was only fourteen years old when he painted this scene.[7] He may have been at school at the time or working in support of his father. The arrival of the foot soldiers in their fine uniforms and the dashing cavalry must have impressed the young Penry who appears to bring a simple apolitical approach to the scene. His painting, confirming the newspaper reports shows, at the right of the picture, some of the 55th regiment from Bristol having had time 'to have a sup of Beer and a little bread', making their

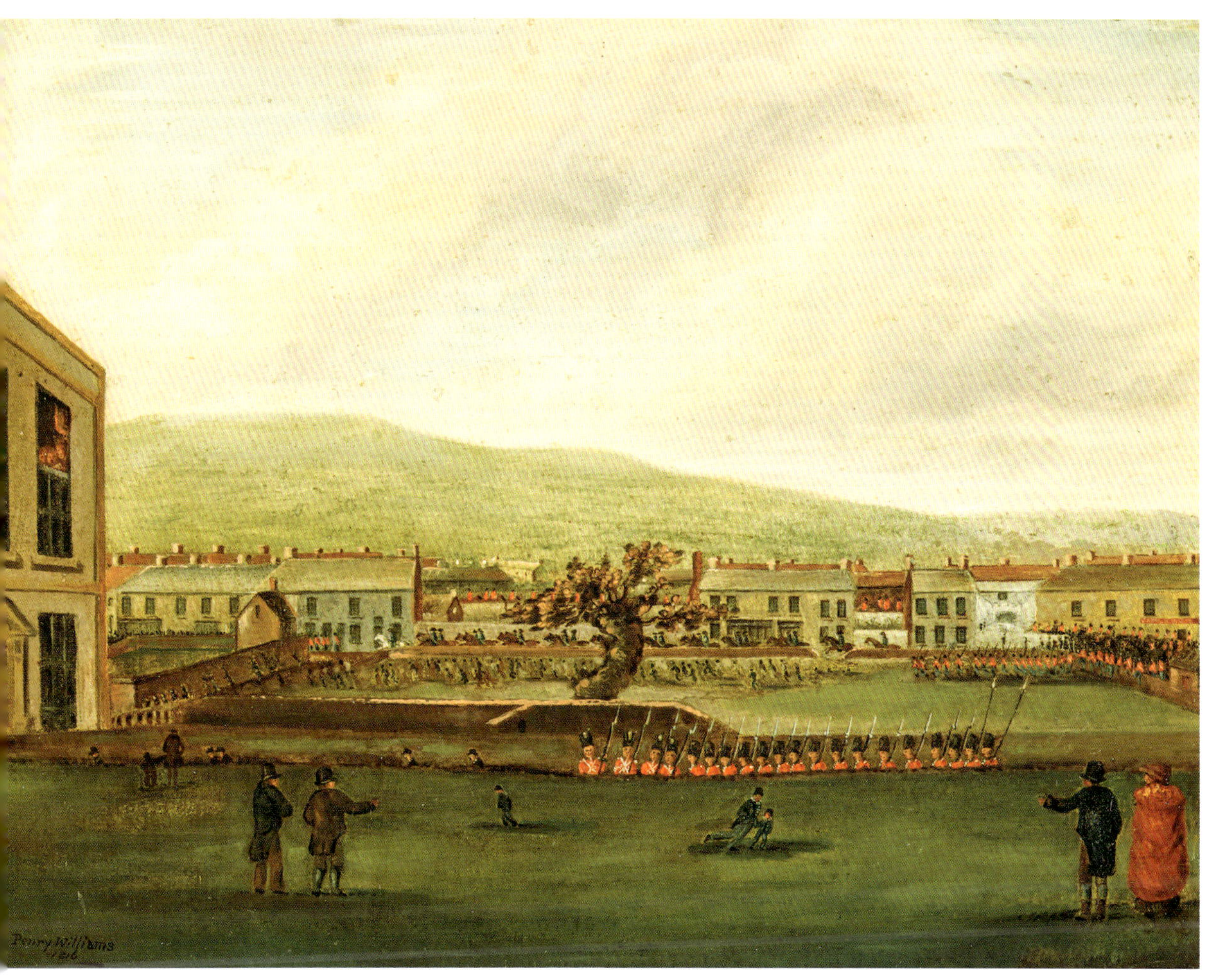

4.1 *The Merthyr Riots*, 1816/17, by Penry Williams, oil on canvas, 41 x 56 cm. Cyfarthfa Castle Museum and Art Gallery, Merthyr Tydfil.

headquarters at the Castle Inn. Foot soldiers parade in the foreground and the cavalry, led by an officer on a white horse with, perhaps, William Crawshay II among them, can be seen in the middle distance. Penry Williams expresses his excitement at the event but the teenager gives us no indication of whether his sympathies lie with the colliers and ironworkers or with the employers and ironmasters who had triggered the riot.

Williams's *Merthyr Riots* was not the first drawing or painting connected with the iron industry at Merthyr but it was the first to represent the unrest which periodically erupted in the new industrial areas of Britain.[8] The painting does not appear to have been commissioned by any of the ironmasters, although the Crawshays, proud of their achievements, had previously invited several artists to make drawings of the ironworks at Cyfarthfa.[9] Their ironworks were the largest in Great Britain in the early 1800s, employing about 1,500 workers

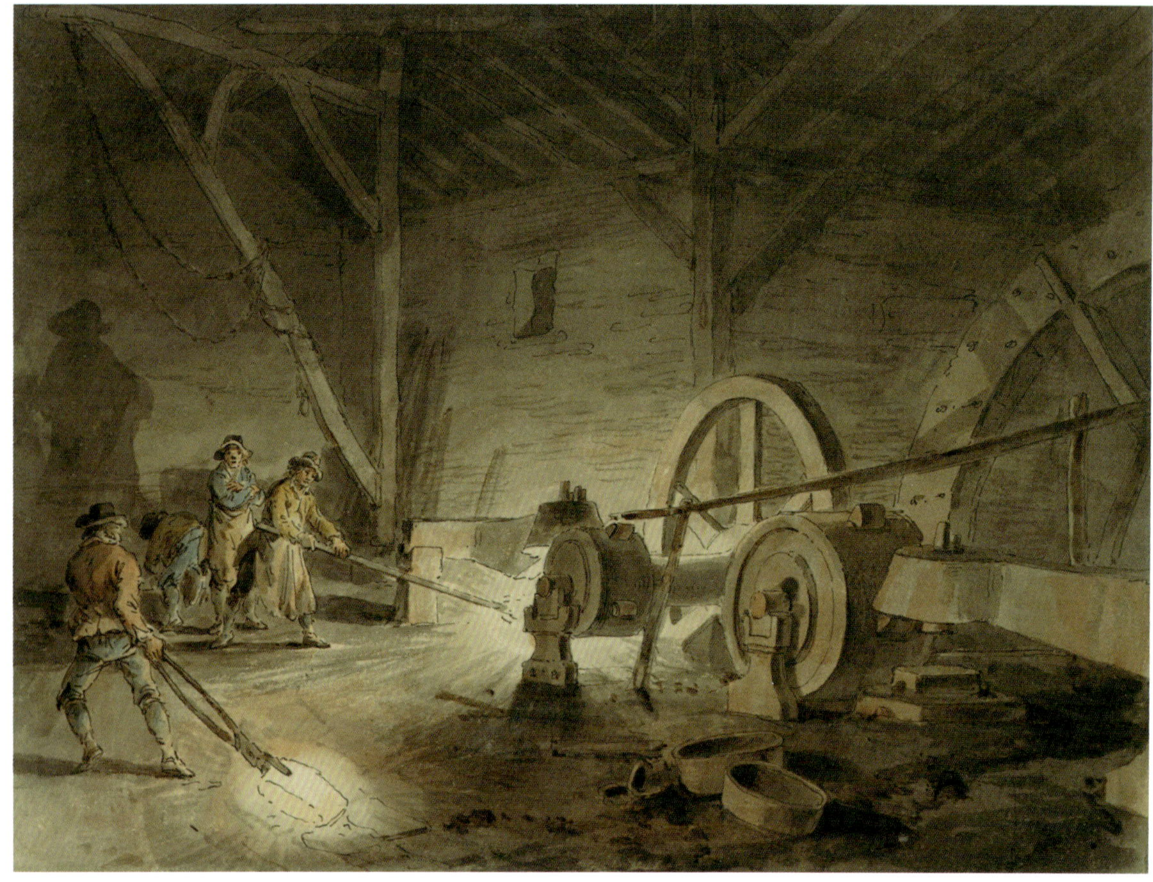

and William Crawshay II's father, Richard Crawshay (1739–1810), the senior partner of the Cyfarthfa ironworks until his death, had been keen to encourage artists to record his success.[10]

A small watercolour of an iron forge at Merthyr Tydfil (Figure 4.2), drawn in 1789 by Julius Caesar Ibbetson who made several drawings in the Cyfarthfa area, is one of the first of these and presents an interior view of operations in the iron industry in South Wales where an iron billet is being brought from the furnace to be forged at the helve or shingling hammer.[11] The drawing takes the viewer inside part of a contemporary industrial forge where the sequential processes in the furnace and forge were brought together in the ironworks. Ibbetson conveys an impression of the dangerous and heroic actions of the men at work and creates an image which radiates the brilliant light and heat of the foundry as the white-hot billets are brought under the water-powered hammer.

Six years later, Richard Crawshay's gardener, William Pamplin, made two landscape drawings at the Cyfarthfa works and in 1798, Anthony Bacon

4.2 *An iron forge at Merthyr Tydfil*, 1789, by Julius Caesar Ibbetson, watercolour on paper, 22 x 29 cm. Cyfarthfa Castle Museum and Art Gallery, Merthyr Tydfil.

(1772–1827), Richard Crawshay's partner at Cyfarthfa, commissioned J.M.W. Turner to draw there.[12] Four of Turner's large graphite drawings, some now sadly faded, show views at or near Cyfarthfa.[13] The drawings come from Turner's third tour to Wales and his first encounter with industrial development in the south of the principality but they were never developed into finished paintings. One includes a sight of the spectacular long elevated wooden aqueduct which fed the great 48-ft diameter Aeolus waterwheel which powered the bellows at four of the works' furnaces, a feature that appears in drawings by Pamplin and later in one by Penry Williams.[14] The early views of the Cyfarthfa ironworks by the young Williams come from a mostly naïve eye and hand but in them Williams proves adept at satisfying his patron, William Crawshay. His drawings have been kept in the collections of successive generations of the Crawshay family.

It is unclear precisely who encouraged Penry Williams to register at the Royal Academy Schools in London at the age of about twenty, but as we have seen his talent had clearly been recognised by J.J. Guest of the Dowlais ironworks, the Crawshays at Cyfarthfa and Michael Faraday. Financial backing for Penry could have come from a number of sources, including William Crawshay II at Cyfarthfa and possibly the owner of the Nantyglo ironworks, Crawshay's cousin Joseph Bailey, who later sponsored and paid for his travel and visit to Rome in 1826.[15] Williams was accepted as a student at the Royal Academy Schools on 4 April 1822 under the supervision of the elderly Johann Heinrich Fuseli (1741–1825) where he served three years as a student. By then Williams had also obtained a post working as an assistant to Sir Thomas Lawrence (1769–1830) in London.[16]

His apprenticeship to Lawrence was influential. During this period he was chosen to help complete some of Lawrence's portrait commissions and he travelled with him to several parts of Great Britain. A new painterly style begins to emerge in his works. This is not the place to discuss in detail Williams's later career after he left Britain for Rome in late 1826 but, before we return to the drawings he produced in Britain immediately after his time at the RA Schools it is worth including a brief summary to put the works of this little known artist in context and to provide a perspective to the industrial drawings he made at Merthyr Tydfil just before he travelled abroad.

In late 1826, encouraged by Thomas Lawrence and sponsored by Joseph Bailey, Williams left Britain for Italy where he was soon one of the British expatriate art establishment. There, except for occasional visits home, he spent most of the rest of his life in Italy. He exhibited regularly at the Royal Academy, however, and in the early 1830s at the Old Water Colour Society.[17] Many of the art establishment visited him in Rome where he achieved great success. His works after he left for Italy mainly exhibit a nineteenth-century romantic view of peasant life in the Roman campagna with a leaning to Arcadian scenes. The young William Blake Richmond (1842–1921) in a letter to his father from Rome in 1866 refers to Penry Williams as the head of the 'old ones' who continue the school of costume model painting.[18] In his *Dictionary of Landscape Painters* Maurice Grant sums up his view of this phase of Williams's working life, 'Royalty, nobility, collectors, dealers all clamoured for his paintings of Italian *festas*, peasants and *banditti*, undeterred by the slick and gaudy manner in which they were rendered … .'[19]

The majority of Williams's known works in the period between him leaving the RA Schools and his departure for Italy are watercolours. They include several portraits, landscape views taken in South Wales and an extensive commissioned set of paintings of Deepdene, Dorking, Surrey, the Seat of the banker Thomas Hope (1769–1830/31). The few landscapes in oil show a marked development in conception and execution from his earlier works. His *View of Lancaster*, for example, exhibited at the Royal Academy in 1826, shows him drawing on the late eighteenth-century approach to landscape painting in Britain introduced by Richard Wilson but Williams's figures in his rural landscapes of this period invariably know their place.[20] Recognising the needs and aspirations of his clients and patrons, Williams responds by creating images which express stability and security in the social order. This image-building avoided any suggestion of conflict and mostly gave support to the established social hierarchy. This is something to which Williams, as a young teenager, does not appear to have worried about when he responded in *The Merthyr Riots*.

On his return to Merthyr Tydfil in 1825, after his apprenticeship at the Royal Academy, Penry Williams produced two drawings of the ironworks at Merthyr Tydfil for William Crawshay II, *Cyfarthfa Iron Works*, and *Cyfarthfa Iron Works, Interior at Night*.[21] These detailed drawings in watercolour and body colour appear to have been commissioned to celebrate an extension to the ironworks and the addition of new rolling mills which were completed that year. They contribute significantly to our understanding of the layout and operations at one of the country's largest ironworks in the early nineteenth century. It is clear from them that there had been a step-change in Williams's artistic development while he was apprenticed to Sir Thomas Lawrence and being tutored at the Royal Academy Schools, but they also demonstrate the constraints that painting an industrial scene put on an artist at that time.

Both of the drawings are explicit in the technical details of the scenes portrayed. In the daytime scene of the *Cyfarthfa Iron Works* the view is taken from a point near William Crawshay II's recently completed Cyfarthfa Castle.[22] In the foreground Williams includes part of the outside of the new rolling mills and the head of the Glamorgan canal which ran from Merthyr Tydfil to Cardiff and was completed in 1794 before being extended to a sea lock in 1798. The canal improved the ironworks' position by allowing easier import to and export from the factory.[23] Penry Williams takes a broad view of the industrial landscape and sets it against the distant hills. The detail is precise and the panorama includes Cyfarthfa's seven furnaces, the buildings housing the steam engines which now powered the furnace bellows, the adjacent foundry buildings and part of the old aqueduct. In the distance, smoke and steam, rising from the furnaces, the steam engines and the mills, partially hide the hills beyond and pollute and darken the sky. Williams shows several hundred labourers and animals at work. Horse-drawn trucks haul material along a rail track for delivery to the rolling mills. This comprehensive scene is illuminating in its detail and appears to offer very little of invention. Williams, who would have been familiar with the ironworks at Merthyr Tydfil, responds with a view which displays the great extent of his patron's ironworks, and the efficiency and effectiveness of the large workforce he employs but Williams also reveals its impact on the natural landscape.

In the companion painting *Cyfarthfa Iron Works, Interior at Night* (Figure 4.3), Williams goes inside the new extension to the ironworks to view the rolling mills. The reverberatory furnaces, where iron was reheated ready for rolling are shown on the right of the picture with the rolling machinery shown in the centre and on the left. The impressive set of large span iron trusses overhead which support the roof, probably manufactured with great pride at Cyfarthfa, take on a prominent role in the painting. Spare parts for the rolling machinery are shown in the foreground below. This finished drawing was the first to show the inside of a large nineteenth-century industrial ironworks, so it is worth a short digression here to examine earlier paintings of foundry works to compare them with the Cyfarthfa painting. There were several at the end of the eighteenth century but few others until Penry Williams's view at Cyfarthfa in 1825.

Sketches and paintings by British artists such as George Robertson (1742–88), Julius Caesar Ibbetson and J.M.W. Turner in the 1780s and 1790s provide several pictorial responses by professional artists to conditions inside foundries in Britain in the early years of the Industrial Revolution. George Robertson's now lost painting *The Inside of a Smelting House at Broseley* was one of a set of six oil paintings of views taken at or near Coalbrookdale. An engraving of it by Wilson Lowry FRS (1762–1824) survives.[24] Foundrymen, small figures in the tall smelting house, are at work but the appearance of the moon in the picture does not just provide a counterpoint to the white light radiating from the molten iron flowing from the furnace, instead it is an acknowledgement that

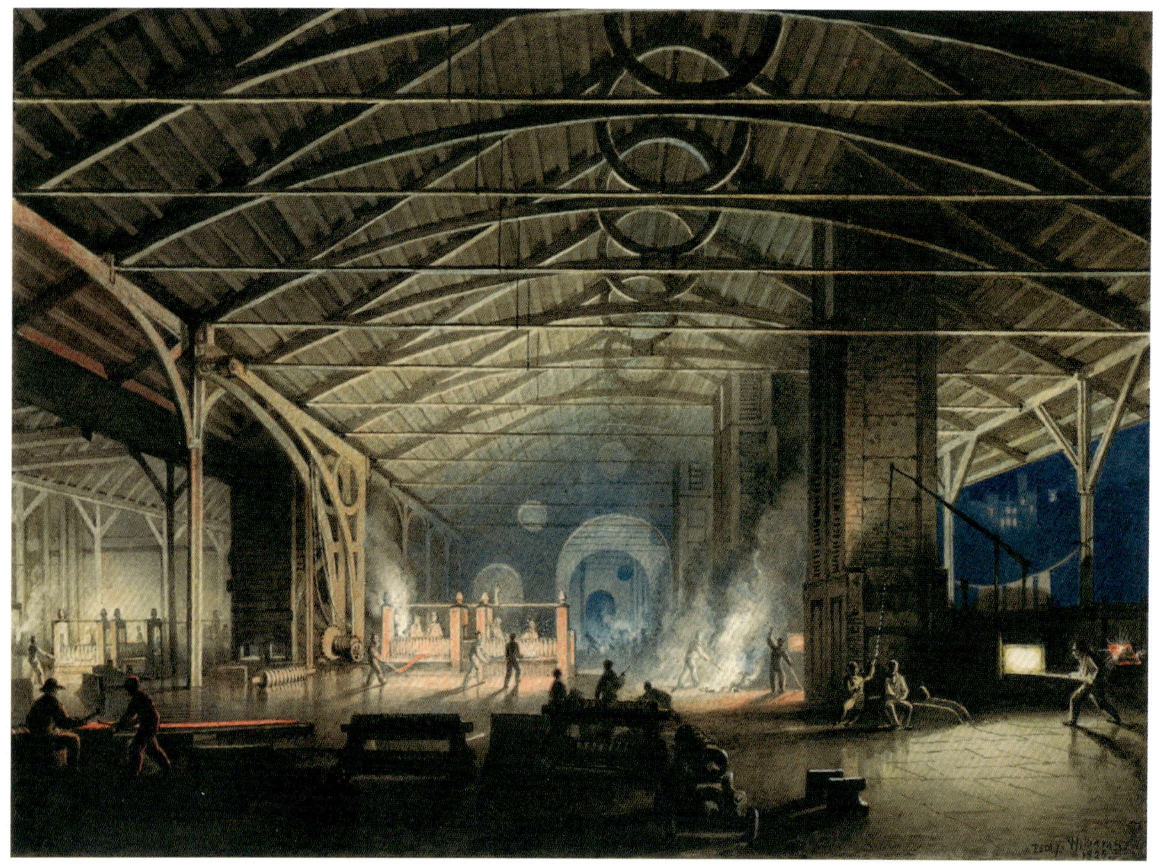

4.3 *Cyfarthfa Iron Works, Interior at Night*, 1825, by Penry Williams, watercolour and body colour on paper, 15.2 x 21.0 cm. Cyfarthfa Castle Museum and Art Gallery, Merthyr Tydfil.

these men are working at night. Ibbetson's more intimate painting of *An Iron Forge at Merthyr Tydfil* (Figure 4.2), salutes the fearless actions of the men at work there but in the images in Turner's sketchbooks he reveals his enthusiasm in recording this subject-matter.

On a double page of the *Wilson* sketchbook Turner includes a small watercolour, *Interior of a Forge, Making Anchors*, 1796–7 (Figure 4.4), in which a smith is shown reheating an anchor fluke at a furnace before it is taken to the anvil. The sketch shows other anchors in varying degrees of finish. Turner has worked up an image which captures the essence of the operations required: the heavy manual labour, the heat from the furnace and the dark recesses of the building. And a year or so later we have Turner's spectacular watercolour of *An Iron Foundry, or Cannon Foundry: ?Interior of Walker's Foundry at Rotherham or Conisbrough, c.1798* (Figure 4.5), which may have been based on a visit to the northeast of England. It presents the drama of what would have been an everyday operation at a large foundry. This is not a new workshop and the men shown at work all look assured in their tasks, whether at the furnace

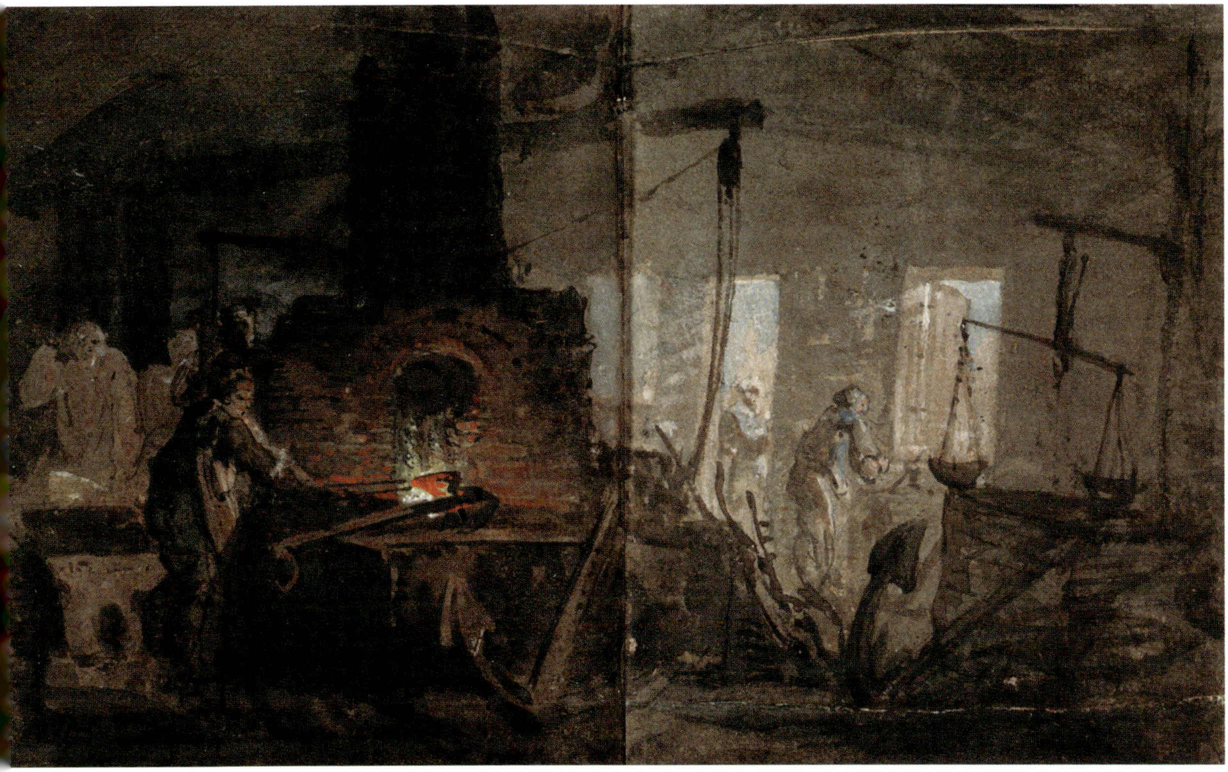

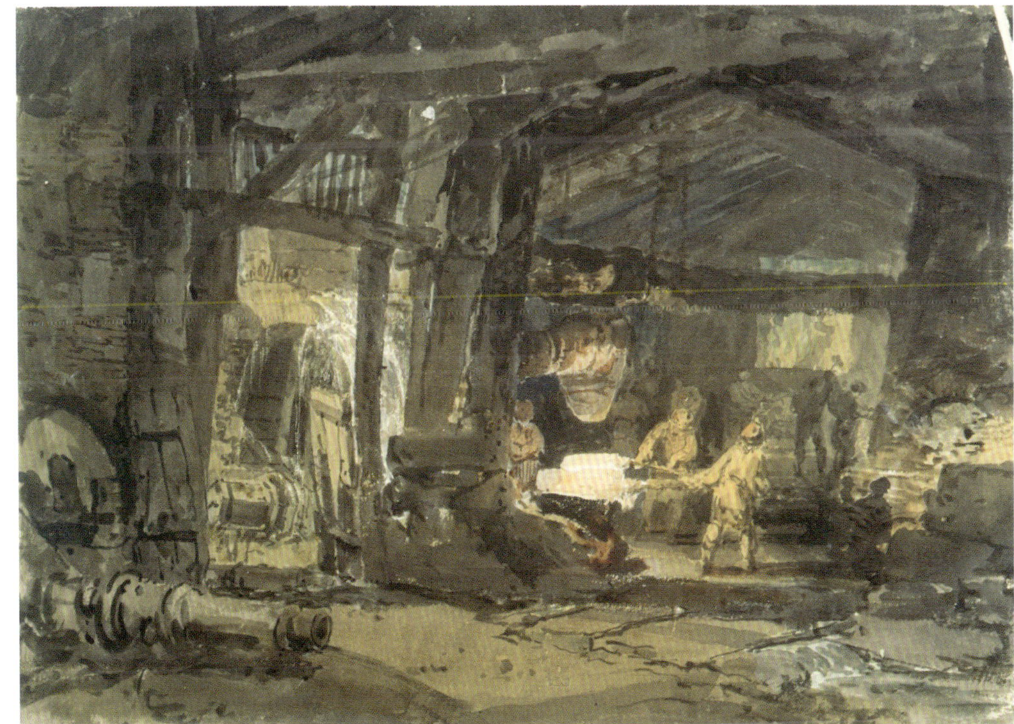

4.4 *Interior of a forge, making anchors*, 1796/7, by J.M.W. Turner, gouache, graphite and watercolour on paper, 22.6 x 9.3 cm. Tate, London.

4.5 *An Iron Foundry, or Cannon Foundry: ?Interior of Walker's Foundry at Rotherham or Conisbrough*, *c*.1798, by J.M.W. Turner, watercolour and graphite on paper, 24.7 x 34.5 cm. Tate, London.

hearth or at the forge. The focus of attention is the white-hot mass of metal being brought under the hammer. This is not the traditional tilt-hammer that we find in Joseph Wright's iron forge paintings nor the shingling hammer of the Ibbetson scene but a large compacting hammer which is being used to forge or weld blocks of iron together to form a large machine component such as a trunnion shaft.[25] The item in the left foreground is not a newly cast iron cannon but appears to be part of an old cannon which is to be re-used as scrap iron. In this drawing, Turner shows the massive hammer, probably weighing 2 or 3 tons, at work in the centre of the picture, the waterwheel in the distant workshop beyond and the channel of cooling water crossing the floor of the foundry. Turner's loose and fluid use of watercolour conveys the heat, light, noise and grime of the workshop. The figures almost appear to be moving. Turner takes the subject beyond simple representation. These late eighteenth-century drawings by Turner were not commissioned and provide an unvarnished picture of working conditions in the foundry and forge at the end of the eighteenth century. It was nearly thirty years later that Penry Williams's paintings at Cyfarthfa demonstrated the development and expansion of the iron industry that had taken place in Britain during that period.

We should not forget that the iron industry on the continent in the 1770s and 1780s was on a par with that in Britain. Pehr Hilleström (1732–1816) in Sweden and Léonard Defrance (1735–1816) in Belgium produced some large oil paintings of scenes taken inside foundries. One of Hilleström's paintings shows the activities at Adolf Ulrik Grill's forge at Södersfors with Grill himself, his back to the viewer, introducing some important visitors to his ironworks.[26] The artist reveals some rather frantic and dangerous working practices but this painting has clearly been commissioned by Grills to demonstrate his position as a successful employer of a workforce dedicated to his cause.[27] Defrance's paintings of the iron industry come from Liège, where he produced more than thirty oil paintings of forges and foundries in the late 1770s and the 1780s. In his *Interior of a Foundry*, 1789, where goods for agricultural and domestic use would have been produced, he shows the foundrymen carrying ladles of molten metal to the casting moulds.[28] The emphasis, as in the Hilleström painting, is on the smartly dressed visitors. In Defrance's painting, he portrays the foundry supervisor addressing the smartly dressed visitors, arms akimbo in an attitude which could be regarded as challenging and almost aggressive. The date, MDCCLXXXIX, under the words 'France, de Liege' can be seen being cast in the ironwork at the bottom right of the picture. It marks the outbreak of the French Revolution which spread to Liege in August 1789 where Defrance had his studio. Léonard Defrance was prominent in the revolutionary movement and became an official of the French revolutionary state.

These works by British and continental artists from the end of the eighteenth century present a variety of messages which provide a useful comparison with Penry Williams's work at Cyfarthfa. In Robertson's picture we see foundry men working at night, a practice that was almost unknown before industrialisation, in Ibbetson's we find him impressed by the courageous actions of the foundrymen and Turner, in his un-commissioned sketches, injects an intensity to the subject which bespeaks a reality but lifts the images beyond simple representation. From Hilleström and Defrance we get something very different. Hilleström's painting has been constructed to demonstrate his patron's success and Defrance's has subtly turned the scene into a propagandist image on the eve of the French Revolution in 1789.[29] Few paintings of this subject-matter emerged in the first quarter of the nineteenth century until those of Penry Williams at Cyfarthfa.

In *Cyfarthfa Iron Works, Interior at Night*, Penry Williams serves his patron William Crawshay II with a fine drawing of the rolling mills but he would have faced a difficult decision in choosing an appropriate view of the interior of the new industrial buildings. Both he and his patron would have been familiar with the rigid geometry and details of the structures and the size of buildings which dwarf the men and boys employed at the furnaces and the rolling machinery. Williams must have asked himself whether he should focus, as earlier artists had done, on the furnaces or on the machinery or whether he should make play with the ironworkers at their several tasks. He does none of these. Instead he looks up and gives half the painted area to the large span wrought-iron tied-arch trusses which support the roof.

This structure was an innovative, cutting-edge design for the period and Williams celebrates this in his painting making use of the geometry of the building. The effect, however, is to reduce the importance of the actions of those working in the rolling mills and we are forced to refocus to take in the operations at hand. Here the furnaces and rolling mills are drawn in great detail but Williams's figures – the furnace-men and ironworkers lose their individuality. In this industrial landscape they are components of a wider enterprise, busily and efficiently performing their allotted tasks, apparently unaware of either the intense heat of the furnaces or the sparks flying from the red-hot rolled-iron bar.

In this painting Williams's primary purpose has been to celebrate his patron's investment in the new works and its operations at night but he introduces a further element which adds another angle to our view of his patron William Crawshay II. At the far right of the picture we can see through the open wall of the rolling mills to the hill beyond and to the outline and lights of Crawshay's recently completed Cyfarthfa Castle which overlooks the ironworks. Williams presents an image of an apparently harmoniously functioning ironworks running like clockwork but is he also revealing the autocratic nature of the ironmasters in South Wales? Is he signalling, intentionally or otherwise, through the image of the ironworkers on the nightshift dwarfed by their surroundings, the beginning of the underlying relationship which underpinned the unrest that was to erupt again a few years later in Merthyr Tydfil? Penry Williams, in satisfying his patron with this image, reveals William Crawshay II as an unseen but not to be forgotten presence, distancing himself from the majority of his employees. Crawshay's castle serves as an emblem of power and prestige and an investment in Crawshay's status while his employees toil through the night; the rich man in his castle, the poor man at the gate.

Whether Williams, recently back from the Royal Academy Schools in London, was raising questions over the disparities between William Crawshay II and the men and women he employed in his extensive ironworks we do not know but he would have been aware from the 1816 strike that Crawshay had to deal with the ups and downs of the iron industry. In 1825 nearly 5,000 people were on the payroll at Cyfarthfa and although the trading conditions then had improved considerably since 1816, five years after Williams painted *Cyfarthfa Iron Works, Interior at Night*, the conditions had again weakened alarmingly.

In late May 1831, Crawshay, repeating his action of 1816, gave notice to those employed at the ironworks at Cyfarthfa that they would suffer a reduction in pay. This sparked riots again in Merthyr Tydfil. Seventy 93rd Highlanders were immediately sent from Brecon. The High Sheriff read the Riot Act. William Crawshay II and J.J. Guest implored rioters to desist, but to no avail. Workers from the surrounding ironworks and collieries gathered together and reports suggest that up to 20,000 men faced the 110 Highlanders, fifty Glamorganshire militia and 300 Yeoman cavalry who had been brought in to secure the town. Twenty-three workers were killed on the spot and many of the military were injured. Rioters destroyed the house of the Court of Requests, some adjacent buildings and furniture, and took to the burning of books.[30] Crawshay gave way and restored the existing wage levels but by doing so was strongly criticised by other employers in the region for encouraging other miners and manual workers to demand increases.[31] Crawshay was stung by this criticism of his perceived weakness in backing down and he responded by writing defiantly a lengthy defence in an article *The Late Riots of Merthyr-Tydfil*, which he had published:

> … the trifling reduction I required, was not founded on rashness
> or avarice, but upon the most mature and rational calculation of
> circumstances; and the fact of my not having complied with the
> demands of my men, but openly defied them while in a state of
> tumult … is a proof that the timidity you attribute to me [in restoring
> the wage cut], is unfounded. … my conduct at all times to my men

has been guided by the most liberal and humane feelings … . The
weight of blame where it is justly due is upon the men themselves;
and not upon the Masters, the Magistrates, or the soldiers, or on my
individual head.[32]

Penry Williams had an intimate knowledge of the iron industry and as an artist familiar with Cyfarthfa and with commissions from Crawshay was content as few other artists of the day to display his talents on industrial subject-matter. In his Cyfarthfa ironworks drawings, he brings a directness of approach to his work but one which raises the questions that were being asked of the conditions that ironworkers and miners were facing in the country. A widening gap was developing between the wealthy industrialists and entrepreneurs and their employees as the iron industry expanded in the nineteenth century.

Illustrations and paintings, like those of Cyfarthfa, were by the early part of the nineteenth century beginning to be commissioned by factory owners and industrialists keen to leave a record of their achievements. They were to become a feature of the mid- and late nineteenth century. The majority of these paintings, by minor artists, were made to adorn the walls of the houses and the offices of those who owned the industrial complexes. The finely executed drawings and paintings by Penry Williams, who had had a long association with Cyfarthfa and who had filled several sketchbooks with views of the ironworks, fall into this category. However, Williams in his Cyfarthfa paintings of 1825 and of other ironworks was perhaps also beginning to recognise the social impact of the Industrial Revolution and the polluting effects of the industries in South Wales.[33] Eighteen months after completing the Cyfarthfa drawings Penry Williams, escaping from Merthyr Tydfil, was writing to Sir Thomas Lawrence from Rome and reporting that he had been in Switzerland where he had '… collected a great number of sketches in Landscape and of the Peasantry, … the country is truly Picturesque and romantic …'. Six months later he was painting pictures of Italian Peasants and views of Rome from the Barberini Gardens, and settling into life in Italy.[34]

Penry Williams is today a little-known nineteenth-century artist, the success of whose industrial paintings stem from his early life experiences at Merthyr Tydfil where the iron industry, at his doorstep, had developed on the edge of the South Wales coalfields in a region which lay close to sources of iron ore. The principal sources of *non-ferrous* ores for the metal industries, however, were to be found principally in Cornwall and on the Isle of Anglesey. In the next chapter we turn to the copper mines on Anglesey, to an oil painting by the young William Havell, and to drawings by artists who visited the mines there and took an interest in the copper industry.

Notes

1   Letter from Michael Faraday to J.J. Guest Esq., Tuesday 20 July 1819. Dafydd Tomos, 1987, p. 147.

2   *Crawshay's Cyfarthfa Ironworks*, 1817; *Cyfarthfa Ironworks seen from the West*, c.1820; *Cyfarthfa Ironworks, Aqueduct*, c.1820; *Cyfarthfa Ironworks, Watkin George's Water-wheel*, c.1820; *Cyfarthfa Ironworks*, 1820; and *Ynysfach Ironworks*, 1820, all by Penry Williams.

3   In 1803 the Cyfarthfa ironworks was the largest in Great Britain. Of the sixteen furnaces at Merthyr Tydfil in 1803, six belonged to the Crawshays at Cyfarthfa.

4   *Sherborne Mercury*, 6 October 1800, p. 3.

5   *London Courier and Evening Gazette*, 21 October 1816, p. 2.

6   *Public Ledger and Daily Advertiser*, 25 October 1816, pp. 2–3.

7   There are two versions of this painting: CCM.30,991 and CCM.31,991 at Cyfarthfa Castle Museum. Also see Derrick Pritchard Webley, 1997, p. 22.

8   1816/1817 saw Luddite agitations, the Prince Regent robbed, the Blanketeers' demonstration and suspension of the Habeas Corpus Act.

9   Derrick Pritchard Webley, 1997, pp. 12 and 22 and nn. 5 and 6, p. 32. discusses the origins of Penry Williams's *The Merthyr Riots*. He records correspondence which suggests that support for Williams came from the Welsh printer-publisher William Williams (c.1795–1844) and George Scale of Llwydcoed iron foundry, Aberdare.

10   See *Richard Crawshay (1739–1810)*, c.1796, by Richard Wilson of Birmingham.

11   E.g. *A Bridge at Cyfarthfa, Iron, Merthir Tidville*, c.1789, by Julius Caesar Ibbetson. This view is probably of the Taf Fechan or Taf Fawr rivers which drain from the Brecon Beacons and which flowed near to Cyfarthfa. At the end of the eighteenth and in the early nineteenth centuries water from the Taf Fechan was used to power the 48-ft diameter Aeolus waterwheel which drove the bellows at the Cyfarthfa iron works.

12   *Cyfarthfa Works and Waterwheel*, c.1795; and *The Head of the Glamorganshire Canal at the Ironworks*, c.1795, both by William Pamplin.

13   *View of Cyfarthfa Ironworks ?from the North-West*, 1798, by J.M.W. Turner, TB XLI-2, Tate, London. See also TB XLI-1, 3 and 4, Tate, London. Andrew Wilton, catalogue entry, May 2013, in David Blayney Brown (ed.), *J.M.W. Turner: Sketchbooks, Drawings and Watercolours, Tate Research Publications, April 2015*.

14   *The Aqueduct, Cyfarthfa*, c.1820, by Penry Williams.

15   Derrick Pritchard Webley, 1997, pp. 14–15. Joseph Bailey, later Lord Glanusk. Derrick Pritchard Webley, 1997, n. 17, p. 32.

16   Derrick Pritchard Webley, 1997, p. 16, suggests that Williams '… had probably been enrolled as his [Lawrence's] pupil-assistant, the customary fee being paid by the patrons; a relationship that must have continued through his time at the RA Schools'.

17   As a long-time expatriate he could not be elected to the Royal Academy.

18   Correspondence: W.B. Richmond, 123 via Felice, Rome to George Richmond, W.B. Richmond papers, 1866.

19   Maurice Harold Grant, 1952, p. 222.

20   *A View of Lancaster*, 1826, by Penry Williams.

21   *Cyfarthfa Iron Works*, 1825, and *Cyfarthfa Iron Works, Interior at Night*, 1825, both by Penry Williams.

22   Construction of Cyfarthfa Castle, designed by Robert Lugar, began in the spring of 1824 and was completed twelve months later. See Margaret Stewart Taylor, 1967, p. 43. William Crawshay II's father, William Crawshay I, who ran the family's iron-trade business in London, disapproved of the building of the castle. See Anon., 'The Welsh Iron Trade' in *Cambrian Quarterly Magazine and Celtic Repertory*, 1830, p. 249.

23   *The Head of the Glamorganshire Canal at the Ironworks*, c.1795, by William Pamplin also shows Richard Crawshay's house, Cyfarthfa House.

24   Six engravings from the paintings by George Robertson and published in 1788 by John and Josiah Boydell, London. The engravings by Francis Chesham, James Fittler and Wilson Lowry are *Lincoln Hill and the Iron Bridge, Coalbrookdale, The Iron Bridge, Coalbrookdale, from the Madeley Side, The Iron Bridge Coalbrookdale from Lincoln Hill* (Robertson's original oil painting of this is at The Ironbridge Gorge Museum), *The Mouth of a Coal Pit near Broseley, The Iron Work for Casting Cannon*, and *The Inside of a Smelting House at Broseley*, 1788, engraved by Wilson Lowry.

25   *An Iron Forge*, 1772, and *Iron Forge viewed from Without*, 1773, by Joseph Wright of Derby.

26   *In the Anchor-forge at Södersfors. The Smiths Hard at Work*, 1782, by Pehr Hilleström.

27   M. Abkund, 'Joseph Wright of Derby in a northern light; Swedish comparisons and connections: Pehr Hilleström & Elias Martin', pp. 33–40, *The British Art Journal*, 2010, XI (1).

28   *Interior of a Foundry*, 1789, by Léonard Defrance.

29   Also see a set of fifty watercolour drawings of 1778 by the master founder Jan Verbruggen [or by his son Pieter] which show the stages of cannon and mortar manufacture at the Royal Brass Foundry, Woolwich. M.H. Jackson and C. de Beer, 1974.

30   *Cambrian Newspaper*, 12 June 1831.

31   *Observer Newspaper*, Sunday 12 June 1831.

32   William Crawshay, 1831.

33   See also *South Wales Industrial Landscape (Rhymney)*, c.1825, by Penry Williams.

34   Correspondence, Penry Williams, 39 Via della Mercede to Sir Thomas Lawrence, 28 March 1827. *Royal Academy of Arts Archive*.

5 William Havell and the Welsh Copper Industry

In 1778 John Whitehurst FRS, a distinguished member of the Lunar Society of Birmingham, recognising that underlying forces had been active in forming the body of Earth but struggling to reconcile his conclusions with his religious faith, published an *Inquiry into the Original State and Formation of the Earth*.[1] In this, Whitehurst included a cross-section of Lincoln Hill near Coalbrookdale, showing the extent of the coal and limestone strata there, providing valuable details for the iron industry. A few years later, Joseph Wright of Derby in his portrait of Whitehurst shows him with his drawing of a cross-section of Matlock Tor, Derbyshire, indicating the important role he had played in revealing the geological strata in the lead mines and caves of that region.[2]

In 1785, following nearly a quarter of a century's research, the natural scientist, geologist and Scotsman James Hutton FRSE (1726–97) in his ground-breaking work *A Theory of the Earth* revealed the results of his study of Earth's evolution. Hutton describes the impact that natural processes such as erosion, transportation, deposition, consolidation and uplift had had on the morphology of the Earth's surface. He challenged the commonly held view of Earth's age and drew attention to the great and continuous forces at work in the creation of an ever-changing landscape.[3] A better understanding of Earth's physical make-up began to emerge as surveyors and geologists began systematically to record details of the strata exposed during the construction of new canals and cuttings, and as they examined the rocks and metallic ores from the deeper strata. William 'Strata' Smith (1769–1839), the 'father of English geology', was among the surveyors to record these details and in 1815 prepared the first national geological map of Britain, *A Delineation of the Strata of England and Wales, with part of Scotland; exhibiting the collieries and mines, … and the varieties of soil according to the variations in the substrata … .*[4]

These geological and man-made features proved alluring, encouraging tourists and some artists during the summer months to visit mines and quarries to see how mineral ores and building materials were being abstracted and processed. Some artists were inspired by the effect that mining and quarrying was beginning to have on natural landforms and by the impressive structures that appeared when the mineral ores of copper, tin, lead and other building materials were removed.[5] For those making sketching tours, watercolour proved convenient as a medium. We find John Webber visiting the Odin lead mine at Castleton, Derbyshire in 1789, William Payne (*c.*1760–1830) at several stone quarries in Devon in the early 1790s and J.M.W. Turner at stone and slate quarries between 1795 and 1813. Thomas Rowlandson sketched extensively in Cornwall in the early 1800s and was fascinated by the Delabole slate quarry and Carclaze tin mine near St Austell but it is, perhaps, the geologist Thomas Webster (1772–1844) in Sir Henry Englefield's *Description of the principal picturesque beauties, antiquities and geologic phœnomena of the Isle of Wight*, published in 1816, who confirms the contemporary fascination with geological structures.[6]

The Parys and Mona copper mines on the Isle of Anglesey proved to have a wide appeal and regularly attracted visitors in the summer months. The mines were one of the principal sources of copper ore in Britain in the latter part of the eighteenth century. Ores could be extracted in part from open-cast excavations there providing competition for the Cornish mines where copper ores were exclusively extracted via underground shafts and adits. The Parys and Mona mines had been worked in both the Roman and Elizabethan periods but the mines' fame and importance grew when a valuable source of ore, the Great Lode (or vein) with 3.5 per cent copper content, was discovered in 1768 and the significant potential of the mine was proved. The mines were conveniently close to the island's port at Amlwch from where the ore could either be shipped to Swansea for processing, sent to be smelted at works near Liverpool or transported onwards via the Sankey navigation canal to works close to the coalfields at St Helens in Lancashire.[7] The mines were the largest copper mines in the world at the turn of the century.

John 'Warwick' Smith (1749–1831) and Julius Caesar Ibbetson, sometimes working side by side, visited Anglesey on several occasions during the early 1790s to sketch the unusual forms of the mines, and the men, women and children working there. Captain and Mrs Hanmer, who visited in 1819, took great interest in the processing of the ore and the various minerals that were to be found. They describe how 'The beautiful ore called Peacock Copper is formed by water running over iron, on its way down the mine, which becoming impregnated with iron, turns the copper all kinds of colours.'[8] 'Warwick' Smith, in particular, produced some fine atmospheric watercolour drawings of the mines and the surrounding landscape, capturing the light and these subtle colour variations. Drawings by the Frenchman François Louis Thomas Francia (1772–1839), who visited the mines at the turn of the century, show the development of the complex underground workings. However, none of

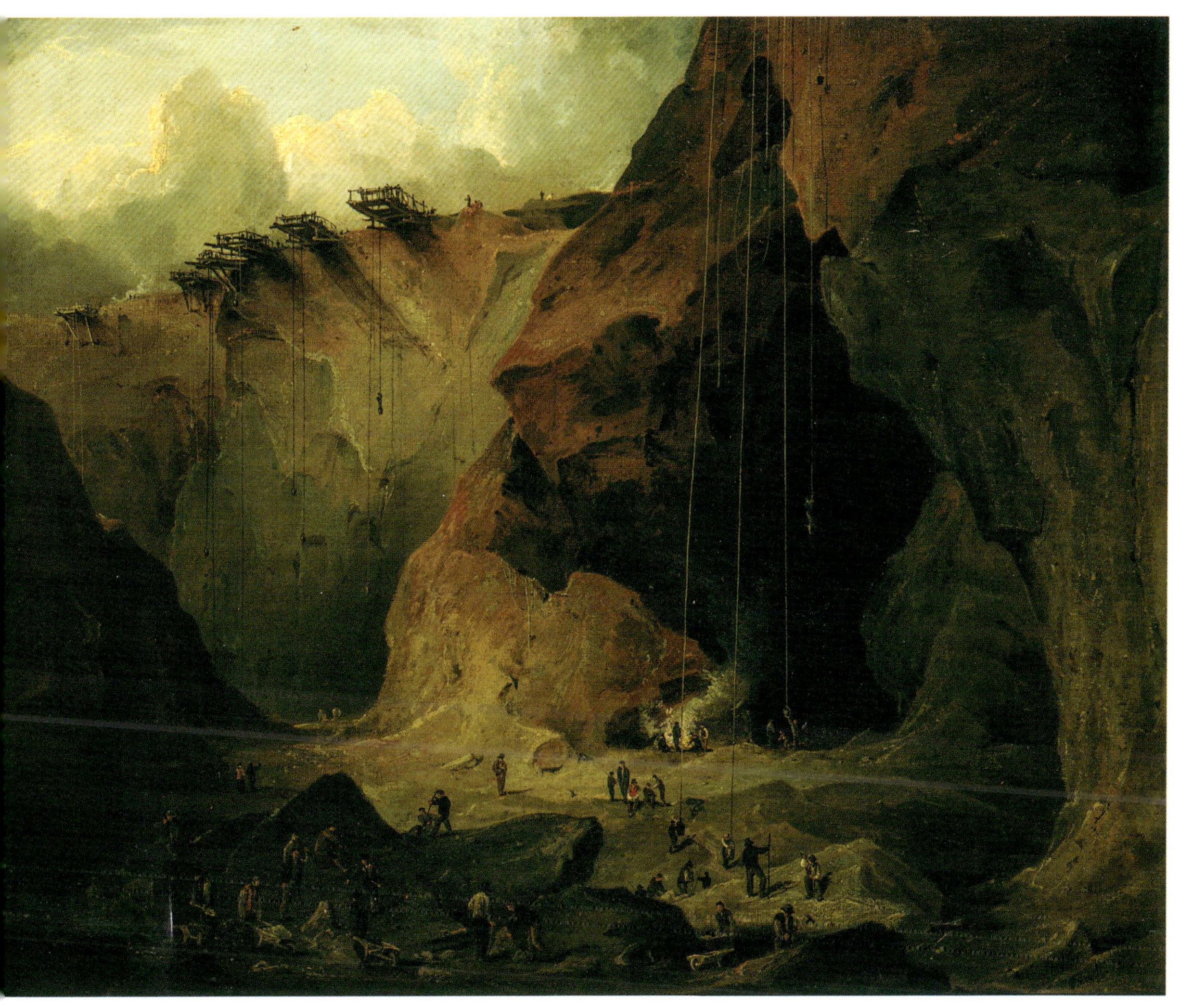

5.1 *Parys Mountain Copper Mine*, c.1803/4, by William Havell, oil on canvas, 84.5 x 104.5 cm. Collection of The Marquess of Anglesey.

these artists developed their views as oil paintings and we must turn to the young William Havell (1782–1857) who in his *Parys Mountain Copper Mine*, *c.*1803–04 (Figure 5.1), takes a view of the main body of the mine and develops a larger and grander picture revealing the immensity of the excavation.

William Havell was born in Reading, Berkshire, one of fourteen children of Luke Havell, a drawing master at Reading Grammar School, and his wife Charlotte, and one of a family of artists. His father at first discouraged him from becoming a professional artist but later relented in the face of his son's enthusiasm and obvious talent. Greater attention was being given to British landscape painting at this time. It had been stimulated by the return to Britain from Italy in 1757 of Richard Wilson and then through the artist and travel writer Rev. William Gilpin and the contemporary discussions and debates on the picturesque, the sublime and the beautiful.[9] William Havell, at first working close to home under these influences, soon began to develop his skills as a landscape painter and widen his range.[10]

Havell's painting of the Parys copper mine on the Isle of Anglesey arises from his first trip to Wales in 1802. It is unclear what took him to Anglesey during his tour of North Wales. In *A History of the Old Water-Colour Society*, John Lewis Roget relates how Havell met the watercolourists and brothers John (1778–1842) and Cornelius Varley (1781–1873), the painter Joshua Cristall (1767–1847) and the geologist Thomas Webster at Dolgelly, as well as a party who were making a geological tour through North Wales. The party included the chemist and mineralogist Arthur Aikin (1773–1854), one of the founders of the Geological Society, and his sister, the novelist and feminist Lucy Aikin (1781–1864).[11] Perhaps he just joined this group to visit the Parys and Mona mines but it is possible that the 2nd Earl of Uxbridge, who owned the Mona mine and had property not far from Reading, may have been aware of the Havell family of artists and commissioned William to paint a view of the mines. The painting is now in the collection of his descendants. Havell's *Parys Mountain Copper Mine* is the only one of his works in which he confronts an industrial scene and one of only a few in which he shows men and women at work.

Thomas Pennant (1726–98), the naturalist and traveller who visited Anglesey in the 1780s, reported that at that time the Parys and adjacent Mona mines employed about 1,200 men and women.[12] Later records show that by 1806 the number working there had shrunk to 200. When Havell visited the Parys mine in 1802, it was already becoming difficult to find profitable areas from which the relatively cheap open-cast ore could be extracted and both the Anglesey mines and the competing mines in Cornwall were suffering from the impact of a dip in the demand for copper. Havell's painting reflects this decline in output but it does not fail to convey the effect that this 'immense excavation', as Michael Faraday describes it, had on visitors.[13]

From his chosen viewpoint Havell captures the vastness of the excavation and the colour variations of the exposed surfaces. He finds a spot for his view high above the figures breaking out and removing the copper ore and well below the timber platforms which overhang the edge of the mine from which buckets and labourers descend and ascend. It is tempting to suggest that Havell made his original sketch or sketches for his final painting after being lowered in a cradle on the end of a rope from one of the working platforms. He finds a place where the view of the massive wall of the excavation and the ant-like figures at work is comparable with that from the upper circle of a theatre.

The sublime natural landscape of Snowdonia was a stone's throw from the Parys mine but Havell conveys the awesome grandeur of a man-made landscape where one may marvel at the impact that the miners, through a multitude of small actions, have had on the natural morphology. However, we may also be tempted to question the entrepreneurial spirits and driving forces behind this business enterprise and the relative financial returns to labour and management.

An unidentified traveller visiting Anglesey in 1792 writes in his journal for Tuesday 13 August:

> View'd the Paris [sic] & Mona Mountains – Smelting houses &c.
> a wonderful production of Nature & of equal advantage – Men
> poorly paid – not more than 14[d] p. day [£18 p.a.] – ab. 1500 persons
> employed. Black bread & water principal diet. The most wretched
> and ignorant poor workers that can be Conceived in human forms.
> The whole of the Mona L[d] Uxbridge's – W[ch] included gives him ¾ of
> the whole profit said to be 40,000 £.p.an – Mr Williams his agent is
> very rich – as is Mr Hughes formerly a Welch Curate … .[14]

Lord Uxbridge referred to by Pennant, above, was Henry Bayley, Lord Paget (1744–1812), who was created the 1st Earl of Uxbridge in 1784. He had taken over the Parys and Mona mines as part of an inheritance on his father's side in 1782 and was the father of Henry William Paget, the 2nd Earl of Uxbridge and 1st Marquess of Anglesey (1768–1854), and the Duke of Wellington's cavalry commander at the Battle of Waterloo. The 'very rich' agent mentioned is Thomas Williams (1737–1802),[15] a successful lawyer from Llanidan, Anglesey who, through his association with the Parys Mine Company and his links with the coal masters of the St Helens District established a successful and profitable copper smelting works adjacent to the Sankey navigation canal at Ravenhead, Lancashire in 1780.

Matthew Boulton had several dealings with Thomas Williams over the supply of copper from the mine for the manufacture of coins and medals. On 10 June 1785 he wrote to James Watt expressing admiration of Williams's energy, comparing him with the Cornish adventurers who, he said, competed with the Anglesey mines, taking their profits at the expense of the Cornish mine workers.[16] However, five years later in 1790, James Watt wrote to Thomas Wilson, one of the Boulton and Watt Partnership's agents, writing: 'Let me advise you to be extremely cautious in your dealings with W [Thomas Williams] he is a perfect tyrant and not over tenacious of his word and will screw damned hard when he has got anybody in his vice.'[17] A year later, Boulton described Williams as: 'the despotick [sic] sovereign of the copper trade'.[18] Thomas Williams became one of the most formidable industrialists of the time with control not only over the Parys and Mona mines on Anglesey but also the Cornish Metal Company, warehouses in London, Birmingham and Liverpool, brass mills in Buckinghamshire and the Chester & North Wales Bank. He had substantial interests in the Stanley Smelting Company, and in copper production at Ravenhead, Lancashire, at Greenfield and Holywell, Flintshire, and at Upper Bank, Swansea.[19]

Swansea was at the centre of the copper processing business, importing ore from both Cornwall and Anglesey. Thomas Williams's export businesses, some linked with the slave trade which he openly supported, maintained links with Europe, North America and Africa where copper Manillas (bangles used as currency in Africa and the slave trade) and Neptunes (salt evaporation pans) were sent, and the Caribbean where copper plate and finished items were shipped for use in sugar refining works and rum distilleries. By the end of the century, Williams controlled one-fifth of British copper smelting and had interests in about half the capital invested in the trade.[20] The portrait (Figure 5.2)

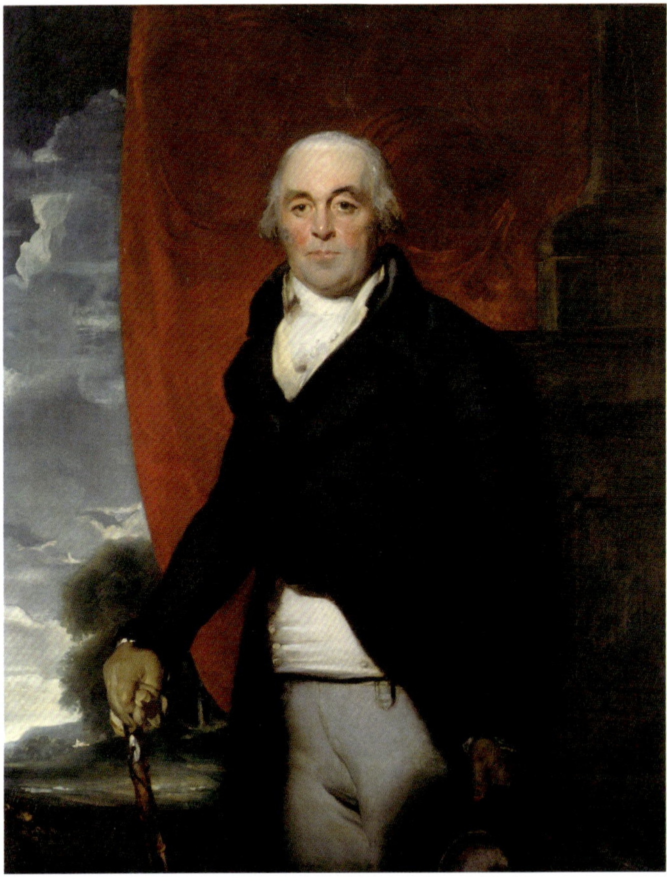

5.2 *Thomas Williams*, c.1792–5, by Sir Thomas Lawrence, oil on canvas, 127.5 x 102.1 cm. National Museum of Wales, Cardiff.

by Sir Thomas Lawrence (1769–1830) shows this tough influential entrepreneur at the age of about sixty.

The portrait was completed a few years after Thomas Williams, with a country seat at Bisham in Berkshire, had become the Member of Parliament for Great Marlow, a constituency he held from 1790 until his death in 1802. Lawrence portrays him, no doubt very much as Williams would have wished, as the established landowner but omits any attributes that would have linked him to the copper industries and the commerce through which he had built his fortune. Havell's *Parys Mountain Copper Mine* was painted some ten years after Lawrence's portrait, just after Thomas Williams's death. When Havell visited the mine, he was to come across an established industry where the workforce used a primitive mining technology. The operations relied principally on manual labour where the employer and his agent managed the risk arising from the fluctuations in the demand for copper by managing the amount of labour employed.

Havell's painting of the Parys copper mine came at the time of a downturn in the demand for copper and is among the few works by artists of this period whose sketches, drawings and paintings provide a record of the men, women and children at work in an industrial landscape. However, questions asked by art historian John Barrell of eighteenth-century images of the rural poor and agricultural workers may be relevant to Havell's images of those working at the Parys copper mine.[21] Are illusory images being employed by William Havell in his *Parys Mountain Copper Min*e to show a contented and harmonious industrial society?

Havell first and foremost seems to have been fascinated, as were other artists visiting the mine, by the sight of the ore being winched from the Parys mine and of materials and men being lowered from or raised to the surface by rope. These were all men and boys, as women were only allowed to work at the surface of the Parys mine. The mining operations clearly required planning, organisation and the employment of a variety of labouring skills. At the time of the painting there had been a downturn in the copper industry and the reduced demand for labour at the Parys mine would have led to many workers being laid off. On the face of it Havell appears to present a view of harmonious operations at the mine but it is one in which he also recognises this downturn. The labourers in the bottom left of the picture in the body of the mine, confined to the shadows, are vigorously and almost frantically breaking out the ore, taking it by barrow and transferring it to buckets which are winched from the bottom of the pit to the staging (or platforms) which overhang the sides of the excavation. Havell also hints, in the centre of the painting, at the consequences of the fall in the demand for copper. Silhouetted against the light, we find a small group of apparently depressed and unemployed labourers. Havell does not shrink from presenting an impoverished and needy workforce in the body of the mine.

Havell was painting at a time when the rationality of Enlightenment thought was being challenged by an incipient romantic movement. Pre-Enlightenment concepts of heaven and hell, however, were still very much alive. At the Parys mine Havell allows us to react with awe at the vast man-made excavation and the men at work, some descending from the heavens above like guardian angels, but he also finds what seems to be a 'hell-like' entrance to the mine's underground workings at the bottom right of the painting. In the view he takes, he appears to hint that, impressive as man's exploitation of the earth's resources at the Parys mine may seem, it is as nothing when compared with the awesome power of God in heaven above or the frightening prospect of an unknown hell which man has begun to explore in the subterranean world below. He places depressed-looking individuals and a group of men on the edge of the shadow in the centre of the painting in the body of the mine where, in a place between heaven and hell, there is no certainty.

The entrance to the underground workings at the Parys mine in Havell's painting is reminiscent of Peak's Hole or The Devil's Arse at Castleton, made famous in the then-frequently revived pantomime, *The Wonders of Derbyshire*, devised by Philippe-Jacques de Loutherbourg and Richard Brinsley Sheridan. This is a comparison unlikely to have been lost on William Havell. Peak's Hole was visited and sketched by several artists during the eighteenth century, including several Royal Academicians.[22] The landscape painter and diarist Joseph Farington (1747–1821) and John Constable (1776–1837) both visited the entrance to the subterranean cavern in 1801, the year before Havell explored the Parys mine.

Michael Faraday records in his journal his visit to the underground workings at the Parys mine in 1819. Faraday was a member of the Protestant Sandemanian sect, one where belief in Christianity was based on the New Testament but which excluded any institutional influence of an established church. Whereas in his scientific research Faraday was prepared to question everything, his religious life was one of complete acceptance. The Parys mine offered a challenge. He writes of his visit to the mine and the precarious descent down narrow passageways via a series of ladders into the bowels of the earth.

In his detailed and rational description, he recounts his experience of the candlelit journey and where explosives were being used in the excavation.

Faraday, led by the miner Captain Leaman, who had told Faraday that he had chosen the shaft because 'it was the most <u>comfortable</u>', eventually arrive at a great chasm more than 100 m below the surface:

> This had been a fine bunch of ore and there were 6 or 7 men with their candles working in it. We did not go down but putting our light aside laid our heads to the aperture and viewed this admirable Cimmerian scene for some time with great pleasure, the continual explosions on all sides increasing the effect.[23]

The dimly lit subterranean chambers would have been enough to strike terror in the minds of those unfamiliar with underground workings and we find Faraday expressing this in his journal:

> Here again it became very narrow and we had in one corner to lay on our backs and wriggle through a rough slanting opening not more than 12 or 14 inches wide. The whole mountain being above us and threatening to crush us to pieces.[24]

François Louis Thomas Francia responds to the remarkable arrangement of the mine shafts at the Parys mine and the unusual chiaroscuro and compositional opportunities presented by the candlelit passageways. In a watercolour *Parys Copper Mine, Anglesey*, c.1800, he illustrates the precarious sets of ladders giving access to the mine and the *ad hoc* disposition of timber supports (Figure 5.3).[25]

John 'Warwick' Smith, who visited the mines frequently, generally presents views at the top of the excavation. His *Junction of Mona and Parys Mountain Copper Mines* reveals the desolation of the site where the tiny distant figures he shows at work reinforce this impression.[26] Sir Richard Colt Hoare, writing in his journal in 1801, recalls the description of the area written by Giraldus de Barri some 600 years earlier, '*Sit autem Mona arida tellus et saxosa, deformis aspectu et inamoena*' [Mona is an arid and rocky region, of a dismal and ugly form] and Captain and Mrs Hanmer describe the road to the mine as 'flat, ugly and rough, the walls on each side are composed of shale of various hues'.[27] A visit to the mines and their surroundings today confirms these views, as well as the unusual light and colours of this corner of the Anglesey landscape which John 'Warwick' Smith captures in his watercolours.

Julius Caesar Ibbetson, 'Warwick' Smith's sometime companion, at the Parys and Mona mines painted an abundance of scenes of rural life. These have earned him nothing more than a rather modest reputation as an artist but most of his drawings contain groups of lively figures at work carrying

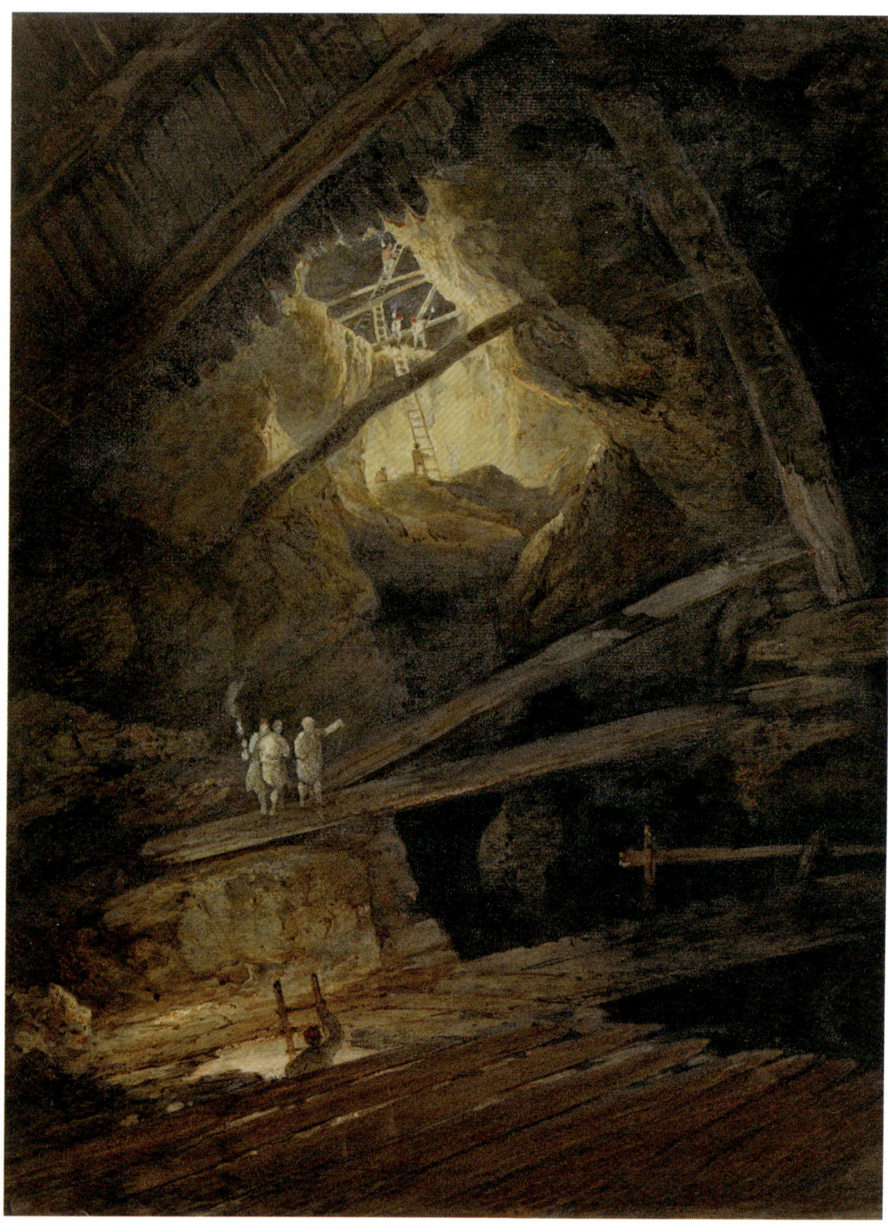

5.3 *Parys Copper Mine, Anglesey*, c.1800, by François Louis Thomas Francia, watercolour over graphite with gum Arabic on paper, 53.0 x 41.1 cm. The Morgan Library & Museum, New York.

out their daily tasks and provide an important picture of the period. They give him 'a greater significance than the more conventional view of him as a trivial painter of amusing genre subjects'.[28] His interest in the occupations of men and women is shown in several of his watercolour sketches of activities at the Parys and Mona mines. In *Miners at Menai* (Figure 5.4), he shows the 'cobbers', principally women and boys, who were employed to break up the copper ore once it had been lifted from the mine to the

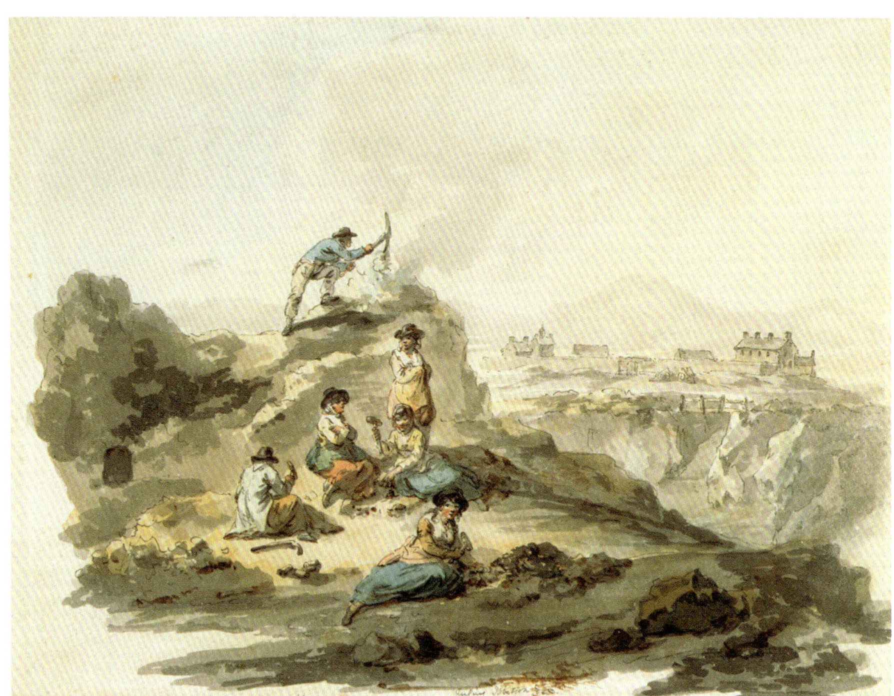

platforms at the top. Ibbetson travelled widely in Wales and the drawing was probably made during a visit to the mine with John 'Warwick' Smith in 1792.[29]

Several visitors to the Parys and Mona mines in the early eighteenth century mention the cobbers. Michael Faraday, more than twenty-five years after Ibbetson's drawing, describes in his journal for Thursday 29 July 1819 a group he came across when visiting the mine:

> The ore is raised from the mine by the whimsy [whim] in large heavy masses and is then thrown over a stage onto the ground below where it comes in charge of the cobbers, principally women and boys. We came up to a large group of these, about 8 or 9 women were sitting on the ground in the midst of heaps of ore of the large and small, their mouths were covered with a cloth to keep the dust of the ore from entering with the breath. The fingers and thumb of the left hand were cased in strong iron tubes forming a sort of glove. A large hammer was handled in the right hand and a block of ore placed before them served as an anvil. Thus furnished they were employed in breaking lumps of ore into small pieces and selecting the good from the bad.[30]

The protective 'iron tubes' can be seen in Ibbetson's drawing.

Captain and Mrs Hanmer, who visited the mine in the same year as Faraday, describe them '… with iron gloves on their left hands, and their mouths and noses covered over to prevent them inhaling the injurious effluvia, that come from the copper'.[31] The same un-mechanised practice was still being employed in 1848 when the 'copper ladies' are described by Enoch Jones either with irony or with an almost total lack of insight: '… the fingers of the hand which grasps the ore are covered with iron and the other gaily handles a hammer of about 4lbs weight, and thus they merrily toil'.[32]

In the same year that Ibbetson prepared his Parys mine drawings he also visited the Lockwood and Morris copperworks at Landore, Swansea. His journey takes us from North Wales to South Wales and to the copper smelting and processing works there. His drawing of the *Coal Staithe on the River Tawe* (Figure 5.5), with a copperworks in the background, provides an image which illustrates the distressing conditions that men and women endured both then and well into the nineteenth century. Here Ibbetson again displays his

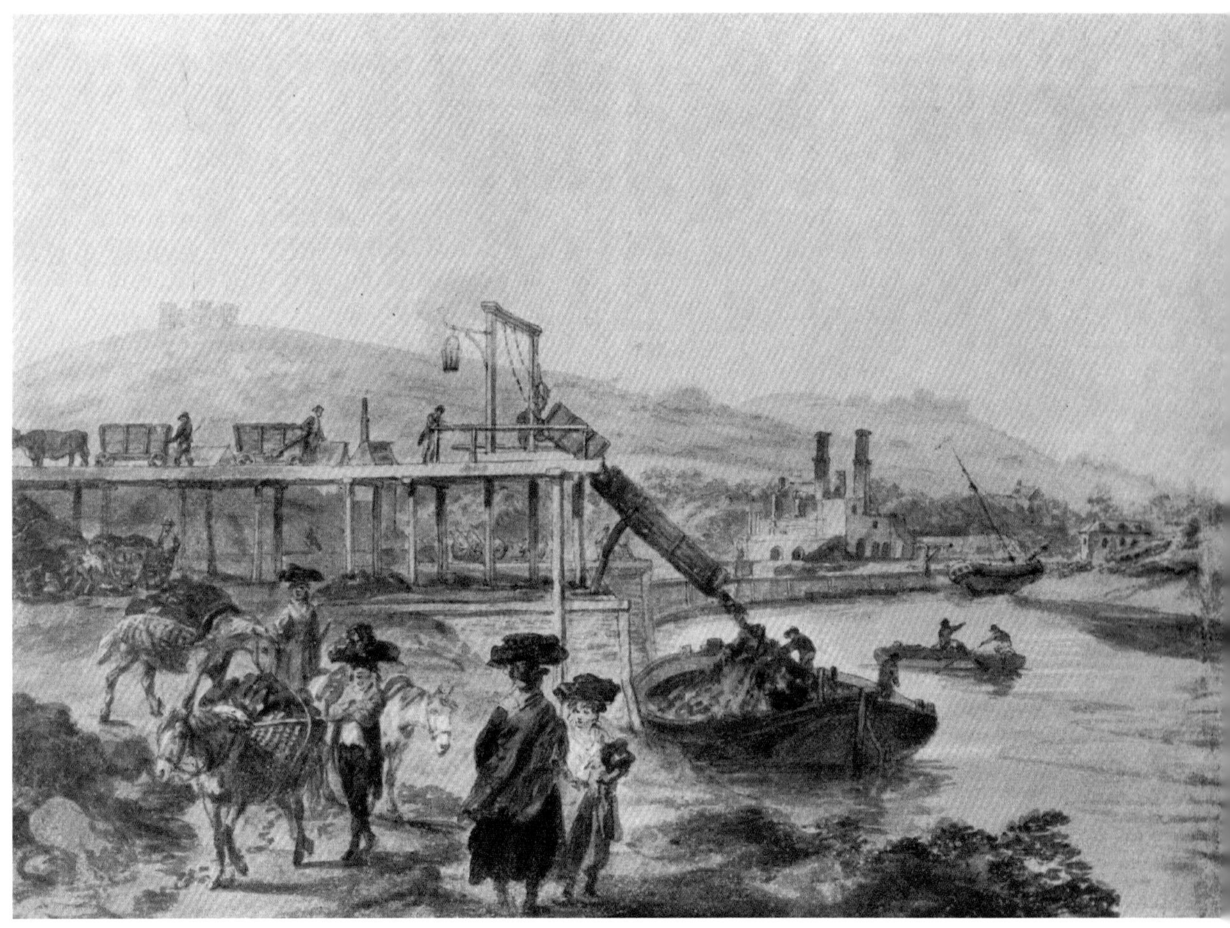

5.5 *Coal staithe on the River Tawe*, 1792, by Julius Caesar Ibbetson, watercolour on paper, 21.0 x 29.5 cm. Formerly Collection of Lady Zia Wernher.

lifetime interest in the working and living conditions of the rural and industrial poor. Images of this directness, which revealed the conditions with which some labourers were faced, were rare during the late eighteenth century and Ibbetson's sketch reveals the impact that the growth of the copper industry was having. In his sketch we see men loading coal on to a barge for delivery to the copperworks and women and children carrying baskets of coal on their heads and leading horses laden with panniers full of coal to other works nearby. William Daniell describes them in his travel journal *A Voyage round Great Britain*:

> On the banks of the canal I saw little companies of them chipping
> the large coals into small pieces for the furnaces, without shoes or
> stockings, their clothes hanging about them, released, for the sake
> of ease, from pins and strings, and their faces as black as coals,
> except where channelled by the streams of perspiration that trickled
> down.[33]

Ibbetson's small sketch, *Coal Staithe on the River Tawe*, also shows the 'castle', now in ruins, on a distant hilltop. This is the building which became known as Morriston Castle, its battlements built from the slag from the copper ore. The 'castle' is one of the first examples of workers' housing built by an employer. John Morris (1745–1819), recognising the effect that the sulphurous fumes issuing from the copperworks was having on his workforce, built the accommodation on higher ground, intending to provide a healthier environment for his employees. The castle flats ultimately fell into decay, however, when accommodation lower down the hill in Morriston, closer to his employees' place of work, became more attractive.[34] In the 1790s, John Morris laid the foundations for Morristown and it is particularly for the development of this village that he is now remembered. The 'castle' flats, built twenty years earlier had been built for about thirty families but the provision of a model village with 141 houses on the slopes of the hill which provided accommodation for the families of those who worked in his Fforest copperworks and the Trewyddfa, Pentre and Glyndu coal mines housed over 600 people in 1796.[35]

Swansea and nearby Neath, close to the South Wales coalfields which provided the energy for smelting the ore and processing the metals, were the destinations for some of the copper ore from the Parys and Mona mines and most of the tin and copper ores mined in Cornwall. Several artists passed through or stopped in Swansea on their tours to South Wales. En route they crossed the River Neath (Nedd) at Briton Ferry, to visit the castles at Llanstephan and Cilgerran or the abbey at St David's. The site of Briton Ferry provided a source of material for nearly all the artists who passed by. Paul Sandby, Julius Caesar Ibbetson, John 'Warwick' Smith, J.M.W. Turner, and Philippe-Jacques de Loutherbourg all stopped to sketch at '… the justly admired spot called Briton Ferry' of which the Rev. Thomas Evans writes, 'The advantages which nature has bestowed on the place baffles all attempts at adequate description … .'[36] However, they made no substantial paintings of the industrial areas of Swansea.

Some sketches by de Loutherbourg of the Swansea copperworks show him collecting information, perhaps for a later larger work, but they do not appear to have been developed further.[37] Other drawings of the Fforest copperworks nearby were made in 1791 by Thomas Rothwell, a Swansea artist who worked primarily as a decorator of pottery and porcelain at the nearby Cambrian Pottery, and by John 'Warwick' Smith in 1792, the year he had been sketching at the mines in Anglesey.[38] None of these sketches or drawings is populated and no artist of the time felt inspired or encouraged to exhibit a painting of the scene which Henry Skrine recalls when he visited Swansea in 1798, '… another Solfaterra exhibited itself, where the numerous forges of Morris-town tinged all the country with the sulphureous [sic] atmosphere of their copper works … .'[39]

The sight of the copper industry in Swansea hardly met the aesthetics of the picturesque, the sublime or the beautiful, and artists did not attempt to bring finished paintings of this industrial landscape to exhibition. Views of the old and established rural industries, the distressed watermill, the dilapidated coal shaft or the smoking kiln often fell quite readily into a 'picturesque' category and astonishment at the sight of some of the industrial processes put them surely among the 'sublime', but the sulphurous and poisonous emissions from Swansea's copperworks were difficult to reconcile with these aesthetic categories. We have, however, Havell's oil painting of the Parys mine and the drawings by Francia, 'Warwick' Smith and Ibbetson as valuable reminders of the conditions that employees endured at that time in this unregulated industry.

In the next chapter we come to an artist who, more than any other artist of the period, showed through his sketches and later compositions the greatest awareness of the Industrial Revolution and the changes that were taking place. In his book *J.M.W. Turner: Romantic painter of the Industrial Revolution*, William Rodner charts how Turner reacted to industrial development in his paintings of the iron and coal industry, the steam railway, the steamship and the canal system. A further look at Turner's drawings and paintings reveals how closely he observed the spread of the canal network, a central feature of the Industrial Revolution, and the striking new structures that the engineers William Jessop, Thomas Telford and John Rennie were building for their clients. Turner's imagination transforms the views of these works into images which enrich our understanding and appreciation of their impact.

Notes

1 John Whitehurst, 1778.

2 *John Whitehurst FRS*, *c.*1782–3, by Joseph Wright of Derby.

3 James Hutton, 1785. The theory was brought to a wider public when the Professor of Mathematics at the University of Edinburgh, John Playfair, 1802, wrote *Illustrations of the Huttonian Theory of the Earth* and through Charles Lyell's classic four-volume text, 1830–33, *The Principles of Geology*.

4 William Smith, 1815.

5 David Stacey, 2010, pp. 62–8.

6 Sir Henry Englefield and Thomas Webster, 1816.

7 See T.C. Barker and J.R. Harris, 1959, pp. 76–89; and T.K. Derry and D.I. Williams, 1960, p. 492.

8 Captain Henry and Mrs Sara Hanmer, 13 October 1819, pp. 69–70.

9 For example: Edmund Burke, 1757; Rev. William Gilpin, 1782 and 1792; Richard Payne Knight, 1794 and 1805; Uvedale Price, 1810.

10 Between 1804 and 1857 William Havell exhibited more than one hundred oil paintings at the Royal Academy and contributed regularly to exhibitions of the Old Society of Painters in Watercolours where he had been one of the founding members.

11 John Lewis Roget, 1891, vol. 1, p. 172. Lucy Aikin wrote under several pseudonyms, including Mary Godolphin.

12 Thomas Pennant, *A Tour in Wales, Illustrations after Moses Griffith (1747–1819)*, vol. III, London.

13 Dafydd Tomos, 1987, p. 89. Parys Underground Group, www.amlwchhistory.co.uk (accessed 4 June 2019).

14 Edited from an autograph in the Pierpoint Morgan Library, New York, in John Gage (ed.), 1980, p. 16. The attribution to Turner was withdrawn see John Gage, 1986.

15 Richard Cavendish, 1 February 1998, pp. 61–3, in *History Today*.

16 Boulton and Watt Papers, MS 3147, 10 June 1785.

17 Thomas Wilson, 1790, *Correspondence: James Watt to Thomas Wilson*, 15 September 1790.

18 Matthew Boulton, 1791, *Correspondence: Matthew Boulton to Messrs Monolron*, 26 December 1791.

19 Barker, T.C. and Harris, J.R., 1959, pp. 77–9.

20 H. Hamilton, 1967, pp. 199–213.

21 John Barrell, 1980; David Solkin, 1982.

22 Thomas Smith of Derby, John Webber and Philippe-Jacques de Loutherbourg.

23 Dafydd Tomos, 1987, pp. 81–5. Faraday explains the fluency he achieves in his journal by saying that he imagines himself writing to his sister. 'My Dear Margaret I will suppose myself scribbling to you.' Dafydd Tomos, 1987, p. 58.

24 Dafydd Tomos, 1987, p. 82.

25 *Parys Copper Mine, Anglesey*, *c.*1800, by François Louis Thomas Francia. Another smaller drawing, a view taken from inside the mine *The Parys Mine in Anglesey* by Francia, *c.*1799, is in the Ironbridge Gorge Museum, Shropshire.

26 John 'Warwick' Smith is reported to have visited the Parys Mountain at least a dozen times between 1784 and 1806. (Peter Lord, 1998, p. 23). His drawings include *Copper Mines on the Parys Mountain*, 1785; *Junction of Mona and Parys Mountain Copper Mines*, 1790; *One of the Copper Mines belonging to the Paris Mountain, Anglesea*, 1790; and *Interior of One of the Copper Mines on the Paris Mountain Anglesea*, 9 July 1792.

27 Richard Colt Hoare's journal entry for Sunday 28 June 1801 in M.W. Thompson (ed.), 1983, p. 185. Captain and Mrs Hanmer, 13 October 1819, p. 69, MS 23996C, National Library of Wales, Aberystwyth.

28 John Mitchel, 1999, p. 22.

29 R.M. Clay, 1948.

30 Dafydd Tomos, 1987, p. 80.

31 Captain and Mrs Hanmer, 13 October 1819, p. 70, MS 23996C.

32 Anon., 1848, p. 7.

33 Ayton, R. and William Daniell, 1814–25. vol. I, p. 64.

34 *Morriston Castle, Swansea* by John 'Warwick' Smith, *c.*1792, shows the castle from a different angle with the copperworks in the distance.

35 J.M. Davies, 1952, pp. 26–30.

36 Rev. J. Evans, 1803, p. 143. In addition to views at Briton Ferry, Paul Sandby also made a watercolour *View of the Copper Works at Neath from Mr Vernon's Garden at Breten Ferry*, 1779, later engraved for *A Collection of One Hundred and Fifty Select Views, in England, Scotland and Ireland*, 1781

37 *Copper Smelting Works at Landore on the River Tawe north of Swansea*, 1786, by Philippe-Jacques de Loutherbourg. Two views, one inscribed *1st Copperworks near Swansea*, 1786, by de Loutherbourg. Turner and de Loutherbourg knew each other as fellow Royal Academicians and between 1807 and 1811 were close neighbours living in Hammersmith, London. These sketches, together with other sketches of Welsh landscapes, are reported to have come to Turner from Dr Monro's collection

are now held in the Turner Bequest, Tate, London. A.J.
Finberg, 1909, *Inventory of the Drawings of the Turner Bequest*.
38 *The Fforest Copper Works* by Thomas Rothwell, 1791. The
drawing, which shows the copperworks and the bridge across
the Tawe from downstream, was also engraved on an oval
plaster plaque. *View of the River Tawe and Fforest Copper Works*
by John 'Warwick' Smith, 1792.
39 Henry Skrine, 1812.

6 Joseph Mallord William Turner's Canals – from Lancaster to Dudley

More than any other artist of the period, Joseph Mallord William Turner (1775–1851) recognised the social and technological changes that were taking place in Britain. He observed an industrial revolution unfolding and understood the transformative impact that these changes were having. In Turner's drawings and paintings of the industrial sector we find him responding to many of the new features that were emerging: the steamboat, the new docks and harbours, the developing towns and cities, and the canal network.[1] The scope of Turner's work is so wide-ranging that this essay has been confined to the discussion of his paintings of the canal network, a fundamental feature of early industrial Britain. Turner's recognition of this subject-matter grew from an initial sketch in 1797 of the new neo-classical aqueduct crossing the River Lune at Lancaster to his response in 1830 to the overwhelming industrial development around the canal network at Dudley, Worcestershire. Turner developed a deep understanding of the role of the canal network in Britain in the early nineteenth century, and his drawings – based on his sketchbook records, his memory and his imagination – fit nicely within the timeframe of this book. The drawings and finished paintings developed from some of his on-the-spot sketches are discussed in this chapter.

As early as 1736 some of the existing river systems were being deepened to make them navigable. The poet James Thomson (1700–48), anticipating the prospect of the country's bright future, was writing enthusiastically:

> See! Long canals and deepen'd rivers join
> Each part with each, and with the circling main
> The whole enliven'd isle …

and the establishment and growth of new industries in the middle and latter parts of the eighteenth century provided the impetus for an improved water transport network.[2] The construction of new canals was promoted by entrepreneurs wishing to gain advantage through the bulk import of raw materials and the export of finished goods to and from their factories. These advantages, which served not only an individual but a group of entrepreneurs, soon became apparent and the call arose for a network of navigable canals and rivers which would, as Thomson dreamed, link the north and south and the east to the west of the country with the oceans beyond. Investors emerged to fund the construction of the Grand Trunk Canal, linking the River Trent to the River Mersey, which was opened in 1777. The route between London and the Midlands followed when canals linking London, Northampton and Leicester to the River Trent near Derby were constructed and these, once established, formed the basis of the Grand Union Canal. The 'canal mania' of the 1790s saw the construction of many new canals, built to serve individual entrepreneurs and the new industrial towns and centres of industry. The network continued to grow until the impact of the railways began to be felt in the 1830s.

Surprisingly, canals which wound through busy towns and unspoilt countryside attracted very few of the artists who toured the country but Turner's continual response can be clearly traced through his sketchbooks and finished works. His interest in the spread of the country's canals revealed in his sketches and paintings of the canals in Britain include five areas of particular interest. The first relates to the Lancaster Canal in the northwest of England, the second to his painting near Kirkstall Lock on the Leeds and Liverpool Canal, the third to the Grand Union Canal at More Park, near Watford, the fourth to the navigable canal built to connect the River Arun and Chichester Harbour in Sussex, and the fifth to the canals in the heart of the Black Country at Dudley, Worcestershire.

It was not until Turner was in his early twenties that he began to confront new industrial development. His early sketching tours took him to Wales. During the 1790s, he visited the principality five times over a period of eight years.[3] From the sketches he made on these visits Turner produced drawings which Andrew Wilton considers are '… of a richness and vitality, a readiness of inspiration and a fecundity of technical invention, that rival those of any other period of his life …' but there is no evidence that he took any interest, during his first two trips to North and South Wales, in the new industries that were beginning to congregate around Neath, Merthyr Tydfil and Swansea.[4]

In 1795, on his third tour to Wales, Turner travelled more widely, visiting, among other historic sites, the castles at Tenby, Pembroke and Llanstephan, the abbey at St David's, and Ewenny Priory. On that trip, he passed through Neath and Swansea but there are no sketches or drawings by him that record any interest in the industrial scene there. His delight in picturesque watermills, shown during his 1794 trip, continued however and his clear open watercolour of the *Aberdulais Mill*, 1796–7, a mill not far from Neath, comes from on-the-spot pencil sketches he made during the 1795 tour.[5] Turner's sketchbooks of 1796/97 and 1798, however, show him visiting iron foundries and forges for the first time, and in 1798 Anthony Bacon (1772–1817), Richard Crawshay's partner at Cyfarthfa, commissioned the twenty-three-year-old Turner to make drawings of the ironworks at Merthyr Tydfil.[6] In the same year Turner travelled further north and we find in his *North Wales* sketchbook a view of Thomas Telford's aqueduct under construction on the Ellesmere Canal in Shropshire, *The Chirk Aqueduct in Course of Construction*.[7] This was his second sketch of a canal structure. In the previous summer Turner had made a trip to the north of England where he had sketched at John Rennie's recently completed aqueduct over the River Lune at Lancaster.

Promotion of the Lancaster Canal began in 1792. John Rennie FRS (1761–1821) was appointed the engineer for its design and construction, and its route was to run from Wigan to Kendal via Preston and Lancaster. The section just south of Preston was never completed, leaving the northern section isolated, but this part of the canal is noted for Rennie's elegant neo-classical aqueduct at Lancaster which was completed in the autumn of 1797.[8] The five-span structure over the River Lune, which still stands today, is the largest masonry aqueduct ever built in Britain.[9]

Turner's sketching tour of 1797, the year the Lancaster Aqueduct was completed, took him first to the northeast of England, and then to Richmond, Durham and Berwick-upon-Tweed. On returning south, he travelled to Penrith, Kendal and then to Lancaster before taking a route via Skipton and visiting south Yorkshire and Lincolnshire on his way home to London. This was the first time that Turner had travelled north of Derby but he would have been aware of the canal building of the previous decades. On his way north he may have seen sections of the Chesterfield and the Leeds and Liverpool canals, where construction had started about twenty years earlier, but there were no more to be seen north of Leeds until he arrived at Lancaster.

Construction of the aqueduct over the River Lune was nearing completion when Turner arrived and a pencil sketch in his *Tweed and Lakes* sketchbook, of the Lancaster Aqueduct with the church and castle seen through the right hand arch, shows the twenty-two-year-old Turner, impressed by Rennie's new structure, recording its details and setting them against the distant town.[10] The sketch shows the two southern-most arches and the abutment of the aqueduct. He shows the full details of the aqueduct up to and including the canal trough but, in the sketch, Turner only indicates a section of the parapet and balustrade, details which he could extend in a painting later if he wished. In this sketch, we see Turner beginning to record and compare details of Rennie's aqueduct, a structure which demonstrates the great ambition of the canal age, with the established buildings of the town beyond.

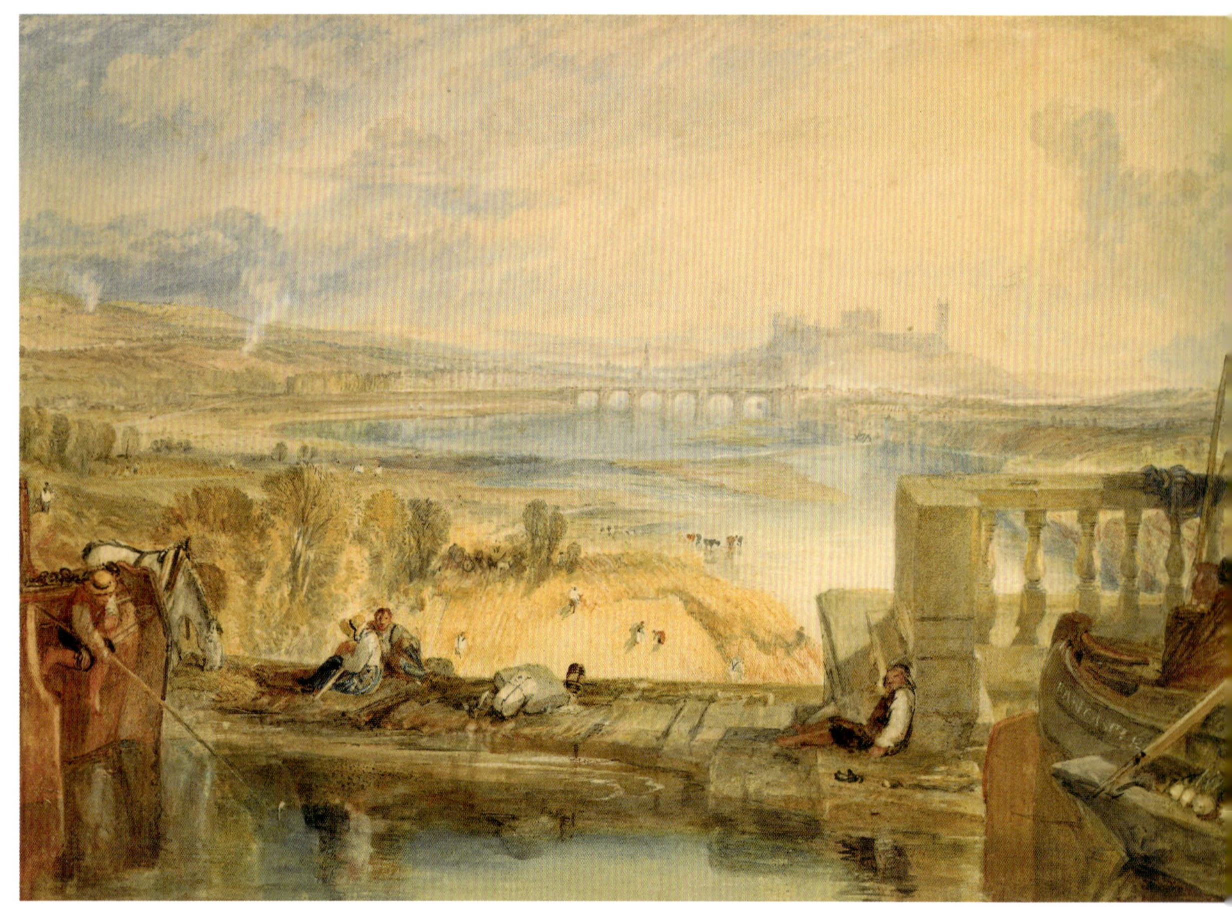

Turner returned to Lancaster nearly twenty years later, in 1816, when the canal was in full use. His sketchbooks during this visit include several views of Lancaster, some of the aqueduct and of the landscape beyond.[11] One in particular in his *Yorkshire 5* sketchbook provides the basis for his watercolour drawing *Lancaster from the Aqueduct* of 1816.[12] The finished watercolour (Figure 6.1) was developed from the sketch. The view is towards Skerton Bridge with the castle in the distance. In the watercolour drawing, Turner revises the perspective of his preparatory pencil sketch and introduces foreground details of the aqueduct that are difficult to interpret but, by emphasising the neo-classical features at the aqueduct's southern abutment and introducing the bargees at rest, he creates a dreamlike image.

Skerton Bridge, over the River Lune, completed in 1788, was designed by Thomas Harrison (1744–1829), who was also responsible for reconstruction of the eleventh-century Lancaster Castle.[13] Turner would have seen the new bridge during his 1797 visit and must have recognised it as a significant

6.1 *Lancaster from the aqueduct*, 1816, by J.M.W. Turner, watercolour and body colour on paper, 28.0 x 39.4 cm. Lady Lever Art Gallery, Merseyside.

structure which would not be out of place in a landscape by Claude Lorrain. It has five semi-elliptical arches with aediculed niches at the bridge piers which at the abutments form entrances to arched tunnels which pass under the bridge. Although twice the size of the bridge at Rimini, the design is reminiscent of the five-arched Ponte d'Augusto (or Ponte di Tiberio) built in 20 BCE, a structure with which Turner was familiar, having copied one of Richard Wilson's drawings of the bridge in his sketchbook in 1796–7.[14]

In *Lancaster from the Aqueduct*, Turner brings together a series of structures through which he recognises the new but reflects on Britain's complex historical past. The eleventh-century Norman castle in the distance which, when Turner was there, was being restored and used as a prison, sits on the site of previous Roman forts. He blends these with the solid neo-classical architecture of Harrison's Skerton Bridge and Rennie's aqueduct and introduces a human element through the contemporary but timeless figures in the foreground. The Industrial Revolution is frequently associated with disruption, exploitation and stress but Turner, while reflecting on change and what might be seen as the country's sometimes troubled past, presents a moment of stillness and calm. He dwells on both an historical perspective and a 'romantic' image of Lancaster. Turner is, perhaps, reminding us of Shakespeare's John of Gaunt, the Duke of Lancaster's 'precious stone set in the silver sea' and his romantic and rhetorical cry, 'This blessed plot, this earth, this realm, this England.'[15]

Many of Turner's later works have come to evoke the term 'romantic'. William Rodner, writing in 1997, was certain enough of the term to subtitle his book *J.M.W. Turner: Romantic Painter of the Industrial Revolution*.[16] The term has been much debated and its relevance with reference to industrial paintings by Turner is worth a short diversion. In the early nineteenth century, writers in Britain were defining 'romantic' as the 'ascendency of the imagination over judgment', and the 'romantic' response to landscape as one in which the 'character' of nature resonates with the viewer's emotions.[17] In the twentieth century, however, we find Arthur Lovejoy writing, '… "romantic", with its derivatives, is possibly the most equivocal in the language …' and '… "romanticism" has no generally understood meaning and has therefore come to be useless as a verbal symbol'. He accepts the use of a 'Romantic period', a period between 1780 and 1830, and a 'Romantic movement', in which a new fashion of thought arose.[18]

The 'Romantic movement', the literary movement emanating from Germany, had established itself in Britain by the end of the eighteenth century and current definitions in this field regard Romanticism's stylistic keynote as 'intensity' and its watchword 'imagination'.[19] The movement with regard to the visual arts has parallels. 'Intensity' and 'imagination' are words that could certainly be applied to many of Turner's works but perhaps he described his work and approach most clearly when he wrote that he was for 'the use of practical observation and reflection … in preference to all the splendid Theory of Art'.[20] Embedded in these few words, Turner shows his belief in 'self' and that artists should trust their own instincts and reactions. The greatness of Turner is that he did. With his curiosity and wide-ranging interests and the intensity he brought to his work, he was able to break from the conventions of the day and respond to his own deeply felt feelings and imagination, creating images which subsequently stimulate the imagination of those who see them.

William Vaughan also discusses the attitudes and ambiguities of the word 'romantic', the evolution of its meaning and the complexities of its application in the visual arts. In relation to Turner, he writes:

> It is not difficult to see how Turner's outlook – his fatalism, love of the elemental, of grandeur and decay – accord with contemporary Romantic preoccupations; but his way of painting, that indistinctness which in a moment of defiance he called his 'forte', seemed to be the epitome of arbitrariness, a brilliant subjectivity only appropriate for those evocative and imaginative subjects known as 'romantic'.[21]

At the turn of the century, when Turner first visited Leeds, two-thirds of the Leeds and Liverpool Canal (comprising the two sections closest to both cities) had been operating for nearly twenty-five years but no agreement had been reached on the route for the central section of the canal between Wigan and Gargrave, near Skipton. This took many years to finalise. James Brindley (1716–72), John Smeaton FRS and William Jessop (1745–1814) were, at different times, involved in surveying and making proposals for the most economic route. The 127-mile long canal between Liverpool and Leeds was finally completed and opened in 1816. The first barge to travel the full length of the canal left Leeds on 19 October 1816. On the following day the *Leeds Mercury* described the event: 'On entering the first lock, the band struck up the national anthem, … all the sloops in the basin were decorated with streamers and the whole formed a truly animated and delightful scene.'[22]

Turner had taken an interest in the Leeds and Liverpool Canal's development in 1797 on his return from Lancaster en route to York. His drawing of a canal tunnel is almost certainly of the 1-mile long Foulridge Tunnel near Skipton which had been completed and opened on 1 May the previous year.[23] In 1816, a few months before the canal was finally completed, and again in 1823–4, Turner returned to sketch views of structures on the canal, this time near Leeds, and he used the later sketches to develop his watercolour known as *Kirkstall Lock on the River Aire* in 1824–5 (Figure 6.2). His sketches provide an

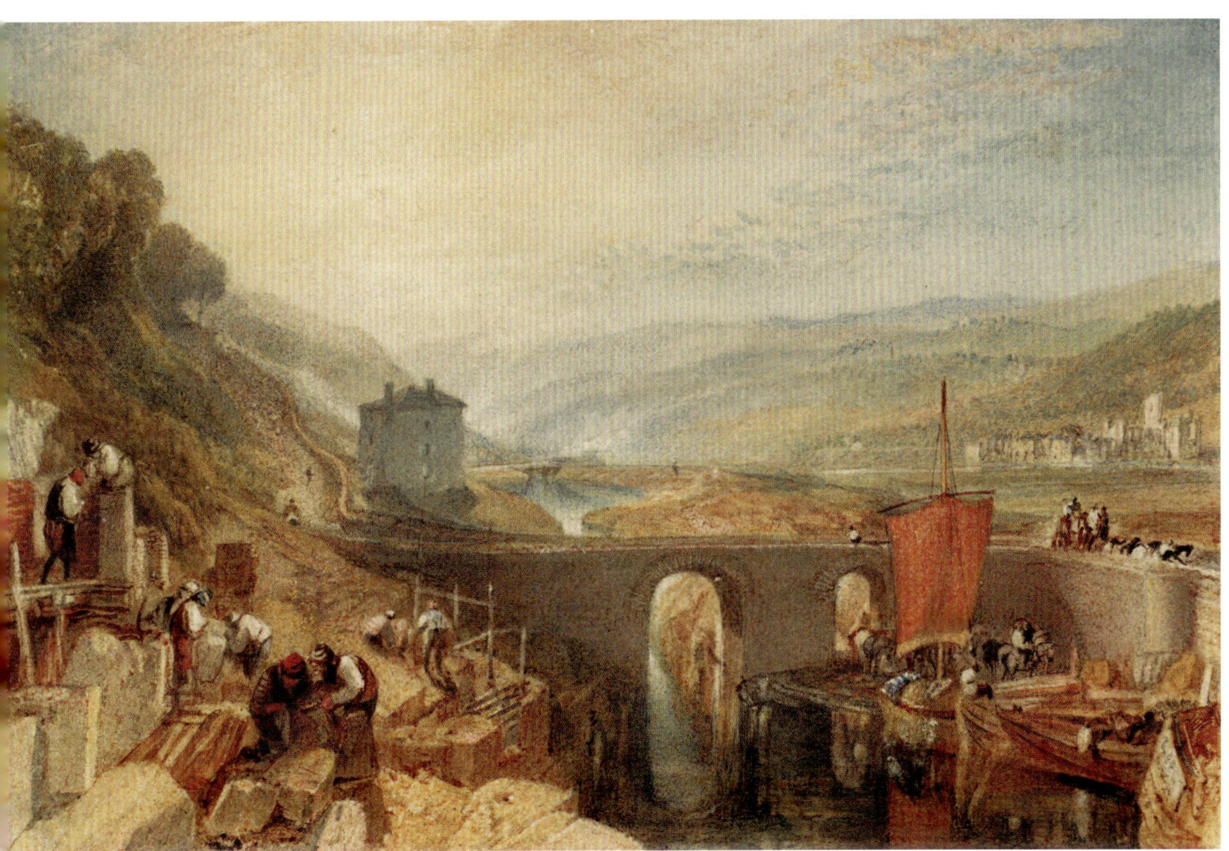

interesting backdrop to the development of the watercolour and to his method of working.

The *Kirkstall* sketchbook of 1816 finds Turner sketching very loosely as he records views of the abbey and of locks on the Leeds and Liverpool Canal from a variety of different angles. From these, we see him building up his understanding of the area by sketching near the abbey, by the River Aire and along the canal at spots within about a mile of one another. The sites where he made the sketches can still be found today, although the area is now over-grown with large trees and shrubs on the hillsides and in the river valley below, obscuring the earlier sightlines. Turner's 1816 pencil sketches include a view from just above the flight of three locks, known as the Forge Locks, just above Kirkstall Lock, with Kirkstall Abbey in the distance, and a small watercol-our of a view down the canal towards Broad Lane Bridge with Leeds in the distance.[24] These sketches are of places on the canal within half a mile of the scene he constructs for the 1824/5 *Kirkstall Lock* drawing. Although there were new buildings to be seen when Turner returned to the area in 1823–4, he was already familiar with the canal and its surroundings.

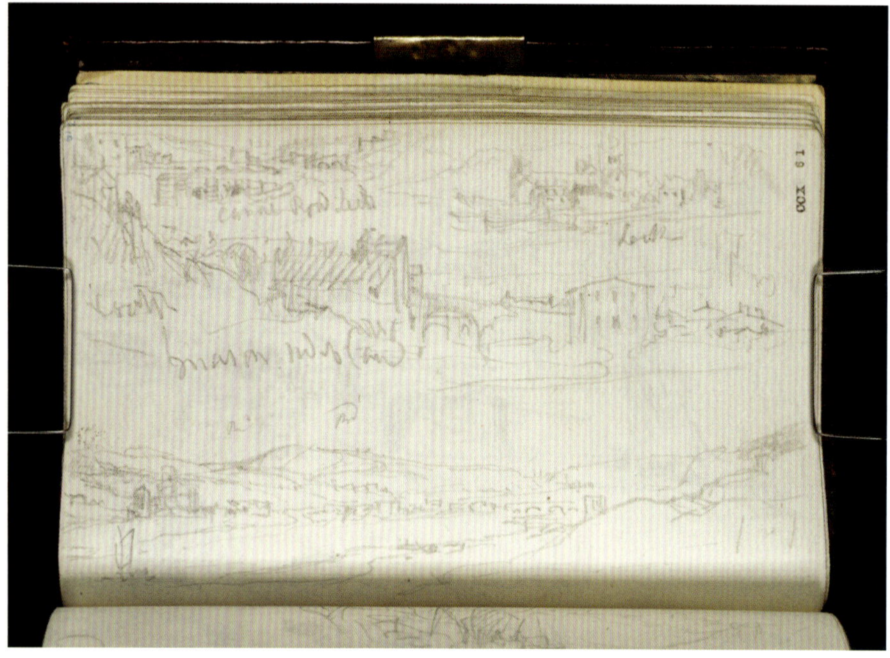

6.3 *Sketches for Kirkstall Lock*, *c.*1823–4, by J.M.W. Turner, graphite on paper. Brighton and Arundel Sketchbook. Tate, London.

Turner's *Brighton and Arundel* sketchbook includes several small pencil sketches which provide the basis on which he was able to construct the final watercolour drawing.[25] Several pages in Turner's sketchbook show views of Kirkstall Abbey but he draws upon two of the sketches, Figures 6.3 and 6.4, in particular. Figure 6.3 contains four, or possibly five, separate views: top right, the abbey; bottom centre-right the Leeds-Bradford road bridge crossing the canal seen through the Broad Lane road bridge; and immediately to the left of this, Turner records the steep canal bank with craftsmen and stonemasons at work in front of the main canal arch of the new Leeds-Bradford road bridge. The last of these views provides the basis for the lower left quarter of the final drawing. The small sketch at the top left of the page shows a distant view of the road over the canal. The sketch at the bottom of the page is a general view from somewhere near the Forge Locks. Figure 6.4 shows three views, two of which are incorporated, in a modified form, into the final drawings; in the centre of the page a view of the Leeds-Bradford road bridge and at the bottom a view over the bridge showing a prominent house, The Ellars, which still stands today, with the steep hillside above the road.

There does not appear to be any single preparatory sketch to provide the outline for the final drawing but on the basis of Turner's sketches of these disparate but key elements, his familiarity with the area and his wish to make a statement about the canal and highway development, he brings them together in the watercolour known as *Kirkstall Lock on the River Aire*. Some of the features

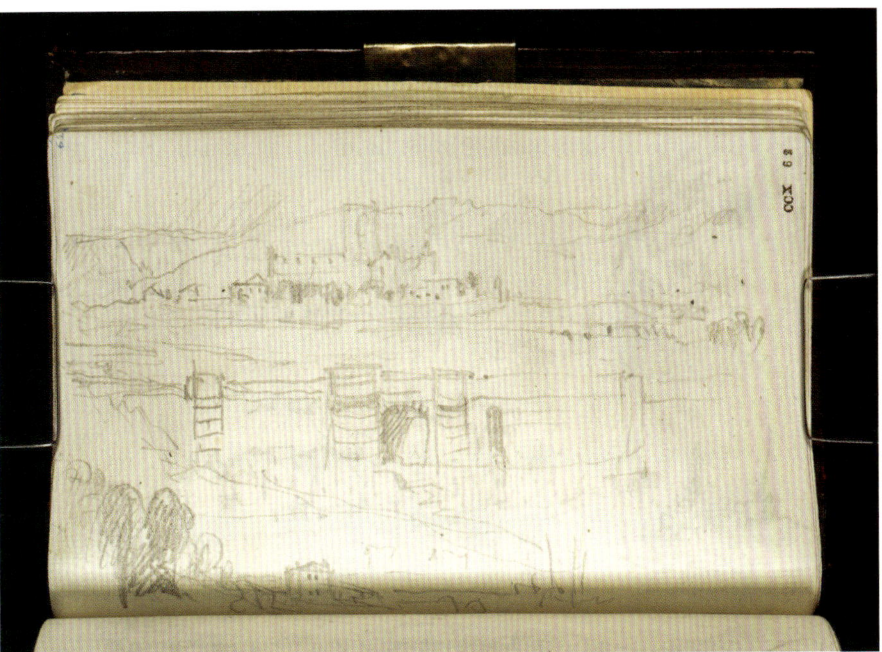

6.4 *Sketches for Kirkstall Lock*, *c.*1823–4, by J.M.W. Turner, graphite on paper. Brighton and Arundel Sketchbook. Tate, London.

in the drawing, particularly the canal water level, may at first glance look rather baffling until we recognise what Turner was trying to express in his watercolour. Turner had found a subject which allowed him to bring together both pastoral and industrial elements, ones he could apply to a scene which showed the recent development of the canal and road network in Yorkshire at the beginning of the nineteenth century. In the final drawing, Turner shows the boats in the holding basin below the bridge, waiting to move through and up the canal when Kirkstall Lock is clear of other traffic. The canal is shown vanishing into the hazy distance of west Yorkshire before continuing its epic route across the Pennines and into Lancashire. He shows the masons at work on the construction of the new brewery and wharf. Turner omits the bridge parapet and supporting piers, losing something of the power of the structure but this allows him to emphasise the benefits of the new turnpike road. He increases the height of the house behind the bridge from the squatness shown in his pencil record to balance the composition with the distant Kirkstall Abbey, allowing us to reflect on both the new and the old.

The title given to the painting, *Kirkstall Lock on the River Aire*, is misleading. The picture shows the new bridge on the Leeds to Bradford road (now the B6157 road) which crosses the Leeds and Liverpool Canal about 3 miles from Leeds. Kirkstall Lock can be seen in the distance about a quarter of a mile beyond the bridge. The River Aire is hidden in the valley to the right of the canal but the title given to the drawing today no doubt suited W.B. Cooke, the

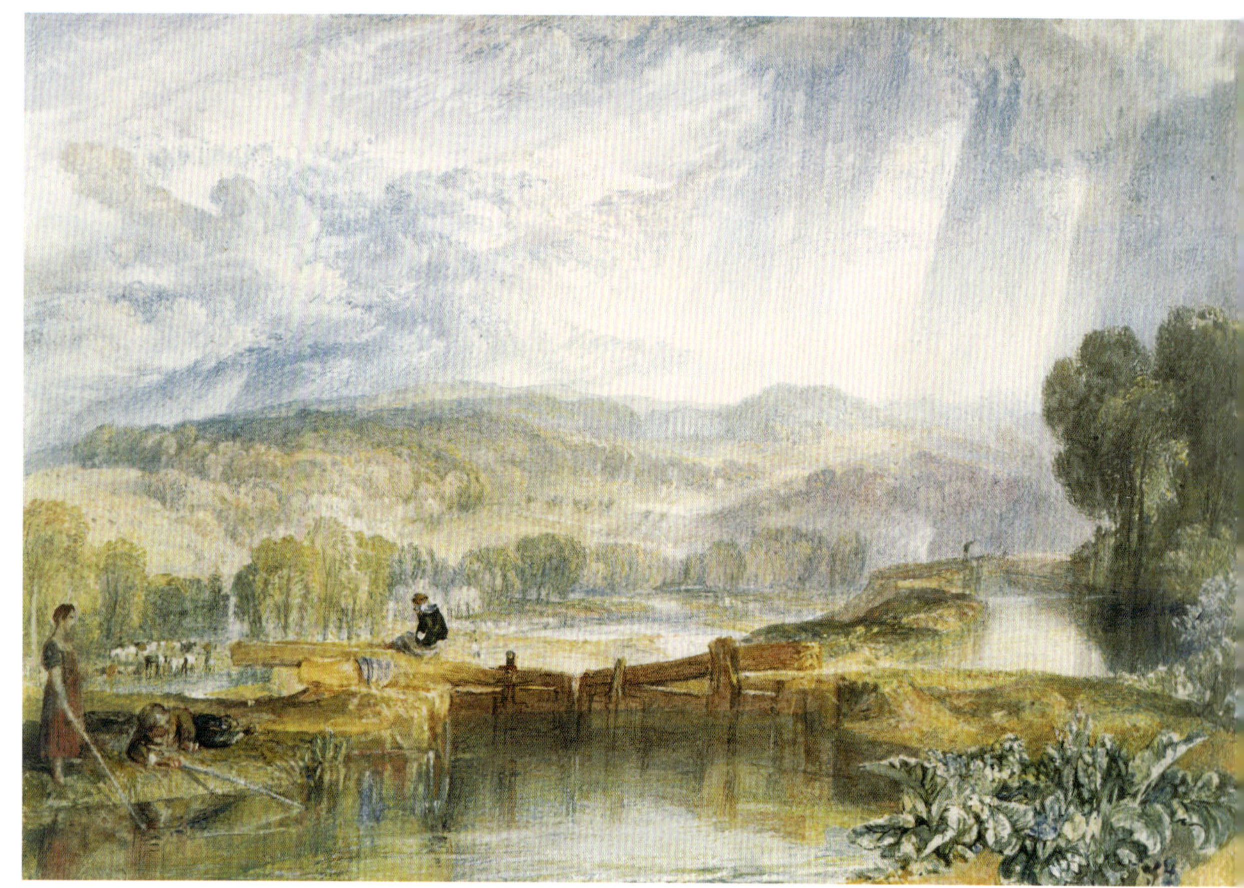

publisher of *Rivers of England*, 1827 in which a mezzotint engraving of the drawing, by William Say, appears.[26]

Cooke's *Rivers of England* includes another fine mezzotint engraving derived from Turner's 1822 watercolour *More Park, near Watford, on the River Colne* (Figure 6.5).[27] This atmospheric watercolour looks towards the 200-hectare estate of More (or Moor) Park, renowned for the landscaping by Capability Brown but, as Eric Shanes has pointed out: 'The title of the work could mislead the unwary into believing that the body of water in the foreground is the River Colne, whereas it is in fact the Grand Union Canal at Lot Mead Lock; the Colne is only just visible beyond the lock gates and below them to the left.'[28] A much earlier sketch of about 1807 in Turner's *Rivers* sketchbook provides the basis for the final drawing.[29]

Turner is not interested here in demonstrating the dynamism of any new industrial development but uses the canal, the pair of lock gates and the figures in the foreground to create an almost Arcadian scene. The watercolour is small, the same size as his *Kirkstall Lock* drawing but, within this area, Turner creates a recession from the lock gates in the foreground through repetitive motifs which lead to the hills beyond. He produces an atmosphere in this space through a full spectrum of colour to create this alluring scene. A proof of the engraved plate by Charles Turner (1774–1857) developed from the water-colour is inscribed by Turner: 'Watch narrowly all the touches and you may calculate upon the best plate, so now for comments, too much Etching upon the left Bank and particularly the Lock. it [sic] will [cause?] the mezzotint to wear. <u>Hold your hand</u> in future, for you compel me to put shadows to support what I could not wish away.'[30] Turner took a close interest in how his drawings were translated by others into prints and it is clear that he was particularly concerned here that the exquisite balance and tonal range of the gouache and watercolour might be lost in the print.

Two years after his first visit to the north of England in 1797, when he had seen John Rennie's aqueduct over the River Lune, Turner was invited by William Beckford (1759–1844) to prepare a set of drawings of Fonthill, Wiltshire. The house and abbey at Fonthill were designed by James Wyatt (1746–1813) and Turner was asked to support Wyatt in preparing impressions of the proposed designs. In Turner's *Fonthill* sketchbook, in addition to the views of Fonthill Abbey, Turner includes a sketch of a somewhat unlikely scene, catalogued as a *Distant View of Fonthill Abbey with Aqueduct in the Foreground* but there are no records or remains of an aqueduct near Fonthill.[31] There are suggestions that an aqueduct may have been built to take water either to Fonthill Splendens or to the new abbey but this is unproven. The canal mania of the period, from which the West Country did not escape, provides a possible explanation.[32] Speculation in the construction of a canal from Bristol to Southampton had begun in 1792 and continued throughout the 1790s, with investors dreaming of making vast gains on the shares they held. Bristol became the centre for pro-moting these canals.[33] The route of a Bristol-Southampton Canal via Salisbury would have passed close to Fonthill and, although the fervour for the route had cooled by the turn of the century, Turner's sketch may show the long aqueduct that would have been required to take a canal across the River Nadder south of Fonthill. It is unusual for Turner to play the architect but for this sketch he seems to have made use of the details he collected during his visit to Lancaster in 1797, where he sketched the aqueduct over the River Lune and those he recorded on his visit to North Wales in 1798 when he saw and made a sketch in the *North Wales* sketchbook of Chirk Aqueduct under construction. Perhaps we see Turner in this Fonthill sketch creating an 'artist's impression'.

The drawings and sketches, discussed above, provide examples of Turner keeping closely in touch with contemporary development in Britain but his

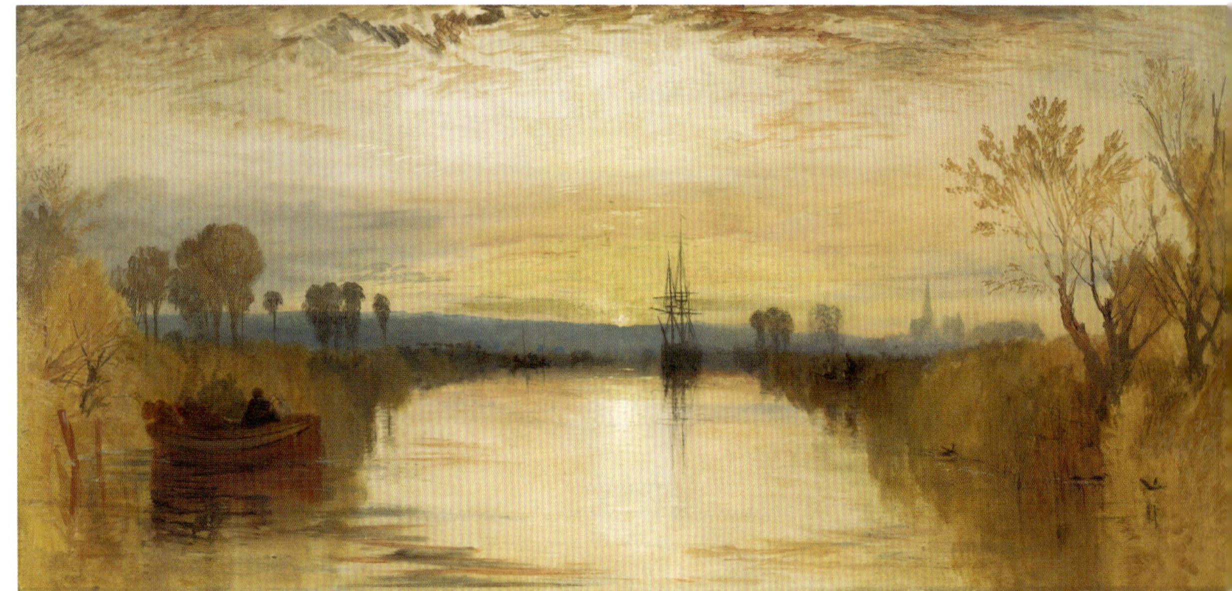

oil paintings of the *Chichester Canal*, one at the Tate Gallery, London (Figure 6.6), and two at Petworth, Sussex, show just how close he was to the issues involved. Turner was commissioned by George Wyndham, 3rd Earl of Egremont to make a painting of the Chichester Canal as one of a set of paintings for the Carved Room at Petworth House. He completed the commission in 1828. Lord Egremont was the largest shareholder in the development of a waterway which, with a short spur to Chichester, ran east-west from Chichester Harbour to the River Arun and was part of the Portsmouth and Arundel Navigation. This, when connected with the Wey and Arun Navigation, provided a continuous waterway from London to Portsmouth. The Bill for the Chichester Canal was presented to Parliament in 1817 and described as:

> Making and maintaining a Navigable Canal from the River Arun to Chichester Harbour and from thence to Langstone and Portsmouth Harbours with a Cut or Branch from Hunston Common to or near the City of Chichester, and for improving the Navigation of the Harbour of Langstone, and Channels of Langstone and Thorney.

The Portsmouth and Arundel Navigation Act was given Royal Assent the same year and the 12-mile canal from the River Arun to Chichester Harbour and the 1-mile long northern branch to the City of Chichester, starting about 3 miles from the west end was completed in 1823. The western end of the canal was wide and deep enough for sailing ships of up to 100 tons displacement but the eastern 9 miles was limited to a depth of 4 ft 6 in and a top width of 33 ft. The largest vessels it could accommodate were 75-ton horse-drawn barges.[34]

6.6 *Chichester Canal*, *c.*1828, by J.M.W. Turner, oil on canvas, 65.4 x 134.6 cm. Tate, London.

The Chichester Canal was another structure to which Turner was asked to turn his attention. The canal had been designed by John Rennie in the last years of his life. It is almost inconceivable that Rennie, a Fellow of the Royal Society, did not meet Turner, the Royal Academician. They had a patron in common in the 3rd Earl of Egremont at Petworth and Turner was to make a painting not only of the Chichester Canal and the aqueduct over the Lune at Lancaster but also of Rennie's bridges at Southwark and Waterloo, and the harbour works at Plymouth and Margate. From 1781, Somerset House on the Strand housed not only the Royal Academy but also the Royal Society. Turner had quite extensive contacts with the scientists of the day, including Michael Faraday and Richard Owen, both Fellows of the Royal Society.[35] Contacts and exchanges such as these with leading scientists and engineers may well have fed into his awareness of the changing face of Britain during the period of the Industrial Revolution. Turner would no doubt have been aware of the ill-fated Chichester Canal before he was commissioned by Lord Egremont to make the painting of the Chichester Canal.

The canal had a troubled history. In the first six months of its operation consignments from the south coast to London mainly comprised timber, marble and Indian cotton, and a combined total of 1,500 tons were transported from London to Portsmouth and Chichester. The quantity of corn and groceries reached nearly 4,000 tons in 1824 but the anticipated return on shareholders' investments was based on transport of more than 55,000 tons a year.[36] The Portsmouth and Arundel Canal Company was soon in financial difficulties and Lord Egremont gave up his financial interest in the company in 1826. Traffic on the Chichester Canal was negligible during the years that followed but efforts were made to revive its use in the 1830s. The canal between the River Arun and the southern end of the branch to Chichester is now filled in.[37]

One might ask why Lord Egremont wanted to commemorate this apparent failure by having a painting of the canal in the Carved Room at Petworth. Some very quick, simple, almost illegible sketches in Turner's *Brighton and Arundel* sketchbook seem to have been enough to provide the basis for the *Chichester Canal* painting.[38] In the painting Turner takes a view to the west along the canal from a spot about 2 miles east of the city. The sun is setting over Chichester Harbour and Chichester Cathedral is shown just to the north. The sailing ship, apparently motionless in the deeper water at the west end of the canal, is close to the entrance to the branch canal to the city. The eastern end of the canal is shown bereft of barges, with only a small skiff, from which figures dabble in the water searching for fish, shown near the canal bank in the foreground. The canal, laid out before the setting sun, has been returned to nature by Turner.

Turner's vision would have appealed to the romantic sensibilities of the period and those who were beginning to have reservations about the impact of industrialisation. Hung at Petworth, the image, reflecting on the nexus of Hope and Memory would perhaps have served a cathartic role after the difficulties that Lord Egremont had experienced. Turner's painting shows him responding to one of the two local ventures which Lord Egremont had wholeheartedly supported: the very successful Brighton Chain Pier, of which Turner also made several paintings, and the ambitious but unsuccessful project to connect London and Portsmouth by an inland waterway.[39]

Finally, Turner's visit to the Midlands in 1830 and his penetrating view of the development around the canal network at Dudley, Worcestershire, takes us to the limit of the scope of this book. His watercolour *Dudley, Worcestershire*, 1832, finds Turner among the canal complex north of Birmingham looking up towards Dudley Castle, where Thomas Newcomen's first steam-powered beam engine was installed for a colliery in 1712.[40] Turner's composition sets thirteenth-century Dudley Castle on the distant hilltop against the dense industrial development, which by the 1830s had become established in the canal basin below. The scene was later engraved by Robert Wallis (1794–1878) and was included, together with Turner's *Coventry*, in the 1835 volume of prints *Picturesque Views in England and Wales*.[41]

The scene is brilliantly sensed by Turner for which, working with both transparent watercolour and body colour, he employs a subtly limited range of colour based on the violet end of the spectrum, to achieve the effects in this drawing. In *Dudley, Worcestershire*, a drawing once owned by John Ruskin (1819–1900), it seems clear that Turner had been on the barges and into the foundries, forges and workshops, and had tasted the smoke and the smell of industry. He understands the people employed in the industries he portrays. In this scene, set below a dusky moonlit sky, a saltire composition draws the viewer in. We are dazzled by the glare of the furnaces from the right, the warehouses and a pumping station which appear from the gloomy atmosphere on the left of the painting as smoke rises from the chimneys to the top of the image. Canal barges fill the lower right. There are awe-inspiring signals here and Turner raises issues that were becoming a significant factor of Britain's industrial development: issues of extreme working conditions and pollution, issues which would not be seriously addressed for more than a century. Turner makes no judgment but, by laying a beguiling veil over the scene, asks the viewer to peer into his painting and seek out and reflect on the issues he raises.

In Turner's canal drawings from the late 1790s to the 1830s he presents his evolving response to the changes that Britain was undergoing at the turn of the century. He ponders the place of the emerging industries in the context of the country's historical development and observes with delight the opening up of pastoral scenery along the canal routes. He recognises the risks that entrepreneurs were taking in pursuit of industrial development but leaves the viewer to consider the effects of pollution and the impact of the concentration of industry in urban areas.

The discussion in this chapter has been confined to Turner's canal drawings but in his wider response to the developing industrial sector we find him recognising the impact of the country's expanding economy in the spread of the steam railway and the steamboat, the new docks and harbours, and in his views of the manufacturing towns and cities. The expansion of towns and cities increased the demand for building materials and in the final essay we will see how the demand for slate from the quarries of North Wales, where quarry owners were slow to adopt new technology, affected the lives of those employed in this industry.

Notes

1 William S. Rodner, 1997.

2 James Thomson: 'Liberty, Part V: The Prospect', 1736, p. 276.

3 In 1792, 1794, 1795, 1798 and 1799.

4 Andrew Wilton, 1984, p. 5. He was attracted during his second visit in 1794 by the traditional technology of the picturesque and decaying rural watermills, however, e.g. *Marford Mill, Wrexham, Denbighshire*, 1794/5, by J.M.W. Turner.

5 *Aberdulais Mill, Glamorganshire*, 1797, by J.M.W. Turner and *South Wales* sketchbook, page 6, *c.*1795, TB XXVI, Tate, London.

6 *Interior of a Forge, Making Anchors*, 1796/7; *The Interior of a Tilt Forge, with Figures*; and *An Iron Foundry*, or *Cannon Foundry: ?Interior of Walker's Foundry at Rotherham or Conisbrough*, *c.*1798; and *Cyfarthfa Iron Works*, 1798 (four drawings), by J.M.W. Turner.

7 *Chirk Aqueduct in Course of Construction*, 1798, by J.M.W. Turner.

8 T. Ruddock, 1979, pp. 129–31.

9 The aqueduct is a Grade I listed structure and underwent rehabilitation in 2012.

10 *Lancaster: The Aqueduct, with the Town in the Distance*, 1797, by J.M.W. Turner. See Andrew Wilton, '*Lancaster: The Aqueduct, with the Town in the Distance* 1797 by Joseph Mallord William Turner', catalogue entry, August 2010 in David Blayney (ed.), *J.M.W. Turner: Sketchbooks, Drawings and Water Colours*, Tate Research Publication, November 2014, https://www.tate.org.uk/art/research-publications/jmw-turner/joseph-mallord-william-turner-lancaster-the-aqueduct-with-the-town-in-the-distance-r1150244 (accessed 22 June 2020).

11 *Yorkshire 2* sketchbook, 1816, graphite on paper, 15.4 × 9.6 cm. D1157, TBCXLV 77; D11165, TB CXLV 81; D11167, TB CXLV 82a; and 1816, graphite on paper, 17.3 × 26.0 cm. Folio 9 verso: D11585, TB CXLVIII 36; and Folio 10 recto: D11583, TB CXLVIII 35.

12 *Lancaster from the Aqueduct*, 1816, 17.3 × 26.0 cm, graphite on paper, *Yorkshire 5* sketchbook, Folio 10 Verso: D11584, TBCXLVIII 35a. Also see David Hill, '*Lancaster from the Aqueduct* 1816 by Joseph Mallord William Turner', catalogue entry, May 2009, in David Blayney Brown (ed.), *J.M.W. Turner: Sketchbooks, Drawings and Watercolours*, Tate Research Publication, December 2013, https://www.tate.org.uk/art/research-publications/jmw-turner/joseph-mallord-william-turner-lancaster-from-the-aqueduct-r1143677 (accessed 22 June 2020).

13 The castle was reconstructed/rehabilitated between 1786 and 1799.

14 *The Bridge of Augustus at Rimini*, 1796–7, by J.M.W. Turner, after Richard Wilson 1796–7. Turner shows the Skerton Bridge with six arches, misinterpreting the sketches in his *Yorkshire 2* sketchbook.

15 William Shakespeare, *King Richard II*, Act II, Scene 1, lines 46 and 49.

16 William S. Rodner, 1997.

17 Rev. Foster, 1805. and see Kriz, 1997, p. 86.

18 A.O. Lovejoy, 1941, pp. 258–61. For other syntheses see William Vaughan, 1978; M. Löwy and R. Sayre, 2001.

19 Margaret Drabble (ed.), 1985, p. 843.

20 Quoted in J. Lindsay, 1966, p. 130.

21 Vaughan, W. 1978, p. 173.

22 *Leeds Mercury*, 20 October 1816.

23 *A canal tunnel near Leeds*, *c.*1799, depicts '… a flat-bottomed canal boat passing through what may be the "great tunnel" of the Leeds and Liverpool Canal at Foulridge, 1,648 yards long…'. William S. Rodner, 1997, p. 95. The drawing is also listed in Andrew Wilton, 1979. See also *A Canal Tunnel near Leeds*, *c.*1799–1801, by J.M.W. Turner.

24 *Lock Gates with Kirkstall Abbey in the Distance*, *c.*1816–22, by J.M.W. Turner and his sketch known as *Kirkstall Lock*, *c.*1816–22.

25 See Alice Rylance-Watson, '*Views of Kirkstall c*1824 by Joseph Mallord William Turner', catalogue entry, February 2015, in David Blayney Brown (ed.), *J.M.W. Turner Sketchbooks, Drawings and Watercolours*, Tate Research Publication, August 2016, https://www.tate.org.uk/art/research-publications/jmw-turner/joseph-mallord-william-turner-views-of-kirkstall-r1181301 (accessed 20 June 2020).

26 *Kirkstall Lock on the River Aire*, mezzotint on steel-faced plate, engraved by W. Say after J.M.W. Turner, in W.B. Cooke, 1827.

27 See Alice Rylance-Watson, '*More Park, near Watford, on the River Colne* c. 1823 by Joseph Mallord William Turner', catalogue entry, March 2013, in David Blayney Brown (ed.), *J.M.W. Turner Sketchbooks, Drawings and Watercolours*, Tate Research Publication, August 2014, https://www.tate.org.uk/art/research-publications/jmw-turner/joseph-mallord-william-turner-more-park-near-watford-on-the-river-colne-r1146207 (accessed 20 June 2020).

28 E. Shanes, 1990, p. 104.

29 *More Park*, *c.*1807, *Rivers* sketchbook, Folio 49 Recto, D06071, TB XCVI 76.

30 Quoted in Luke Herrmann, 1990, p. 155. And see *More Park, near Watford on the River Colne* by Charles Turner, mezzotint engraving on steel after J.M.W. Turner, 1824.

31 *Distant View of Fonthill Abbey, with an Aqueduct in the Foreground*, 1799, by J.M.W. Turner. See Andrew Wilton, 'Distant View of Fonthill Abbey, with an Aqueduct in the Foreground', 1799, by Joseph Mallord William Turner', catalogue entry, March 2013, in David Blayney Brown (ed.), *J.M.W. Turner Sketchbooks, Drawings and Watercolours*, Tate Research Publication, April 2015, https://www.tate.org.uk/art/research-publications/jmw-turner/joseph-mallord-william-turner-distant-view-of-fonthill-abbey-with-an-aqueduct-in-the-foreground-r1174231 (accessed 20 June 2020).

32 See previous note.

33 J. Latimer, 1893. The canal nearest to Fonthill, the Kennet and Avon canal, is some 20 miles north was completed in 1810.

34 A.H.J. Green, 2009, p. 20.

35 James Hamilton, 1998.

36 P.A.L. Vine, 2007, p. 60.

37 Between 1973 and 1977 The Sussex Canal Trust sought to re-establish the canal, excavating a length of a few hundred yards. The Sussex Industrial Archaeological Society aims to uncover and conserve some of the lost structures on the Sussex line. See Green, 2009.

38 *Brighton and Arundel* sketchbook, *c.*1824, D18331, TB CCX 12A and D18332, TB CCX 13, Tate, London appear to be Turner's possible starting points for the painting.

39 *Brighton from the Sea*, 1828, by J.M.W. Turner.

40 *Dudley, Worcestershire*, *c.*1832, by J.M.W. Turner. The industry has now disappeared from the area apart from a number of relict buildings and canals which are preserved as part of the Black Country Museum.

41 *Coventry, Warwickshire*, *c.*1832, by J.M.W. Turner. See Hannibal Evans Lloyd, 1838, *Picturesque views in England and Wales*.

7 Henry Hawkins and the Penrhyn Slate Quarry

The spectacular view of *Penrhyn Slate Quarry*, 1832 (Figure 7.1), was painted by Henry Hawkins (1800–81), one of a group of British Victorian artists of whom little is recorded and whose works are rarely seen. This painting is one of only a handful of Hawkins's known paintings and was either commissioned or bought by George Hay Dawkins-Pennant, the owner of Penrhyn Quarry, in the earlier nineteenth century.[1] The painting passed by descent to the Douglas-Pennant family and the Lords of Penrhyn, and is now held in the National Trust collection at Penrhyn Castle.[2]

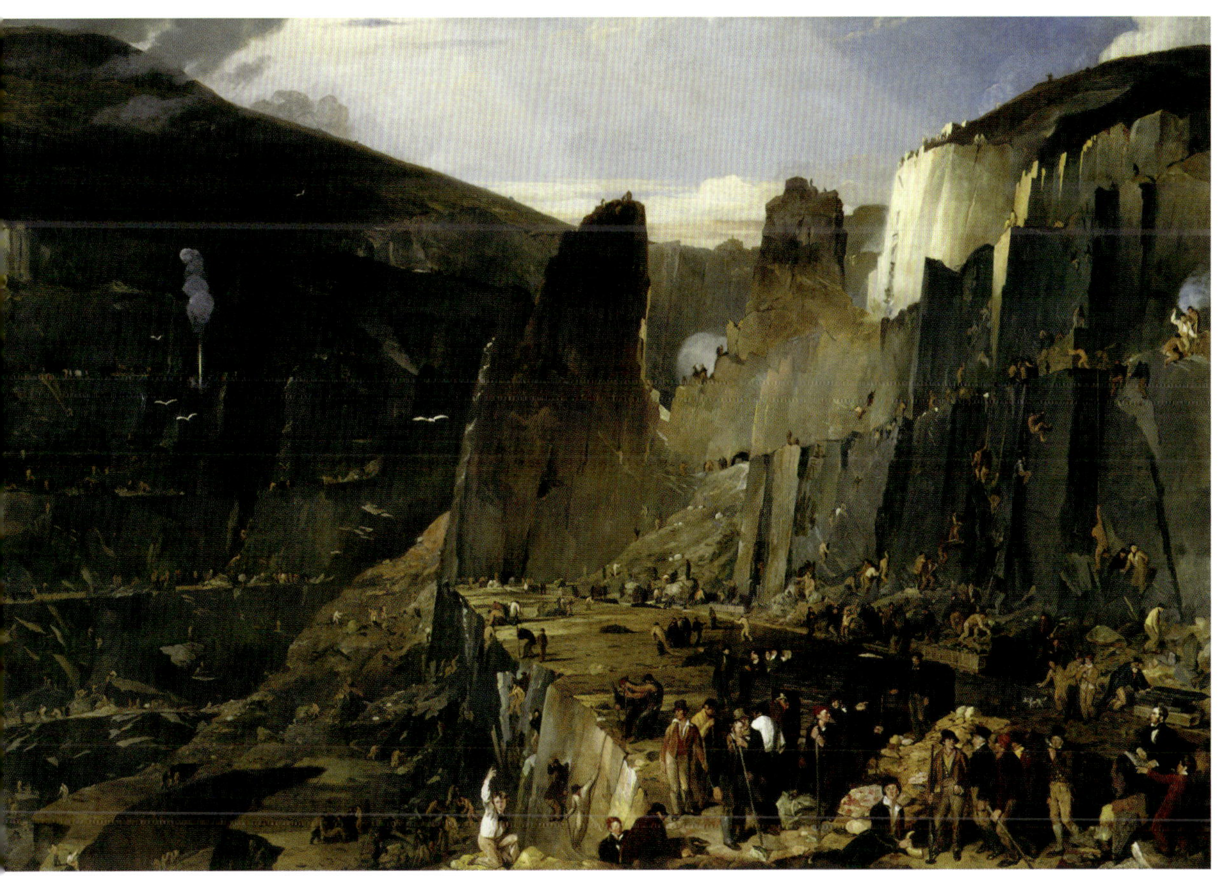

7.1 *Penrhyn Slate Quarry*, 1832, by Henry Hawkins, oil on canvas, 132 x 188 cm. Penrhyn Castle, Gwynedd, Wales.

The lives of the artists referred to in previous chapters, who like Hawkins painted industrial scenes during the early years of the Industrial Revolution, are mostly well-documented. The record of Hawkins's career is patchy and would not suggest that he would produce such a significant work as *Penrhyn Slate Quarry*, so I have prefaced this chapter with details of what is known of him both in the periods before and after he painted this work to provide background and context. The chapter then continues with discussion of Hawkins's patron, George Hay Dawkins-Pennant, the reputation of the Penrhyn Quarry in North Wales and the symbolism of Hawkins's painting.

No friends or relatives appear to have kept records of Hawkins's life and the details garnered from census records, the archives of the Society of British Artists and a brief survey of the few known paintings by Hawkins still only offer a rather sketchy picture of his career. Extracts from contemporary reviews of his works supplement these and reveal the struggle that this apparently unappreciated and mostly unsuccessful artist faced during his working life.

Nineteenth-century census returns show Henry Hawkins giving his profession as 'portrait painter' or 'artist'. In 1851, the earliest census in which he appears, he is found lodging in the household of Frederick Beighton, a wax chandler, at 8 Great Marylebone Street, Marylebone, London. In 1861 we find him lodging in the household of Martha Putman, a widow and a plaiter, at Manor Street, Great Berkhamstead, Hertfordshire, and giving his birthplace as Bourne End, near Hemel Hempstead. In 1881, the year Hawkins died, he was living at 18 Crowndale Road, St Pancras, a visitor in the house of Thomas B. Banyard, house decorator, at the age of eighty-one. Henry Hawkins was born around 1800 at Bourne End and was the second child of Edward and Catherine Hawkins. He was christened on 8 March 1801 at the church in Kings Langley, not far from his place of birth. He never married and does not appear to have had any children.[3]

Hawkins was closely associated with the Society of British Artists (later the Royal Society of British Artists) where he was a founder and lifelong member. A long list of addresses is recorded for him in the catalogues of exhibitions at the Society and the Royal Academy of Arts. He appears to have rented an apartment or studio for a year or so in London before moving to another.[4] In the first twenty years of his career, he lodged in the area north of Oxford Street in London now known as Fitzrovia where many artists lived at that time. Hawkins enrolled at the Royal Academy Schools in 1821 and between 1822 and 1849 exhibited eight works at the Academy's annual exhibitions. He was a more regular and prolific contributor to the exhibitions of the Society of British Artists.[5]

The Society of British Artists was founded on 21 May 1823 at a meeting held at the Freemasons' Tavern, Great Queen Street, Lincoln's Inn Field where the participants argued that a new society should be formed on the grounds that the Royal Academy and the British Institution were inadequate to meet the needs of British artists and that it would give '… publicity to the numerous works of talent which are annually presented for exhibition'.[6] At a General Meeting of the Society on 23 December 1823, in the first year of its existence, the twenty-three-year-old Henry Hawkins was elected to the committee as one of the auditors. He was among the young un-established artists on the committee which included Clarkson Stanfield (1793–1867) and David Roberts (1796–1864) who were working as scene designers at the Theatre Royal, Drury Lane.[7]

The minutes of committee meetings from the early years show that financial matters were of central importance to the Society as it began to develop. The Society had to meet expenses in establishing a gallery at Suffolk Street in London, and Hawkins played a role in these activities. He was not re-elected as an auditor at the end of December 1824, however, but was co-opted on to the committee in 1825 and is to be found in the Society's records with an active role on the hanging committee for the 1825 summer exhibition. He remained a committee member until the end of 1826.[8] Hawkins exhibited almost 150 works in oils and watercolour at the Society's exhibitions between their inception in 1824 and his death in 1881.

Despite these contributions to the exhibitions, his name rarely appears in reviews of them. The review in the *Art Journal* of April 1858 of a painting he exhibited at the Society of British Artists' Summer Exhibition at the Suffolk Street Gallery, Pall Mall East, is one of the few positive ones of his work:

> The [Society of] 'British artists' are not in the habit of covering their walls with portraits, The small number of pictures of this class that are now exhibited possess no claims for particular comment: they are very fair portraits, No. 6 for example, Mr Hawkins's portrait of *Lady Mary Grimstone (now Viscountess Folkestone), a sketch* [hung in the Great Room] being something much better than a very clever and effective 'sketch'.[9]

Some reviews of his work are damning. The *Spectator* ran an aggressive campaign against the Society of British Artists between 1840 and 1844, asserting that the Society, although inferior, was trying to compete with the Royal Academy and was not encouraging good young artists, as it had originally professed it would:

'Vulgar Arts' would be the proper heading of a notice of the
disgraceful exhibition of conceit, incapacity and unfairness on the
part of the 'Society of *Bad* Artists' who have got possession of the
Gallery in Suffolk Street, and who seem bent on perpetrating its
nickname 'Refuge for the Destitute' by driving away the few clever
painters who continue to send their works there.[10]

And if Henry Hawkins, who had by then been a Member of the Society for
more than twenty years, had read the review of the 1845 exhibition in the
Spectator, he would have been distressed:

> … The two newly-elected members, Messrs H.M. Anthony and
> H. Hawkins, are such prodigies, the one of incapability, the other
> of vicious mannerism, that their productions are curiosities in
> their way. *Sheep-washing* (240), by Mr Hawkins, is a rare specimen
> of ploughboy painting; but his portraits of *Twin daughters of the
> Honourable Granville Ryder, M.P* (286) are indescribably ludicrous.[11]

Hawkins ploughed on during the 1840s and 1850s and seems to have made
a living from commissioned portraits, including some of the aristocracy, but
the lists of his exhibited works in this period also show him attempting to
widen the scope of his subject-matter. Two years after the 1845 review in the
Spectator, a critic in the *Art-Union Monthly Journal* reviewed his painting *The
Morning of Life* at the Society of British Artist's exhibition: 'Groups of nude
"bambini" busied in sports as we find children of Albano and Rubens occupied
in. The subject is not for the tastes of the present day.'[12] This comment appears
to confirm the central problem Hawkins faced; although dedicated and serious
in his endeavours as an artist, his works were unpopular with the critics who
found him failing to capture the mood or fashion of the period.

The cruellest comment on his work is found in a review in the *Echo* on 5 April
1879. A reference is made to a work Hawkins exhibited at the Society of
British Artists at the end of his life when he was nearly eighty, his painting *The
Progress of Time: Sun-Dial in Aldbury Churchyard, Herts*:

> Perhaps the most ambitious and the most wretched picture in this
> exhibition is Mr H. Hawkins's 'The Progress of Time, Sundial in
> Aldbury Churchyard, Herts' (425), which from the motto appended
> to the title in the catalogue would seem to be intended to illustrate
> a passage in Shakespeare. From whatever point of view this work is
> regarded, it must be pronounced to be the most foolish failure. The
> idea is as feeble and foolish as its execution …[13]

and the next day in *The Era*, the work

> … is one of those pictures which we hope in 'progress of time' will
> cease to be hung in galleries of English Art.[14]

Unfortunately the painting cannot now be traced but the 'motto' submitted by Hawkins and entered in the catalogue is from the scene in *As You Like It* when Jaques tells of his meeting with a motley fool in the Forest of Arden, the scene in which he describes the seven ages of man.[15] Henry Hawkins was born some 5 miles from Aldbury Churchyard, the site of the painting, and the elderly Hawkins was no doubt reflecting on the ups and downs of his own life and career.

Among Henry Hawkins's few known works we have his *Crucifixion*, a painting which may have been inspired by John Martin's (1789–1854) mezzotint *The Crucifixion* published in 1834. Hawkins's *Crucifixion* was exhibited at the Royal Academy in 1835 to no known critical response.[16] The scene draws on the description from the New Testament when at the ninth hour in darkness '… the earth did quake and the rocks rent; and the graves were opened; and many bodies of the saints which slept arose' (Matthew, XXVII, 45-53).[17] The list of Hawkins's exhibited works includes several religious paintings, including *The Parting of Elijah and Elisha* (1833) and *The Ascension of our Saviour* (1848) and significantly, as we shall see later, his painting of *Dante in Florence*.[18] *The Crucifixion* is the only work of a similar scale as his *Penrhyn Slate Quarry*, the whereabouts of which can be traced today.[19]

Around the time Hawkins exhibited *Penrhyn Slate Quarry*, there are a few references to him in the daily press. In 1832, he is listed as one of the Stewards for the Artists' General Benevolent Institution for the Relief of Decayed Artists, their Widows, and Orphans' Seventh Anniversary Festival celebrated at the Freemasons' Hall on Saturday 26 May 1832. The event was attended by the President of the RA, Sir Martin Shee (1769–1850) and the institution's patron HRH Prince Augustus, Duke of Sussex (1773–1843).[20] In 1836 Hawkins is listed among the subscribers making a contribution (£5, equivalent to about £60 in 2020) with George Hay Dawkins-Pennant (£100, equivalent to about £1,200) to fund the statue by Matthew Cotes Wyatt (1777–1862) of King George III riding his favourite horse Adonis.[21] In the 1830s, at the time Hawkins painted the Penrhyn Quarry scene, he appears to have been at the height of his career and these references show him maintaining his contacts and relationships with his patrons and established figures of the time.

In the period before he painted *Penrhyn Slate Quarry* in 1832, Hawkins had exhibited more than two dozen works in oil and watercolour and several miniatures at the Society of British Artists and two paintings at the Royal Academy. These included animal portraits, several sentimental and romantic scenes including *The Fisherman's Return, Evening, 'O mother see 'tis him'*, and a work inspired by James Thomson's description of Musidora in his poem *The Seasons*, as she is secretly observed by her youthful lover Damon: *Musidora, 'With fancy blushing at the doubtful breeze, Alarmed and starting like the peaceful fawn.'*[22] This does not suggest that Hawkins would, in *Penrhyn Slate Quarry*, produce a work in which he reveals and comments with such force on the social order and conditions at the celebrated slate quarry near Bangor, the largest of its kind in the world.

In 1736, almost one hundred years before Hawkins's painting, the small scattered quarries on the Penrhyn Estate produced less than 2,000 tons of slate per year. A more focused approach to slate extraction was taken from about 1770 when Richard Pennant, later 1st Baron Penrhyn of County Louth (*c.*1739–1808), inherited the extensive workings through his marriage to Anne Susannah Warburton, Lady Penrhyn. Richard Pennant recognised the commercial value of the quarries and the increasing demand for slate for roofing and cladding in the new towns and cities, and in schools for blackboards and writing-slates. They and their architects, the Wyatts, actively promoted the use of Welsh slate for use in buildings.[23]

In 1820, a few years after the Dowager Lady Penrhyn died and after George Hay Dawkins-Pennant had inherited the estate, the quarry produced 40,000 tons of slate and provided employment for more than 1,000 men. Production continued to grow in the 1820s and 1830s and was boosted further by the repeal of Pitt's wartime slate duty in 1831. By 1836, the Penrhyn quarries produced about 75,000 tons of slate annually and provided employment for nearly 1,800. Slate from the quarry was transported to Port Penrhyn on a narrow-gauge railway track and exported to London, Dublin and Liverpool for use there or for onward distribution. Profits from the quarry added substantially to the income accruing from the Dawkins-Pennant's Jamaican sugar plantations and contributed to the cost of building the mighty neo-Norman Penrhyn Castle.

Richard Pennant, 1st Baron Penrhyn of County Louth's Irish title permitted him to represent Liverpool as a Member of Parliament. He sat in the House of Commons from 1784–90. Liverpool was at one of the corners of the triangular trade route which connected Britain, West Africa and the West Indies and by which the export of goods to West Africa, the purchase and transport of slaves to the West Indies and the return of sugar from plantations was made possible. Although Richard Pennant never visited the plantations, he was noted for his numerous and vigorous speeches in defence of slavery.[24] His successor at Penrhyn, George Hay Dawkins-Pennant, who was Member of Parliament for Newark, Nottinghamshire between 1814 and 1818 and for New Romney, Kent, between 1820 and 1830, also opposed the emancipation of slaves within the British Empire.[25] Despite the ban on the slave trade from 1807, the total emancipation of all British slaves was not concluded until the 1830s. The announcement in the *London Evening Standard* in July 1833 made it clear that Hawkins's patron, Dawkins-Pennant, had not by then freed his slaves. Announcing the engagement of his daughter to Captain Gordon Douglas of the Grenadier Guards, the reporter in the *London Evening Standard* wrote, 'Mr. Pennant (the most extensive proprietor of slaves in the West Indies) has made handsome settlement on the lady …'.[26] Seven hundred and sixty-four slaves were working on his plantations in 1833.[27]

Not only was Dawkins-Pennant able to make a handsome settlement on his daughter but also to put on an event to mark the occasion '… such as has never been witnessed before in this district by the oldest man living'. The festivities to celebrate the wedding on 6 August 1833 are described in the *North Wales Chronicle* when through '… the munificence of the proprietor of Penrhyn … not less than 3,000 persons partook of his bounty, and kept joyful festival in honour of the happy event'. At the first peep of dawn, the firing of salvos of artillery was heard at Port Penrhyn and the vessels there 'hoisted every flag they had'. Marching bands accompanied a procession of about 700 children who were served cake and a cup of spiced ale. There was a dinner at the slate quarry which 1,700 attended and ate 'prime roast and boiled beef, mutton, plumb [sic] pudding …' and drank '… a plentiful supply of *cwrw da*'.[28] There was a dinner at Penrhyn Castle for 260 workmen, 120 tradesmen and others, and a public dinner for fifty at the Penrhyn Arms, Bangor. A band played 'the usual mess-room air "The Roast Beef of Old England"' at a dinner for 150 workmen at Port Penrhyn.[29]

The Penrhyn Quarry became a well-known landmark and attracted tourists and artists from both Britain and abroad from the late eighteenth century onwards. It was noted for both its size and depth and for the unusual landforms that the excavations produced. Geologists and natural scientists were interested in the near vertical planes of slate and the inclusions in the uplifted metamorphic rock. The young Charles Darwin (1809–82), a few months before he set out on his voyage on *The Beagle* in 1831, with the geologist Professor Adam Sedgwick (1785–1873) visited the quarry during their travels in North Wales. Prince Hermann von Pückler-Muskau (1785–1871) visited in 1828 and records in his journal, 'Above the blasted walls of slate, smooth as a mirror and several hundred feet high, scarcely enough of the blue heaven was visible to enable me to distinguish mid-day from twilight … .'[30] The young Princess Victoria visited with her mother the Duchess of Kent on Saturday

8 September 1832. She records in her journal how she saw the men, some hanging from ropes, split and cut the slate and how others used wedges to split and separate blocks of slate from the rock face.[31]

Artists have visited the Penrhyn Quarry over a period of more than two centuries to capture the forms of this man-made landscape. John Nixon (*c.*1750–1818), in *Bangor Slate Quarry*, 1807, gives us a view of men at work in a small section of the quarry; Thomas Hosmer Shepherd (1793–1864), in a wood engraving *Chwarel Cae-Braich-y-Cafn, Ger Bethesda, c.*1830, delivers a view taken from a place not far from Hawkins's viewpoint, and later images by other artists include topographical views of the quarry terraces.[32] Henry Hawkins's more complex and populated picture of 1832, from an artist of no great reputation, comes as something new.[33]

Hawkins appears to have travelled to Wales in 1831. He exhibited portraits at the Society of British Artists in that year, indicating that he had been in Wales but his connections to Penrhyn or anything which might have suggested to Dawkins-Pennant that he should choose Hawkins to paint a view of the quarry is difficult to establish.[34] If we assume that Henry Hawkins was commissioned by the elderly George Hay Dawkins-Pennant to paint the quarry scene, we may also assume that he was given an indication of what he would like to see in the painting. Hawkins's response, however, is personal and gives an artist's interpretation of a scene which goes beyond the probable wishes of his patron. The quarry, as we have seen, was an important piece of Dawkins-Pennant's estate. There can be little doubt of the coincidence of the date of the painting and the visit of Princess Victoria to the quarry in 1832, which Dawkins-Pennant would have wished to have had commemorated.

The visit of their Royal Highnesses is described in the *North Wales Chronicle* of 11 September. On a 'delightfully fine and beautiful morning', the shipping at Port Penrhyn and in the Bay was decked out with flags and bunting. Guns saluted as the royal party passed by. Flags were flying all along the route to the quarry and the horses pulling the slate trucks had ribbons about their heads. Near the village of Bethesda (which chiefly comprised the homes of quarrymen) '… triumphal arches had been erected across the road, whilst every Cottage was more or less ornamented'. At the Penrhyn Slate Quarry, flags flew on the high points of the quarry. The royal party came in their carriages to the quarry, where over 1,500 quarrymen were at work. Batteries of guns announced the arrival of the royal party followed by a twenty-one gun salute. The royal party then visited Penrhyn Castle '… to view that magnificent and interesting structure' where Mr and Mrs Dawkins-Pennant held a reception

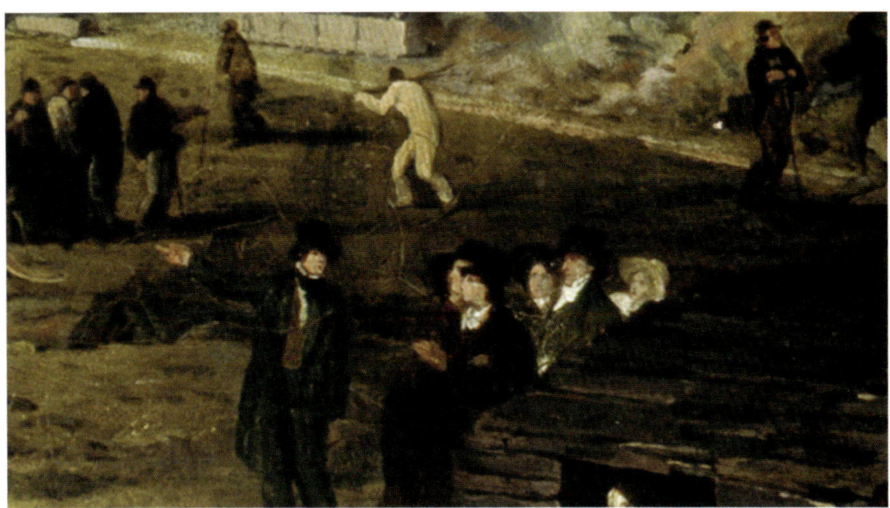

before their Royal Highnesses left to return to Plas Newydd, the home of the Marquess of Anglesey.[35]

Hawkins seems to refer to their visit to the quarry. In the group of five visitors partly hidden behind the quarrymen's shelter on one of the main terraces of the quarry, Hawkins includes a figure that certainly matches an earlier portrait of the sixty-eight-year-old George Hay Dawkins-Pennant.[36] We find his wife Sofia Mary by his side, with perhaps their younger daughter standing behind. In front of them we see two women who appear to be the young Princess Victoria with the Duchess of Kent being shown the extent of the quarry workings (Figure 7.2). Hawkins could have painted a celebratory painting showing flags flying on the high points of the quarry and batteries of guns being fired as the royal party and their attendants view the quarry. He does not do this. In this seemingly secular painting, Hawkins puts great emphasis on the quarrying process itself and the principal actors in the quarry.

In the bottom right of the picture a group of quarrymen, ignoring the important visitors, are discussing the terms of a contract to work a new part of the quarry with a quarry manager. Another group nearby, some of whom lean on their slate-splitting tools, await the outcome of the negotiations (Figure 7.3). In the mid-nineteenth century, quarrymen in North Wales were not generally full-time employees but worked, often within a family structure, to provide the skills required by the quarry owner. A group, perhaps men and boys from the same family and some friends, would agree 'a stake' with the quarry manager for the right to work a face or an area of the quarry. The system led to the setting up of slate splitters' shelters, one of which can be seen in Hawkins's painting, providing a base for individual groups. The labourers, who undertook

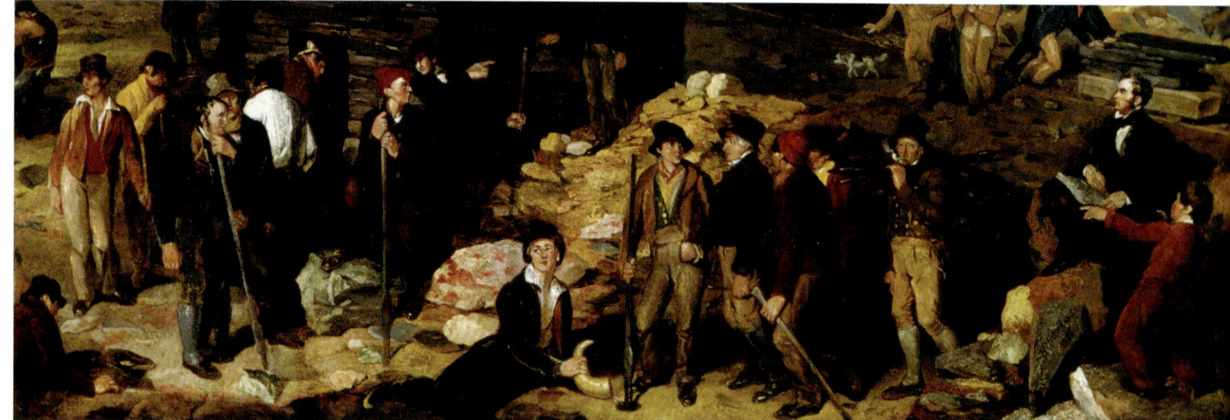

the unskilled work such as clearing rubble, were employed on a day-by-day basis.

Dafydd Gwyn has suggested that the slate industry was technically self-contained, formed of self-confident and literate communities, strongholds of the Welsh language and that 'The spirit [of the quarrymen] was sustained by the traditions of the chapels, which claimed the allegiance of some 80 per cent of the people of Wales, where individuals had their own say in the running of their places of worship and could make up their minds on matters of doctrine.'[37] Bethesda, a few miles from the quarry, with its independent chapel built in 1820, provided much of the housing and facilities for the families and employees who worked at the Penrhyn Quarry.[38] The village was built on land which was not part of the Penrhyn Quarry estate, giving those who lived there some sort of independence.

Hawkins shows several hundred quarrymen and labourers, some hanging precariously from or clambering up a smooth rock face, others at work prising large blocks of slate from the faces of the quarry. Day labourers can be seen moving rubble and slabs of slate from the quarry to be transferred by rail to the splitters' yards. The painting reveals the vastness of the quarry, the types and extent of human activity and the mixture of resignation and enthusiasm with which the labourers perform their tasks. Visitors to the quarry mention the '… bustle of the workmen on the various ledges, the breaking up of the Strata, and the noises of the splitting, and shaping with at intervals the roar of a blast, and the subsequent crash of the pieces, thrown in every direction …'.[39] Henry Hawkins includes in the painting a man with a bugle (Figure 7.3), whose job would have been to alert workers to an imminent blast. He shows him lounging on the terrace in the foreground, perhaps suggesting the somewhat casual approach to safety that was adopted in the quarry. In the early

7.3 *Penrhyn slate quarry*
(Detail II, Quarry manager and quarrymen, and the artist Henry Hawkins far right), 1832, by Henry Hawkins.

1800s an overseer reported that 150 workers were wounded and seven or eight were killed in accidents at the quarry each year.[40] Contemplating Hawkins's painting today, the conditions at the quarry are shocking.[41]

Henry Hawkins recognises and presents in this painting the hierarchy of this enterprise in a picture which includes the quarry owner, his agents and managers, the quarrymen and day labourers, and a portrait of himself sketching in the bottom right corner of the picture. Just under this portrait on a slab of slate he has signed the painting 'Hy Hawkins, 1832'. By including this portrait of himself, Hawkins expresses his self-confidence as an artist and the creator of the work, and could be recalling a practice found in the religious imagery of the Renaissance where the artist includes his patron and himself among others in the picture. However, here Hawkins, holding his sketchbook with a young guide by his side, positions himself in the corner of one of the most explicit images of some of the deplorable conditions endured by quarry workers at this time.

Religious paintings by Hawkins suggest he was a devout member of the church and that he pondered Christian teachings and religious painting by other artists. His painting of *Dante in Florence*, its whereabouts now unknown, also indicates that he was familiar with the poet and his *Divine Comedy*.[42] Perhaps we also see Hawkins, in *Penrhyn Slate Quarry*, recognising a parallel with the image of Mount Purgatory in the painting of *La commedia illumina Firenze* by Domenico di Michelino (1417–91) which hangs on the north wall of Florence Cathedral (Figure 7.4). As far as we know Hawkins did not visit Italy and would not have seen the original painting but it is possible that he would have seen the recent line engraving by Vincenzo Gozzini (1760–1831) of Domenico's painting in a copy of *La Metropolitana Fiorentina Illustrata* which had been published in Florence in 1820.[43]

In *La commedia illumina Firenze*, Domenico bases his painting on descriptions from *The Divine Comedy* by Dante Alighieri (1265–1321) to create a tribute to the poet. In the painting Dante is seen holding a copy of his poem in which he, guided by Virgil, describes the path he takes and the sights he sees as he passes through Hell and climbs Mount Purgatory on the ascent to Paradise. Dante describes those struggling on Mount Purgatory as they serve their punishments on the different levels or terraces and attempt to reach the summit. Domenico shows Dante's home, the city of Florence, on the right of the fresco, his vision of hell on the left and Mount Purgatory in the distance.

With this in view, Henry Hawkins, the artist holding his sketchbook at the right of the painting, appears to signal a correspondence with Domenico's

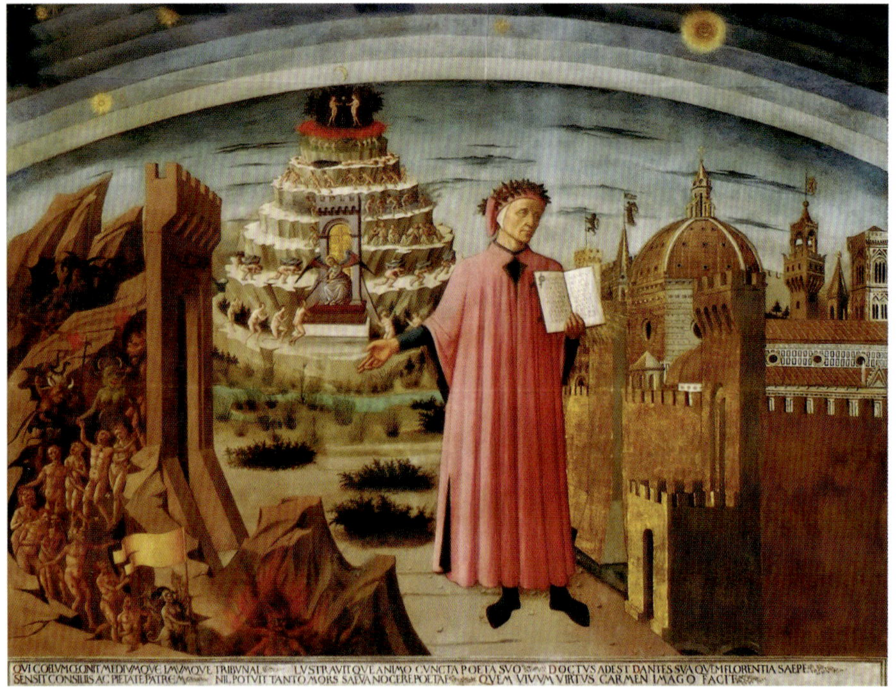

7.4 *La commedia illumina Firenze*, 1465, by Domenico di Michelino, tempera on panel, 232.5 x 292 cm. Santa Maria del Fiore, Florence.

image in which Dante holds his *Divine Comedy*. Alistair Laing has pointed out that the boy in the white shirt with hand upraised, in the bottom centre of the painting, emerging from the lower levels of the quarry and echoing the outline of the strange rock form at the end of the main terrace, takes on the pose of Joshua Reynolds's *John the Baptist in the Wilderness*, c.1776.[44] Hawkins appears to refer here to John the Baptist, the patron saint of Florence, '… del gran Giovanni,/ che sempre santo il deserto e il martiro/ sofferse, e poi l'Infermo da due anni …' in Dante's *Il Paradiso*.[45]

The quarry terraces and rock faces begin to assume a modern and present purgatory. The main terrace, representing the contemporary socio-economic hierarchy, includes the visiting royal party, the Dawkins-Pennants, the quarry managers, the quarrymen and the day labourers. On the face of the rock below this terrace, men cling on to life, attempting to avoid the descent into the hell of the lower regions. Hawkins shows a group tending an injured or dead man below and another group close to the young John the Baptist look up in consternation as another labourer is about to fall. On the terraces and rock faces above we see quarrymen and labourers undergoing the terror and torment of repetitive and dangerous tasks in a purgatory of their own which they may never manage to escape. The forms of some of the labourers are almost replicas of those seen on the lower terrace of purgatory in Vincenzo Gozzini's engraving of Domenico's *La commedia illumina Firenze*.

Dante's concept of Purgatory rests on the premise that life in the Garden of Eden before the fall of man was to have been the perfect heavenly life and that only by finding a way through purgatory could mankind regain the Garden of Eden and Earthly Paradise, knowledge of earthly wisdom and a consciousness and nearness to God. Hawkins imitates this in the Penrhyn Quarry painting. At the top of the slate mountain, a shaft of light illuminates the uppermost rock face where at the final ascent there appears to be a rock fall. Perhaps this is the metaphorical and final fire of Dante's Purgatory that must be passed through before entering the sunlit uplands of the Earthly Paradise of the Garden of Eden.

We have in *Penrhyn Slate Quarry* a manifest image of the conditions that labourers of the period endured and of which Hawkins's patron, Dawkins-Pennant, who features in the painting, appears to have been either completely oblivious or in denial. The quarry owner appears to have been quite unconcerned to have the canvas hung on the walls of his castle, which was built on the proceeds from this slate quarry at Penrhyn and his plantations in Jamaica.

This is not a work which speaks of new technology – rather the reverse – but it illustrates how the impact of the early years of the Industrial Revolution made increasing demands on the manual labour employed in mines and quarries to match the complementary demands of those working in the new towns and cities. The painting comes from the hand of a little-known and often derided artist who had the vision to present a scene which expresses a nineteenth-century vision of Britain in the context of a Divine Comedy. Hawkins's painting of the quarry should have served as a prescient warning to its owner. Penrhyn Quarry holds a significant place in the history of the British Labour Movement. It was the site of a strike in 1873 and two prolonged strikes, one in 1896 and a second in 1900 which lasted for three years.

Notes

1 Alastair Laing, 1995, p. 95. Painting accepted in lieu of death duties from the estate of Hugh Napier Douglas Pennant, 4th Baron Penrhyn of Llangedai, and allocated to the National Trust in 1951.

2 The painting was exhibited in *Paintings from National Trust Houses* at the National Gallery, London in 1995, see Alastair Laing, *In Trust for the Nation*, 1995.

3 The consistency of the census returns suggests that the Royal Academy Schools entry of 1821 (note 5, below) giving Henry Hawkins's age as twenty-five (i.e. born 1796) is an error.

4 *Morning Post*, Friday 12 February 1836, reports on a court case in which Henry Hawkins is a witness and living at 105 Titchfield Street, London.

5 Ref. RAA/KEE/1/1/1/51 (1809–22), p. 51-H, 31 October, 1821, Royal Academy Archives. Algernon Graves, 1906, Reprint 1970, vol. IV, p. 32.

6 Royal Society of British Artists [RSBA], 1823–7, Ref BA-M1.

7 Royal Society of British Artists [RSBA], Council Minutes (M1), 1823–27, Ref AAD/1997/8/1, and RSBA Deed of Establishment, 27 December 1823, Ref AAD/1997/8/47. The President was Thomas Heaphy, the Vice-President Thomas Hofland, the Treasurer John Glover and the Secretary William Linton.

8 RSBA Minutes of General Meeting, 3 March 1825, record that 'Mr Hawkins be desired to come to town to attend his duties.'

9 RSBA *Catalogues including Press cuttings* (Cat 3), 1855–63, Ref. AAD/1997/8/37. Mary Augusta Frederica Playdell-Bouverie (born Grimstone) (1820–79) daughter of Sir James Walter Grimstone, 1st Earl of Verulam and Lady Charlotte Harriet Grimstone, Countess Verulam. Hawkins's miniature portrait of Mary Grimstone's mother, The Right Hon. Charlotte Grimstone, Countess of Verulam was engraved by T.A. Dean (1801–60) and published as No. 69 of a Series of Female Nobility *c.*1830.

10 *The Spectator*, Saturday 27 March 1841, p. 307.

11 *The Spectator*, Saturday 25 March 1845, p. 306–07. The Honourable Granville Ryder JP (1799–1879) was a Tory MP for Hertfordshire at that time.

12 *The Art-Union, Monthly Journal*, London, 1 May 1847.

13 *The Echo*, 5 April 1879, Ref AAD/1997/8/60.

14 *The Era*, 6 April 1879, Ref AAD/1997/8/60.

15 "'It is ten o'clock; Thus we may see", quoth he, "how the world wags; Tis but an hour ago since it was nine; And after one hour more 'twill be eleven; And so, from hour to hour, we ripe and ripe, And then, from hour to hour, we rot and rot, And thereby hangs a tale.'" William Shakespeare, *As You Like It*, Act II, Scene vii.

16 *Crucifixion*, 1835, by Henry Hawkins.

17 See C. Forbes, in *The Magazine Antiques*, December 2001, vol. clx, no. 6, pp. 794–803, illus. p. 798, text pp. 800–01.

18 Algernon Graves, 1906, vol. IV, p. 32 and Anon., *Works exhibited at the Royal Society of British Artists 1824–1893*, 2 vols, 1975.

19 A later painting by Henry Hawkins, *The Great Bangor Slate Quarries, North Wales* (the Penrhyn Slate Quarry) was exhibited at the Royal Academy Exhibition in July 1848. This appears to have been a smaller work based on his visit to Anglesey in 1832. The painting was condemned by the reviewer in *The Morning Post* of 12 July 1848, who compared it with a work by Royal Academician, painter of military scenes, and sometime Keeper of the Royal Academy, George Jones (1786–1869). 'Mr. G. Jones, R.A. … He can now only execute sepia sketches, and even if these were good of their kind we would not complain, but they are monstrous in their iniquity. … (1017). This is a pitiable specimen of what it is possible for an academy to produce, and it required the introduction of such trash as (1077) "The Great Bangor Slate Quarries, North Wales" by H. Hawkins, to justify its exhibition, and lend it a false appearance of comparative merit.'

20 *Public Ledger and Daily Advertiser*, Saturday 19 May 1832.

21 *Morning Post*, Friday 17 June 1836. The statue can still be seen today just off Cockspur Street, near Trafalgar Square, London. Matthew Cotes Wyatt was one of the sons of Samuel Wyatt, the architect, who contributed significantly to the designs for the interior of Dawkins-Pennant's Penrhyn Castle.

22 James Thomson, 1730, pp. 1–168, in G. Gilfillan (ed.), 1853, pp. 75–8.

23 Alastair Laing, 1995, p. 94.

24 Anon., 2018, p. 46.

25 Anon., 2018, p. 48.

26 *London Evening Standard*, Saturday 13 July 1833.

27 University College London, *Legacies of British Slave-ownership*, https://www.ucl.ac/lbs (accessed 20 June 2020). Dawkins-Pennant received £14,684-11s-9d in compensation for release of these slaves in 1835.

28 *Crwr da* translates as good beer.

29 *North Wales Chronicle*, Tuesday 13 August 1833.

30 Hermann von Pückler-Muskau, 1832, pp. 46–9.

31 Alastair Laing, 1995, p. 94 and p. 204, n. 6.

32 These include *The Penrhyn Slate Quarries*, 1842, by W. Crane of Chester. The Penrhyn quarries continued to attract attention and a fine woodcut *Penrhyn Slate Quarries* by Harry Fenn, illustrating the quarry, is in Bayard Taylor (ed.) *Picturesque Europe*, 1875.

33 *Lord Penrhyn's Slate Quarry near Bangor*, 1807, by John Nixon.

34 George Hawkins the younger (1809–52) made a number of lithographs in 1846 at Penrhyn Castle but there appears to be no familial connection between Henry and George. The presumed commissioning of this painting is described in Alastair Laing, 1995, p. 95.

35 *North Wales Chronicle*, Tuesday 11 September 1832.

36 *George Hay Dawkins-Pennant*, *c.*1820, by John Jackson.

37 Dafydd Gwyn, pp. 12–13, in British Archaeology, July 1998, No. 36.

38 Bethesda or 'house of mercy'. Capel Bethesda was first built *c.*1820, rebuilt in 1840 and remodelled 1872–5. This is the chapel from which the town, having previously been known as Glanogwen, took its name.

39 Captain Henry and Mrs Sara Hanmer, 11 October 1819, pp. 65–6.

40 Hermann von Pückler Muskau, 1832, pp. 46–9, reports that 'An hospital exclusively devoted to workmen on this property, receives the wounded.'

41 Alastair Laing, 1995, p. 94.

42 *Dante in Florence*, by Henry Hawkins, oil on canvas, 31 × 50 in, Sotheby's auction 8 October 1992, New Delhi, Indian, European and Oriental paintings. INR 125,000 (£2,600).

43 G. Baccini *et al*, 1820, *La Metropolitana Fiorentina Illustrata*, Plate XXXVII. A fifteenth-century engraving attached to the inner binding of an old Laurentian manuscript exists but this would not have been seen by Hawkins. See Rudolph Altrocchi, 1931 'Michelino's Dante', pp. 15–59, *Speculum*, January, Vol. 6, No. 1, p. 22 and Plate III.

44 Alastair Laing, 1995, p. 95. *John the Baptist in the Wilderness*, *c.*1776, by Joshua Reynolds, Minneapolis Institute of Art.

45 '… the great John who ever holy endured the desert and the martyr death and thereafter Hell for two years' space …', Dante Alighieri, *Paradiso*, Canto XXXII, p. 389, ll.31–3.

Epilogue

In the preceding chapters we have seen how seven artists about 200 years ago were among the few who, through their paintings of industrial scenes, reacted to the changes they saw during the early years of the Industrial Revolution. They responded in a variety of ways. Joseph Wright of Derby's enigmatic painting of Sir Richard Arkwright's mills at Cromford indirectly invites us to consider the lives and working conditions of those employed. John Opie's early life in the tin and copper mining areas of Cornwall and his early success as an artist in London led him to comment on new technology, the use of capital and the hierarchy in the mining industry. Philippe-Jacques de Loutherbourg, while responding to the sublimity of the industrial scene at Coalbrookdale, reveals the impact on labour of an industry no longer subject to the diurnal and seasonal rhythms of nature that attended agricultural production. Penry Williams's close association with the iron industry in South Wales leads him to reveal the widening gap that was emerging between the employer and the employed as the iron industry expanded. William Havell's grandstand view of the excavation at the copper mines on the Isle of Anglesey and drawings by Julius Caesar Ibbetson portray the uncertainty of employment and the cheerless working conditions. J.M.W. Turner's response to the spread of the canal network finds him contemplating the historical context of the new canals and the pastoral views they opened up. He observes the risks faced by those investing in these enterprises and the pollution from the industries that the canals served. And Henry Hawkins provides a parallel between conditions that prevailed at Penrhyn Quarry and a Renaissance image of Purgatory.

These works can all be seen today in galleries or museums or as backlit images on websites but when they were painted most went into private hands and were not seen by the general public for several generations. Of them, only Turner's canal drawings, which could be found as engraved prints in books of the period, were to contribute to the wider visual culture of the day. Until the middle of the twentieth century, reactions to them were mostly limited to the owners of the paintings and the few who knew and visited them: the Cokes, the Oakes, the Daniells, the Crawshays, the Earls of Uxbridge, the Dawkins-Pennants and Lords Penrhyn.

Today we have the advantages and disadvantages of hindsight. From our encounters with vastly greater developments since the Industrial Revolution, we may not be so impressed by the scale and complexity of the industries of that time. Nevertheless, as most of the artists appear to have done, we may view with distress the lives of those employed, dismay at the polluting effects of industry and disquiet at the destruction of the natural landscape. Restricted circulation of the paintings limited their influence in the nineteenth and early twentieth century but today these works reveal artists who did not shrink from portraying the impact of industrial development and the working conditions and relationships that were becoming established in a rapidly evolving industrial society. They raise issues that were increasingly to occupy the minds of independent thinkers in the nineteenth century; the impact of industrial capitalism and its effect on the employment and living conditions of industrial workers. A brief summary of how industrial imagery occupied the visual culture from the second half of the eighteenth to the end of the twentieth century follows in this Epilogue, to put the work of our seven artists in context.

From the middle of the eighteenth century artists had been commissioned to prepare sequences of images to illustrate rural industries and industrial processes. Most of these series were published in encyclopaedias and craft manuals such as John Barrow's *New Universal Dictionary and Supplement*, Henry Croker's *Complete Dictionary of Arts and Sciences* and Diderot's *Pictorial Encyclopedia of Trades and Industry – Manufacturing and the Technical Arts*.[1] The images in these publications from the 1750s and 1760s pre-date the Industrial Revolution and the plates, which broadly serve to demonstrate a particular manufacturing process, generally portray anonymous and impersonal images of the artisan at his or her craft. Some later series lean towards a sentimental portrayal of an otherwise tough industrial workplace. At the same time most professional artists were only prepared to sketch the picturesque old watermill, the blacksmith shop or the local iron forge. They were reluctant to address the new industrial landscape. Paul Sandby, for example, showed a passing interest in rural industry and technology. Early wash drawings by him in the 1750s include a water-powered fulling mill with a family group in the foreground and a scene of a waterwheel being employed at a lead mine.[2] In his series of aquatints of 1776, he includes a small stone chafery forge by a small river, where water power is being used to drive the forge's tilt-hammer.[3] This type of forge was an established feature of eighteenth-century iron-making. Thomas Hearne in the 1790s gives us views of the outside of an iron forge at Tintern, Monmouthshire, and the unloading of pit props near a horse whim at Coalbrookdale.[4] Joseph Wright of Derby's images of blacksmiths and iron forges excepted, these types of scenes were overwhelmingly presented as picturesque rural scenes.

From the early nineteenth century illustrations of industrial scenes began to appear in published travel and county history books. Individual workers represented in these publications are essentially symbolic and the associated texts, although they may describe the industry, seldom refer to those employed.[5] By the 1830s we find scenes which celebrate new buildings, factories and urban infrastructure but although in views of municipal buildings a well-dressed middle-class person may appear, there was generally a reluctance to fully populate industrial scenes. The publications of the period satisfied the growing interest of the bourgeoisie in the impact of the spread of industry and the development of towns and cities, but illustrations revealing the unacceptable face of industrial development, other than in satirical cartoons, are rare.

The authors of *Lancashire Illustrated*, for example, published in 1832, although principally interested in illustrating grand houses, churches, new municipal buildings and the fashionable squares of Liverpool and Manchester, also present several images of new industrial development.[6] These illustrations, dedicated to factory owners, include engravings of the six-storey cotton factory in Union Street and the Twist Factory in Oxford Street, Manchester. Figures are in short supply; a couple wait in a canal barge near Union Street, carters and women carry bales of cotton on their heads near the twist factory. The illustrations illustrate the polluted atmosphere but do not tell, as the publication *Observations of the State of Children in Cotton Mills* relates, of the conditions endured by the 'pale-faced', 'stunted', 'scrofulous' children with 'swollen joints', suffering a 'hoarseness and hollowness of voice', who were employed in the mills up to fourteen hours a day.[7] Illustrators of such books almost always looked for ways of softening the images, 'air-brushing' from them the grime, dirt and oppressive conditions of the factory floor. Polite society did not want to be confronted with the societal ills which accompanied the rapidly expanding industrial scene. When viewed in this context, the paintings discussed in the previous chapters assume a greater significance.[8]

To citizens of the twenty-first century, who can fly around the world in less time than it took our artists to travel from London to North Wales, and where the monthly tonnage of steel production in the United Kingdom in the 1970s equalled roughly fifty times the monthly production of iron production in 1830, the scale of the achievements in the period 1780–1830 may seem relatively small. However, in these years which preceded the coming of the steam railways, nearly all the fundamental inventions and processes which characterised the Industrial Revolution had found a place. Their impact was transformative and set in train an evolving developmental process through which a further tranche of research and discovery and an increasing rate of technological advance ensued during the Victorian period.

Many paintings of industrial subject-matter from the 1830s and 1840s relate to the steam engine, employed both on land or at sea. After the opening of the Stockton and Darlington Railway in 1825, the railways spread relentlessly throughout Britain. The line from London to Birmingham was constructed in 1838, to be followed by Isambard Kingdom Brunel's Great Western Railway and by ever more rapid development during the 1840s. Fine drawings of the construction of the Great Western Railway by John Cooke Bourne (1773–1854) in the late 1830s compare favourably with the type of 'work in progress' photographs that are taken today.[9] Other artists also took an interest in the new steam railways but the subject-matter appeared to demand an attention to technical detail that dulled their wider response. Turner's celebrated *Rain, Steam and Speed – The Great Western Railway*, 1844, and David Cox's *The Birmingham Express*, 1848, lifted the subject above the level of illustration.[10]

The introduction of the steamboat did not go unnoticed. Turner's response to it was the most consistent. The part it played in his work is most intense in the period between 1822, when he exhibited the watercolour *Dover Castle from the Sea*, and 1842 when he painted *Snow Storm – Steam-boat off a Harbour's Mouth*.[11] The majority of Turner's steamboat paintings come from the 1830s and early 1840s and his seascapes and river views provide a fascinating account of the efforts to combat the forces of nature. Until the end of the eighteenth century, sailors had had to work with wind, wave and current but the new steam technology provided the means of confronting these. For Turner, the subject also provided elements that would feed into his exploration of the diffusion of light and the emotive nature of colour.

The end of the 1840s saw preparations in Britain for the Great Exhibition of the Works of Industry of All Nations, 1851 and the construction of Joseph Paxton's Crystal Palace in London's Hyde Park. This provided the opportunity for Britain to display its pre-eminence among the industrialising nations as well as the benefits of its empire. The impressive showcase of achievement was relished by the entrepreneurs, manufacturers and professional middle classes but, despite the mid-Victorian public discourse celebrating the dignity and value of labour, there was little to be seen of those labouring in the mills and factories, or in the construction industry.[12] By the mid-nineteenth century, social commentators such as Thomas Carlyle (1795–1881) and John Ruskin were celebrating the fortitude of manual labourer and debating the comparative values of physical and intellectual work. The invention of new machines and the expansion of the coal, iron, steel and manufacturing industries all revealed a new perspective on manual labour which had, through its concentration in industrial centres, become more visible than in the previous predominantly rural economy. *Work*, 1852–65, by Ford Madox Brown (1821–93) which includes a portrait of Thomas Carlyle looking on as a group of labourers excavate a pit for new drainage works in a Hampstead street in London, brings together a complex of issues and concerns of the day; the nobility of physical labour and its redemptive effects, class division, poverty and the roles of men and women.[13]

The coeval painting *Iron & Coal on Tyneside*, 1856–61, by William Bell Scott (1811–90) celebrates Newcastle's contribution to industrial Britain.[14] Four muscular smithies at an anvil, forging an iron wheel for a railway engine, extoll the virtues of manual labour. Scott includes Newcastle's busy port with its new steamships, Robert Stephenson's high-level combined road-railway bridge and the recently developed telegraph. He pays tribute to the individual and suggests the great industrial achievements of the day have come from separate but happy relationships between workers and management. Uplifting and optimistic themes run through the painting. Scott includes a pit boy with his Davy lamp and a bright-eyed but apprehensive looking schoolgirl with the 'First book of Arithmetic' in her hand, who looks forward to a life lifted from the drudgery which many women were being forced to endure. Both Brown and Scott's works have elements which appear to have been painted to assuage the increasing levels of guilt that the middle classes were beginning to feel for the plight of labour and the disadvantaged, conditions that our artists had witnessed several decades earlier.

The spread of education, the growth of the press, the publication of a wide range of new periodicals and the appetite for the Victorian novel all called for illustrators. Many able artists devoted their time to providing artwork for engravings. The demand for paintings to decorate the houses of the expanding middle class and for exhibition in national and provincial galleries grew but industrial images were rarely to be seen other than in periodicals and educational publications. By the mid-nineteenth century, rapid demographic and social changes inspired several artists to comment on the changing social conditions and the growth of the middle class. William Powell Frith (1819–1909), sometimes derided by his contemporaries and later critics for what they considered to be vulgar paintings of the bourgeoisie, addressed issues which appealed to them in his paintings *Life at the Seaside (Ramsgate Sands)*, 1854, and *The Railway Station*, 1862.[15] However, if these paintings were popular with the gallery-going classes because they portrayed images of situations with which they could identify, and in which they sensed a secure place in a world that was undergoing rapid change, there was also an underlying sense among some and indignation among others that the expanding capitalist economy was breeding a largely exploited, often unhealthy, and downtrodden underclass.

Despite the restrictions on child employment in the 1844 Act and the Factory Act of 1847, an eight-year-old child could still be expected to work six and a half hours and an adult up to fifteen hours per day in Britain's expanding industrial cities. Improvements were introduced during the second half of the nineteenth century. The Factory Act of 1878 prohibited employment of children under the age of ten and by the end of the century nearly all children under the age of twelve were at school. Rapid urban expansion required complementary provision of clean water supplies, adequate sanitation and sewerage and drainage systems. These often failed to keep pace in the poorly served and slum areas. Conditions of work were often dangerous and unhealthy in mills and the manufacturing industries.

Some of the less welcome aspects of industrialisation and urban life were becoming increasingly evident. Pneumonia, bronchitis and asthma were widespread, diet was often poor and water-borne diseases were not understood. The conditions endured by the poor were widely and routinely described in the daily press but paintings portraying the conditions of the poor and unemployed, unless they could be romanticised, were rare until social-realist painters such as Luke Fildes (1844–1927), Frank Holl (1845–88) and Hubert von Herkomer (1849–1914) began to illustrate urban poverty in published journals. It was not until 1874 that Luke Fildes exhibited a painting at the Royal Academy that addressed the conditions of the poor in *Applicants for Admission to a Casual Ward*.[16] Fildes was prepared to demonstrate to his middle-class audience at the Academy that despite the benefits of industrial development which they mostly enjoyed, there were serious consequences for those less fortunate.

At about this time John Atkinson Grimshaw (1836–93) in Britain was painting some startling photo-realist images of nocturnal urban and industrial landscapes while Claude Monet (1840–1926), in the same year that Fildes exhibited *Applicants for Admission to a Casual Ward*, exhibited *Impression, Sunrise*, a view of the docks and hazy industrial areas of Le Havre. Industrial subject-matter by then was being viewed by artists as part of contemporary life. We find images of industry appearing quite naturally among the works of Camille Pissarro (1830–1903) and Monet, and Van Gogh (1853–90) provides a ruthlessly uncompromising view of the spread of industrial development in *Factories of Asnières*, 1887.

By the end of the nineteenth century, paintings of the urban and industrial landscape were becoming commonplace, but from that time on the influences from continental Europe and later the United States held sway. New approaches to perspective, colour, line and form began to influence western art and design. The visual arts evolved from the inspirational work of the Post-Impressionists through revolutionary new analyses and interpretations, which challenged established concepts. Pablo Picasso (1881–1973) and Georges Braque (1882–1963), seeking new pictorial spaces in their Cubist phase, led others to explore plasticity and discontinuity and draw strength from their urban lives and industrial surroundings. Among the artistic movements of the early twentieth century, the Constructivists in Russia and the Futurists in Italy embraced the new technologies and reflected on them in their works. In Britain the Vorticists, enthusiastic about relating their art to the machine age, aimed to express the energy of the contemporary world.

Marcel Duchamp (1887–1968), by exhibiting his ready-mades, demonstrated that machine-made and manufactured objects could be used to challenge the concept of art. In the works of Vladimir Tatlin (1885–1953), Naum Gabo (1890–1977) and others we find artists taking the properties and qualities of industrial products, iron, steel, glass, celluloid and concrete, as their starting points. Electricity provided opportunities for Gabo, László Moholy-Nagy (1895–1946) and Lucio Fontana (1899–1968) to explore the boundaries of space and light in their works, and as the electronic age took hold some artists turned to video and computer art.

The twentieth century's revolution in the visual arts, with the radical analyses of the period, has seen artistic movements drawing heavily on the technology of their day, not only to form the subject of their art but also to comment and ask questions of our lives, our world and our livelihoods. Technology has penetrated deeply into the world and works of artists today, providing the flipside to the images of technology and industry that entered the field of fine art 200 years ago. However, it is through our seven artists, who confronted these scenes and provided the first flicker of interest in the changes being wrought by the Industrial Revolution that we are able to muse today on the impact of them on the lives of men, women and children living at that time.

Notes

1 John Barrow, 1751–4; Rev. Temple Henry Croker, 1764–6; Charles Coulston Gillespie (ed.), 1959; Denis Diderot and Jean Le Rond d'Alembert, 1754–72.

2 *A Fulling Mill, Fife*, c.1750, and *Lord Hopetoun's Lead Mine, Leadhills*, c.1751, by Paul Sandby.

3 *The Iron Forge between Dolgelli and Barmouth in Merioneth Shire*, 1776, by Paul Sandby.

4 *Iron Forge at Tintern, Monmouthshire*, c.1796 and *Unloading of Pit Props at Coalbrookdale*, 1790s, by Thomas Hearne.

5 See, for example, John G. Woods, 1813.

6 Anon., *Lancashire Illustrated*, 1832.

7 Anon., 1825.

8 Marx and Engels, reflecting on the division of labour in factories in the 1840s, observe that '… the work of the

proletarians has lost all individual character, and, consequently, all charm for the workman. He becomes an appendage to the machine …', Karl Marx and Friedrich Engels, p. 12.

9 Examples include *Hampstead Road Bridge*, 1836, and *Great Ventilating Shaft, Kilsby Tunnel*, *c.*1836–8, by John Cooke Bourne.

10 *Rain, Steam and Speed – The Great Western Railway*, 1844, by J.M.W. Turner; *The Night Train*, 1848, by David Cox.

11 *Dover Castle from the Sea*, 1822, by J.M.W. Turner; *Snowstorm – Steam-boat off a Harbour's Mouth*, 1842, by J.M.W. Turner.

12 Tim Barringer, *Men at Work*, 2005, pp. 1–10.

13 *Work*, 1852–65, by Ford Madox Brown. Tim Barringer, *Men at Work*, 2005, pp. 20–29.

14 *Iron & Coal on Tyneside*, 1856–61, by William Bell Scott.

15 *Life at the Seaside (Ramsgate Sands)*, 1854, and *The Railway Station*, 1862, by William Powell Frith.

16 *Applicants for Admission to a Casual Ward*, 1874, by Luke Fildes. The picture was first published as an engraving in the *Graphic* in 1869 under the title *Houseless and Hungry*. The casual ward was the accommodation provided at a workhouse.

Appendix A – Timeline 1750–1835

	Technological developments	National and international events	Paintings or drawings of industrial scenes
1750	Westminster Bridge opened; [Old] Walton Bridge opened		Paul Sandby, *A Fulling Mill*; John Boydell, *Crumford near Matlock* [before Arkwright's mills were built]
1751			Paul Sandby, *Lord Hopetoun's Lead Mines, Leadhills, South Lanarkshire*
1752			
1753			
1754		Royal Society of Arts founded	
1755			
1756	Pont-y-Pridd Bridge opened	Start of Seven Years War	
1757	Sankey Canal opened		
1758	Strutt's ribbed hosiery		Francis Vivares after George Perry and Thomas Smith, *Views of Coalbrookdale*
1759			
1760	Smeaton's Eddystone lighthouse; Carron ironworks founded	Accession of George III	William Taverner, *Sand Pits, Woolwich*
1761	Worsley-Manchester (Bridgewater) Canal opened		
1762			
1763		End of Seven Years War	
1764	Hargreave's Spinning Jenny invented		
1765			
1766	Cranage patent for refining pig-iron in reverbatory furnace		
1767	First iron rails at Coalbrookdale		
1768		Royal Academy of Arts founded	
1769	Arkwright's spinning frame patented; Blackfriars Bridge, London, completed		
1770	Jesse Ramsden's screw-cutting lathe		Joseph Wright, *A Blacksmith's Shop*
1771	Arkwright's first cotton mill at Cromford	Smeatonian Club (Society) founded	Joseph Wright, *A Blacksmith's Shop*
1772	Lees's carding machine feeder mechanism invented		Joseph Wright, *An Iron Forge*
1773			Joseph Wright, *An Iron Forge Without*
1774	John Wilkinson's cannon-boring machine invented		

	Technological developments	National and international events	Paintings or drawings of industrial scenes
1775		Start of American War of Independence	
1776	James Watt's steam engine in use	Adam Smith, *An Inquiry into the Nature and Causes of the Wealth of Nations*	Paul Sandby, *The Iron Forge between Dolgelli and Barmouth*
1777	Arkright's second cotton mill at Cromford opened		William Williams, *Morning View and Afternoon View of Coalbrookdale*
1778	Strutt's South Mill at Belper, Derbyshire opened		
1779	Samuel Crompton's Spinning Mule and water-frame used		Edward Dayes, *Bedlam Furnace*; Zachariah Boreman, *Cromford's Second Mill from the East*
1780	Samuel Harrison's first steel pen nib		Edward Dayes, *Bedlam Furnace*
1781	Iron Bridge at Coalbrookdale opened; Strutt's mill at Milton opened		Michael Angelo Rooker, *The Iron Bridge*
1782			Joseph Wright, *Arkwright's Cotton Mills by Night* – version 1
1783	Thomas Bell's fabric printing machine invented	American War of Independence ends; Montgolfier's hot-air ballooon (France)	
1784	Cort's patent for puddling in reverbatory furnace; Boulton and Watt's first steam whim at Cornish mines		
1785			Philippe-Jacques de Loutherbourg, *Lead Mine near Matlock Bath*; John Warwick Smith, *Copper Mines on Parys Mountain*
1786	Albion steam-powered flour mills, London, opened; Meikle's threshing machine invented		John Opie, *A Gentleman and a Miner*; Philippe-Jacques de Loutherbourg, *Iron Foundery near Machynlleth*
1787	Cartwright's power loom in commercial use		
1788	Matthew Boulton's coin-making machine invented		George Robertson, *Six Views of Coalbrookdale*
1789		Start of French Revolution	Julius Caesar Ibbetson, *An Iron Forge at Merthyr Tydfil*; John 'Warwick' Smith, *Junction of Mona and Parys Mountain Copper Mines*
1790	Brunswick Dock, Blackwall, London, opened		Joseph Wright of Derby, *Sir Richard Arkwright with spinning frame*, 1789–90; Mather Brown, *Sir Richard Arkwright*
1791			
1792			Julius Caesar Ibbetson, *Miners at Menai*; *Coal Staithe on the River Tawe*
1793		Eli Whitney's cotton gin (America)	Paul Sandby, *A View of Vintners at Boxley, Kent, with Mr Whatman's Turkey Paper Mills*
1794			
1795			Joseph Wright, *Arkwright's Mills* [by day], *c.*1795–6; *A View of Cromford Bridge*; *Arkwright's Cotton Mills by Night*, *c.*1794–5 - version 2
1796	Sunderland Bridge across the River Wear opened; Maudslay's screw-cutting machine invented		J.M.W. Turner, *Interior of Forge, Making Anchors*; Thomas Hearne, *Iron Forge near Tintern*
1797	Newbold's patent for first cast-iron plough; River Lune Aqueduct, Lancaster, opened		J.M.W. Turner's sketch, *Lancaster Aqueduct with Church and Castle seen through the Right Hand Arch*

	Technological developments	National and international events	Paintings or drawings of industrial scenes
1798			Colt Hoare, *Blaenavon Ironworks*; J.M.W. Turner, *Chirk Aqueduct under Construction*; sketches of *Cyfarthfa Ironworks*; sketch of *Interior of a Tilt Forge*
1799		Royal Institution founded	J.M.W. Turner, *A Canal Tunnel near Leeds*
1800	Trevithick's high-pressure steam engine invented; Trevithick's steam road-carriage opened	Acts of Union of Great Britain and Ireland	F.L.T. Francia, *Parys Copper Mine, Anglesey*
1801	Chirk Aqueduct completed		Philippe-Jacques de Loutherbourg, *Coalbrookdale by Night*
1802	Steam tug-boat *Charlotte Dundas* tested on rivers Forth and Clyde; West India docks opened		William Daniell, *New Docks and Warehouses … on the Isle of Dogs*; John Crome, *Slate Quarries*
1803			William Daniell, *Brunswick Dock, Blackwall*; Paul Sandby Munn, *Bedlam Furnaces*
1804	Trevithick's railway locomotive in use	Napoleon Bonaparte – Emperor of France	William Havell, *Parys Mountain Copper Mine*, c.1803–4
1805	Pontcysyllte Aqueduct completed	Battle of Trafalgar	John 'Warwick' Smith, *Pontcycyllte Aqueduct*; John Glover, *Lead Mills near Hexham*
1806	Gas lighting of cotton mills begun		
1807		Slave Trade Act passed	John Nixon, *Lord Penrhyn's Slate Quarry near Bangor*; Thomas Rowlandson, *Carclaze Tin Mine*
1808			
1809			
1810			John Glover, *Pontcycyllte Aqueduct with Cysyllte Bridge in the Foreground*
1811	Bell Rock lighthouse opened		
1812	Steamboat *Comet* on River Clyde		John Sequier, *Excavating Regent's Canal with View of Marylebone Church*
1813			John Crome, *The Steam Packet* (Norwich–Yarmouth) c.1813–17
1814	Steam cylinder-press printing begun		
1815		Battle of Waterloo and Napoleonic wars end	
1816	Davy lamp invented		J.M.W. Turner, *Lancaster from the Aqueduct*; *Leeds*; Penry Williams, *The Merthyr Riots*
1817	Waterloo Bridge opened		William Daniell, *Steam-boat on the Clyde near Dumbarton*
1818		Institution of Civil Engineers founded	
1819			Thomas Honor, *Rolling Mills*; J.M.W. Turner, *Bell Rock Lighthouse*
1820		Death of George III; ascension of George IV	Penry Williams, *Views of Cyfarthfa Ironworks*
1821			
1822	Steam packet-boat between Brighton and Le Havre		J.M.W. Turner, *Dover Castle from the Sea*; *More Park, near Watford, on the River Colne*
1823	The Royal Suspension Chain Pier, Brighton opened; Chichester canal completed	Society of British Artists founded	J.M.W. Turner, *Newcastle-on-Tyne* and *Shields, on the River Tyne*

	Technological developments	National and international events	Paintings or drawings of industrial scenes
1824		Trades Unions legalised	J.M.W. Turner, *Kirkstall Lock on the River Aire*, 1824–5
1825	Stockton-Darlington railway opened		Penry Williams, *Cyfarthfa Ironworks*; *Cyfarthfa, Ironworks Interior at Night*
1826	Telford's Menai Bridge opened		
1827			John Constable, *Chain Pier, Brighton*
1828			J.M.W. Turner, *Brighton from the Sea*; *Chichester Canal*
1829	George Stephenson's steam engine *Rocket* invented		
1830	Liverpool-Manchester railway opened	George IV dies	
1831			
1832		The Great Reform Act	Henry Hawkins, *Penrhyn Quarry*; J.M.W. Turner, *Dudley, Worcestershire*; *Coventry*
1833		The Slavery Abolition Act, Britain	
1834			
1835			J.M.W. Turner, *The Thames above Waterloo Bridge*

Appendix B – List of illustrations

Sketches, drawings and paintings illustrated in text

1.1 *Sir Richard Arkwright (1732–92) with spinning frame*, 1789–90, by Joseph Wright of Derby, oil on canvas, 241.3 × 152.4 cm. Derby Museum and Art Gallery. On loan to Derby Museums from a private collection, UK.

1.2 *Sir Richard Arkwright*, 1790, by Mather Brown, oil on canvas, 128 × 102 cm. New Britain Museum of American Art, Connecticut. Image from Wikimedia Commons.

1.3 *Arkwright's Mills* [by day], *c.*1795–6, by Joseph Wright of Derby, oil on canvas, 58.8 × 76.2 cm. Photograph: R Tailby / Derby Museum and Art Gallery. Image courtesy of Derby Museums collection.

1.4 *Arkwright's Cotton Mills by Night*, *c.*1794–95 by Joseph Wright of Derby, oil on canvas, 86 × 111 cm. Photograph: © 2020 Philip Mould & Co. / Bridgeman Images.

2.1 *A Gentleman and a Miner*, 1786, by John Opie, oil on canvas, 99.5 × 112 cm. The Royal Institution of Cornwall, Royal Cornwall Museum, Truro.

2.2 Matthew Boulton (in Chasewater) to James Watt (in Birmingham), 23 September 1785. Boulton & Watt Papers (MS 3147/3/9), reproduced with the permission of Birmingham Library and Archives.

2.3 *A Gentleman and a Miner*, 1786, by John Opie (detail from Figure 2.1).

3.1 *Colebrook Dale [Coalbrookdale] by Night*, 1801, by Philippe-Jacques de Loutherbourg, oil on canvas, 68 × 106.7 cm. Image © Board of Trustees of the Science Museum.

3.2 *A View of the Upper Works at Coalbrookdale*, 1758, by Francis Vivares after Thomas Smith of Derby, etching and engraving, 39.3 × 54.3 cm. Plate I in G. Perry and T. Smith, *A Description of Coalbrookdale in the County of Salop* (published according to Act of Parliament, 1758). Image © 2020 The Trustees of the British Museum.

3.3 *The Resolution Steam-Engine, Coalbrookdale, Seen from the New Pool*, 1786 or 1800, by Philippe-Jacques de Loutherbourg, pen and ink on card, 7.3 × 9.5 cm. Tate, London. Photo © Tate.

3.4 *Bedlam Furnace*, *c.*1780, by Edward Dayes, gouache, graphite and watercolour on paper, 31.6 × 44 cm. TB CCCLXXIJ, D36352, Tate, London. Photo © Tate.

3.5 *Boiler, Engine House and Casting Halls, Coalbrookdale*, 1786 or 1800, by Philippe-Jacques de Loutherbourg, pen and ink, graphite and watercolour on card, 7.3 × 9.5 cm. Tate, London. Photo © Tate.

3.6 *Bedlam Furnaces, Madeley Dale*, 1803, by Paul Sandby Munn, watercolour on paper, 32.5 × 54.8 cm (T04172). Tate, London. Photo © Tate.

4.1 *The Merthyr Riots*, 1816, by Penry Williams, oil on canvas, 38.5 × 54 cm. CCM.30.991, Image © Cyfarthfa Castle Museum and Art Gallery, Merthyr Tydfil.

4.2 *An Iron Forge at Merthyr Tydfil*, 1789, by Julius Caesar Ibbetson, watercolour on paper, 22 × 29 cm. Image © Cyfarthfa Castle Museum and Art Gallery, Merthyr Tydfil.

4.3 *Cyfarthfa Iron Works, Interior at Night*, 1825, by Penry Williams, watercolour and body colour on paper, 15.2 × 21 cm. Image © Cyfarthfa Castle Museum and Art Gallery, Merthyr Tydfil.

Sketches, drawings and paintings mentioned in the text but not illustrated, and other relevant works

Abbott, John White (1763–1851)

Slate Quarry at Widdecombe, Devon, 1792, inscribed July 18, 23.8 × 19.1 cm, pen and brown ink and watercolour on paper. B1975.3.1082, Yale Center for British Art, Paul Mellon Collection.

Allan, David (1744–96)

Lead Processing at Leadhills, South Lanarkshire, four cabinet pictures showing lead processing, *c.*1786, oil on canvas, each 38.3 × 58 cm. NG 2834–7, National Gallery of Scotland.

Allom, Thomas (1804–72)

Carclaze Tin Mine near St. Austell, Cornwall, engraving, 38.1 × 26.3 cm. in John Britton (ed.), 1829, *Devonshire & Cornwall illustrated … with historical and topographical descriptions by J. Britton and E.W. Brayley.*

Artist unknown

A Prospect of Derby (Derby and the Silk Mill), 1725, oil on canvas, 64 × 126 cm. Derby Museum of Industry and History, Derby.

View of Soho Manufactory near Birmingham, *c.*1770, watercolour on paper, 34.5 × 26.5 cm. King's Topographical Collection XLII, 82 n & o, British Library, London. Drawings by the same artist from the same collection (LXII p & q) show, respectively, *View of Soho House near Birmingham* and a *View of Mr Eggington's House near Soho.*

Arkwright's First Mill at Cromford, *c.*1775. Derbyshire Archaeological Society.

Boreman, Zachariah

The Second Mill at Cromford, *c.*1780, 20-cm diameter ceramic plate decoration based on a watercolour drawing *Cromford's Second Mill from the East*, *c.*1779, by Zachariah Boreman. Derby Museums Trust.

From a series of fifty-five watercolour drawings:
10. *View of the Side of Sir Richard Arkwright's Cotton works at Cromford*
16. *Mr Strutt's Cotton Mill on the Derwent from Hopping Mill*, 1787
20 & 21. *Cotton Mill near Matlock Bath*
25. *Mr Arkwright's Cotton Works, Cromford*, 1786
On loan to Derby Museum and Art Gallery, Derbyshire Archaeological Society.

Boydell, John (1719–1804)

A View in Crumford near Matlock Bath in Derbyshire, 1750 (a view taken before Arkwright's Mills were built), engraving, 31.3 × 45.7 cm, drawn, engraved and published by John Boydell, London. King George Book, Derby, XI/42-e, British Library, London.

Bourne, John Cooke (1814–96)

Hampstead Road Bridge, 1836, wash drawing on paper, 25.8 × 43 cm. 1990–7196, Science Museum Group.

Great Ventilating Shaft, Kilsby Tunnel, *c.*1836–8, wash drawing on paper, 24 × 34.2 cm. 1990–7239, Science Museum Group.

Brown, Ford Maddox (1821–93)

Work, 1852–65, oil on canvas, 137 × 197.3 cm. Manchester City Art Galleries.

Buck, Samuel (1696–1779)

South Prospect of the Llangyfelach Copperworks, *c.*1730, engraving. *King George III's Topographical Collection, Vol XLVII, 51-1*, British Library, London.

Constable, John (1776–1837)

A Lead Mine at the Foot of Mam Tor (Odin Mine), inscribed August 12 [1801], pencil and sepia wash on paper, 17.6 × 26.4 cm, Inv. 247e-1888, Victoria and Albert Museum, London.

Marine Parade and Chain Pier, Brighton, 1824, pencil with pen additions on paper, 11.1 × 42.5 cm. Victoria and Albert Museum, London.

Cotman, John Sell (1782–1842)

Coal Shaft at Coalbrookdale (previously called *The Brick Kiln*), *c.*1804, watercolour over pencil (now faded), 22.2 × 33 cm. Leeds City Art Gallery.

Coal Shaft at Coalbrook, 1802, pencil on paper, 12.6 × 24 cm. Private Collection.

Coalbrook Dale, 1802, pencil on paper, 16.1 × 28.1 cm. Leeds City Art Gallery.

Bedlam Furnace, *c.*1802, watercolour on paper, 26.1 × 47.7 cm. Private Collection.

Cox, David (1783–1859)

Dudley Castle with Lime Kilns and Canal, *c.*1830, charcoal and sepia wash, 17.8 × 26 cm. Dudley Art Gallery, Dudley, West Midlands.

The Night Train, 1848, watercolour on paper, 28.4 × 38.2 cm. 1925P67, Birmingham Museum and Art Gallery.

Crane of Chester, W.

The Penrhyn Slate Quarries, 1842, lithograph 18.5 × 27.5 cm, pub. T. Humphreys, Bangor. 1982–572, Science Museum Group.

Crome, John (1768–1821)

Slate Quarries, *c.*1802/5, oil on canvas, 123.8 × 158.7 cm. Tate Gallery, London.

Daniell, William (1769–1837)

An Elevated View of the New Docks & Warehouses now Constructing on the Isle of Dogs near Limehouse for the Reception and Accommodation of Shipping in to the West India Trade, published 15 October 1802, London, hand-coloured aquatint and soft-ground etching, Sheet 46.4 × 77.6 cm. G,13.17, British Museum.

Hull, Yorkshire; July I, 1822, coloured aquatint and etching, engraved surface, 16.2 × 23.8 cm, in *A Picturesque Voyage Round Great Britain*, vol. 6, London, 1822.

Day, William (1764–1807)

Richard Arkwright's Cotton Mill, Cromford, *c.*1789, watercolour on paper, 47.7 × 34.3 cm. Derby Museum and Art Gallery.

Defrance, Léonard

Interior of a Foundry, 1789, oil on panel, 48.5 × 61.5 cm. Walker Art Gallery, Liverpool Museums.

de Loutherbourg, Philippe-Jacques (1740–1812)

An Engine to Draw the Water out of a Lead Mine near Matlock Bath, Derbyshire (or *An Aqueduct from Lead Mine near Matlock Bath, Derbyshire*), 1785, oil on canvas, 90.5 × 144.5 cm. B1981.25.225, Yale Center for British Art, Paul Mellon Collection, New Haven, Connecticut.

Iron Foundery nr. Machynlleth, *c.*1786, pen and ink on paper, 12.5 × 21 cm. PA 8821, Ex vol 61, No 52, National Library of Wales, Aberystwyth.

Mill at Aberdulais, 1786, pen and ink and graphite on three linked cards, 7.7 × 10.9 cm, 7.8 × 11.3 cm and 7.8 × 11.8 cm. TB CCLXX 9–11, D36367–9, Tate, London.

A Large Copper-smelting Works at Swansea (Perhaps the Copper Works at Landore on the River Tawe North of Swansea), 1786 or 1800, pen and ink and graphite on paper, inscribed *1st copperworks near Swansea*, 8 × 11.9 cm. TB CCCLXXII 16, D36374, Tate, London.

A Large Copper-smelting Works at Swansea (Perhaps the Copper Works at Landore on the River Tawe North of Swansea), 1786 or 1800, pen and ink and graphite on paper, inscribed *Copper works near Swansea*, 8 × 12 cm. Turner Bequest CCCLXXII 46, D36406, Tate, London.

A Copper Works near Swansea, 1786 or 1800, pen and ink and graphite on card, two linked cards 8 × 11.9 cm. and 8 × 11.4 cm. TB CCCLXXII 13 D36371 and TB CCCLXXII 12, D36370, Tate, London.

Hillsides and Buildings near the Fforest Copper Works, 8 × 10.5 cm. *Fforest Copper Works, Clase*, 8 × 10.9 cm and *Part of the Fforest Copper Works, Clase*. 8 × 11.3 cm. Pen and ink and graphite on paper, 1786 or 1800. D36382–4, TB CCCLXXII 23–25, Tate, London.

The Engine Building at John Morris's Copper Works, Clase, 1786 or 1800, pen and ink and graphite on paper, 8 × 12 cm. TB CCCLXXII 50, D36410, Tate, London.

The Attack on Valenciennes, 1793, 1794, oil on canvas, 260 × 370 cm. Naval and Military Club, London, Collection of Lord Hesketh.

The Victory of Lord Howe, 1st June 1794, 1795, oil on canvas, 266.5 × 373.5 cm. inv. BHC0470, National Maritime Museum, Greenwich, London.

The Battle of Camperdown, 1799, 1800, oil on canvas, 147.5 × 210 cm. inv. T01451, Tate Britain, London.

The Battle of Aboukir, 1800, 1800, oil on canvas, 147.5 × 210 cm. inv. T01452, Tate Britain, London.

A View of Conway Castle, 1800, oil on canvas, 67.2 × 102.8 cm. National Maritime Museum, Greenwich.

The Boiler House and Casting House of a Furnace, c.1800, pen and ink, pencil and watercolour, 7.9 × 12.2 cm. TB CCCLXXII 47, D36407, Tate, London.

A View of Harlech Castle, 1801, oil on canvas, 41.9 × 58.4 cm. Location unknown.

The Hafod Copperworks, Swansea, c.1819, pencil on paper, 23.6 × 37 cm. West Glamorgan Archive.

Farington, Joseph (1747–1821)

The Iron Bridge near Coalbrookdale, Sept 25-1789, 1789, pencil on paper, 38.4 × 59.7 cm. Ironbridge Gorge Museum Trust, Shropshire.

Coalbrookdale, Sept 26-1789, 1789, pencil on paper, 45.4 × 58.8 cm. Ironbridge Gorge Museum Trust, Shropshire.

Curclaze Tin Mine, engraved by S. Middiman, published 1 May 1813, T. Cadell & W. Davis, Strand, London.

Fildes, Luke (1843–1927)

Applicants for Admission to a Casual Ward, 1874, oil on canvas. THC 0021, Royal Holloway, University of London.

Francia, Francois Louis Thomas (1772–1839)

The Parys Mine in Anglesey, c.1799, watercolour on paper, 25.6 × 17.6 cm. Ironbridge Gorge Museum, Trust, Shropshire.

Frith, William Powell (1819–1909)

Life at the Seaside (Ramsgate Sands), 1854, oil on canvas, 77 × 155.1 cm. RCIN 405068, Royal Collection Trust.

The Railway Station, 1862, oil on canvas, 46 × 101 cm. Royal Holloway, University of London.

Gastineau, Henry G. (1791–1876)

Chirk Aqueduct, 10.5 × 15 cm, engraved by Thomas Barber, pub. 1830, London; Jones & Co

Nant-y-glo Ironworks, watercolour and body-colour over graphite, 14.1 × 19.9 cm. The Library, University of St Andrews.

Nant-y-glo Ironworks, *c.*1830, 9 × 14.2 cm, engraved Samuel Lacey, after H.G. Gastineau, pub. London: Jones & Co. Ref. vtls 003374995, National Library of Wales, Aberystwyth.

Hafod Copper Works, *c.*1830, *Swansea*, watercolour on paper, 20.2 × 29.6 cm. Swansea Museum.

Glover, John (1767–1849)

Lead Mills near Hexham, 1805, pencil on paper, 11.5 × 16.5 cm, *Yorkshire/Ullswater Sketchbook No. 61*, pp. 25–6. British Library.

Hawkins, Henry (1800–81)

Crucifixion, 1835, oil on canvas, 114.5 × 183 cm. Graves, A. 1906, vol. IV, p.3 2. Sold at auction, Forbes Collection at Battersea House, 1 November 2011, lot 277.

Dante in Florence, oil on canvas, 78.7 × 127 cm. Sotheby's auction 8 October 1992, Indian, European and Oriental Paintings, New Delhi, INR 125,000 (£2,600).

Hartover, Peter

Coal Staithes on the River Wear and Lumley Castle, 1680, oil on canvas, 113.5 × 219.3 cm. Collection of Viscount Lambton.

Hearne, Thomas (1744–1817)

Iron Forge at Tintern, Monmouthshire, *c.*1796, pencil and watercolour on paper, 18.5 × 24.8 cm, at sale of Old Master & British Drawings and Watercolours, 5 July 2017, Christie's London.

Unloading of Pit Props at Coalbrookdale, 1790s, graphite and grey wash on paper, 21.6 × 19.1 cm. B1975.4.1244, Yale Center for British Art, Paul Mellon Collection, New Haven, Connecticut.

Hilleström, Pehr (1732–1816)

Interior of the Falun Copper Mine, 1780s, oil on canvas, 79 × 65.5 cm. Nationalmuseum, Stockholm.

In the Anchor-forge at Södersfors. The Smiths Hard at Work, 1782, oil on canvas, 137 × 185 cm. NM 961, Nationalmuseum, Stockholm.

Hincks, William

The Irish Linen Industry, twelve etchings each 35 × 42.5 cm, pub. 1791. Robert Polard, 1877,0113.370–81, The British Museum. See https://www.youtube.com/watch?v=kzBYNUHcqrs (accessed 20 June 2020).

Hoare, Sir Richard Colt (1758–1838)

Ironbridge, Colebrooke dale, 1801, pencil on paper, 23.5 × 27 cm, sketchbook *Worcs. Glos. Salop & N. Wales*, 13 May 1801, Item 68, p. 12. Cardiff Libraries.

Colebrook Dale, 1801, pencil on paper, 22.9 × 30. 2 cm, sketchbook *Worcs. Glos. Salop & N. Wales*, 1801, Item 68, inserted p. 8, Cardiff Libraries.

Blaenavon Ironworks, 1798, engraved William Byrne, in W. Coxe, 1801, *An Historical Tour through Monmouthshire, illustrated with views by Sir R.C. Hoare, Bart.*, London: T. Cadell Jun. & W. Davies.

Hornor, Thomas

Rolling Mills, *c.*1819, watercolour on paper, 27.9 × 47.6 cm. National Museum and Galleries of Wales, Cardiff.

Ibbetson, Julius Caesar (1759–1817)

A Bridge at Cyfarthfa, Iron Works, Merthir Tidville, *c.*1789, pen and ink and watercolour on paper, 32.6 × 49.9 cm. D.1926.211 (IRN:1188), Whitworth Art Gallery, Manchester.

Martin, Elias (1739–1818)

The Iron Bridge under Construction, 1779, watercolour. Museum of the Scandia Company, Stockholm, Sweden.

Munn, Paul Sandby (1773–1845)

Limekilns at Coalbrookdale, 1802, watercolour on paper, 24.2 × 35.6 cm. Ironbridge Gorge Museum Trust, Shropshire.

The Iron Bridge, 1802, pencil on paper, 12.3 × 24.9 cm. Victoria and Albert Museum, London.

The Iron Bridge, 1802, pencil on paper, 14.5 × 24.7 cm. Victoria and Albert Museum, London.

Great Wheel at Broseley, Salop, c.1802, watercolour on paper, 21.9 × 32.7 cm. Ironbridge Gorge Museum Trust, Shropshire.

On Lincoln Hill, Coalbrooke, July 20, 1802, grey wash over pencil on paper, 15 × 23.7 cm. Ironbridge Gorge Museum Trust, Shropshire.

Nixon, John (1760–1818)

Lord Penrhyn's Slate Quarry near Bangor, 1807, watercolour on paper, 14 × 20.7 cm. Science Museum, London.

Padley, Paul

A Panoramic View of Swansea from Mayhill, c.1790, pen and ink on paper. Swansea Museum.

Pamplin, William

Cyfarthfa Works and Waterwheel, c.1795, pen and ink on paper. 823.992, Cyfarthfa Castle Museum and Art Gallery, Merthyr Tydfil.

The Head of the Glamorganshire Canal at the Ironworks, c.1795, pen and ink on paper, Cyfarthfa Castle Museum and Art Gallery, Merthyr Tydfil.

Parry, Joseph (1744–1826)

The West View of Mellor Mill – Derbyshire (Samuel Oldknow's Mill of 1790), 1803, aquatint by Francis Jukes, 36.8 × 48 cm. King George Book, Derby, XI/17, British Library, London.

Petherick, John

The Ironworks Manager Dozing, c.1830, watercolour and gouache on paper, 24.5 × 17.2 cm. Cyfarthfa Castle Museum and Art Gallery, Merthyr Tydfil.

Pocock, Nicholas (1741–1821)

Merioneth Slate Quarry at Llanberis, 1795, watercolour on paper, 42.5 × 60 cm. National Library of Wales, Aberystwyth.

Pugh, Edward (*c.* 1761–1813)

Paris Mines in 1804, grisaille watercolour for *Cambria Depicta*. National Library of Wales, Aberystwyth.

Paris Mines in 1804, June 1813, coloured aquatint by Thomas Cartwright, in Edward Pugh, *Cambria Depicta*, 1814.

Pont Cysyllty Aqueduct, coloured aquatint by J. Havell, 1814, in *Cambria Depicta*, 1814.

Robertson, George

Lincoln Hill and the Iron Bridge, Coalbrookdale, 1788, engraved by James Fittler (1758–1835).

The Iron Bridge, Coalbrookdale, from the Madeley side, 1788, engraved by James Fittler.

The Iron Bridge from the Bottom of Lincoln Hill, 1788, engraved by Francis Chesham (1749–1806); the original oil painting for this is with The Ironbridge Gorge Museum Trust, Shropshire.

The Mouth of a Coal Pit near Broseley, 1788, engraved by Francis Chesham.

The Iron Works for Casting Cannon, 1788, engraved by Wilson Lowry (1762–1824).

The Inside of a Smelting House at Broseley, 1788, engraved by Wilson Lowry.

All the above are with the Ironbridge Gorge Museum Trust, Shropshire.

Rooker, Michael Angelo (1743–1801)

The Cast Iron Bridge near Coalbrook Dale, 1781, pen, ink and watercolour on paper, 39.4 × 62.2 cm. Aberdeen Art Gallery.

Rothwell, Thomas (1740–1807)

The Fforest Copper Works, 1791, engraving on plaster plaque, oval 19.7 × 24.4 cm. Swansea Museum.

The Cambrian Pottery, pen and ink on paper, 19.7 × 24.4 cm, oval, published according to Act of Parliament 31 August 1791 by Coles and Haynes, Swansea. Ref SWASM-SM, Swansea Museum.

Rowlandson, Thomas (1756–1827)

Carclaze Tin Mine, 1807, pen and ink, tinted watercolour on paper, 20.3 × 32.1 cm. The Huntington Library Art Collection, and Botanical Gardens, Gilbert Davis Collection, San Marino, California.

Meadow Wharf, Coalbrookdale, c.1797, aquatint, in H. Wigstead, *Remarks on A Tour to North and South Wales in the year 1797*, 1800, London: W. Wigstead.

Iron Smelting (? A Foundry), pen and ink with wash, 14.5 × 20.9 cm, c.1797. PD9393, National Library of Wales, Aberystwyth.

Sandby, Paul (1725–1809)

The Royal Foundery, Woolwich, etching by James Fitter, 17 × 21.5 cm, published 1 December 1779. 1870,1008.447, The British Museum, London.

A Fulling Mill, Fife, c.1750, pen and watercolour over graphite on paper, 16.5 × 30.5 cm. D136, National Gallery of Scotland, Edinburgh.

Lord Hopetoun's Lead Mine, Leadhills, South Lanarkshire, c.1751, pen, ink and watercolour over graphite on paper, 12.3 × 23.7 cm. B1978.39.3, Yale Center for British Art, Paul Mellon Collection, New Haven, Connecticut.

The Iron Forge at Barmouth, c.1775, watercolour on paper, 20.3 × 29.8 cm. 1904,0819.21, The British Museum, London.

The Iron Forge between Dolgelli and Barmouth in Merioneth Shire, 1776, etching and aquatint, 23.9 × 31.4 cm, in Paul Sandby, *Views in North Wales*, 1776, Part 2, Plate XVIII. British Library, London.

View of the Copper works at Neath from Mr Vernon's Garden at Breten Ferry, 1797, pen and ink with wash, 15.7 × 21 cm. National Library of Wales, Aberystwyth.

Mr Whatman's Paper Mills nr Maidstone, c.1793, graphite on paper, 24.7 × 46.1 cm. British Museum, London.

A View of Vintners at Boxley, Kent, with Mr Whatman's Turkey Paper Mills, 1794, body colour and watercolour with graphite on wove paper, laid down on canvas on a wooden strainer, 67.3 × 101.6 cm. Yale Center for British Art, Paul Mellon Collection.

Scott, William Bell (1811–90)

Iron and Coal on Tyneside in the Nineteenth Century, 1856–61, oil on canvas, 186.6 × 187.9 cm. Wallington Hall, Northumberland.

Shepherd, Thomas Hosmer (1793–1864)

Chwarel Cae-Braich-y-Cafn, Ger Bethesda [branch of quarry near Bethesda – Penrhyn Quarry], *c.*1830, wood engraving, 10.5 × 17 cm. National Library of Wales, Aberystwyth.

Sequier, John (1785–1856)

*Excavating the Regent's Canal with a View of Marylebone Church, c.*1812, oil on canvas, 25.4 × 30.5 cm. Yale Center for British Art, Paul Mellon Collection, New Haven, Connecticut.

Smith, John 'Warwick' (1749–1831)

Copper Mines on the Parys Mountain, 1785, watercolour on paper. National Museum of Wales, Cardiff.

One of the Copper Mines belonging to the Paris Mountain, Anglesea, 1790, watercolour on paper. National Library of Wales, Aberystwyth.

*Morriston Castle, Swansea, c.*1792, watercolour on paper. Swansea Guildhall.

*Pontcysyllte Aqueduct, c.*1806, watercolour on paper, 37.5 × 45 cm. PB3825, National Library of Wales, Aberystwyth.

Interior of One of the Copper Mines on the Paris Mountain Anglesea, July 9, 1792, watercolour on paper, 17.5 × 22.5 cm. PD 9620, National Library of Wales, Aberystwyth.

Stanfield, William Clarkson (1793–1867)

Botallack Mines, Cornwall, engraved by William Miller in W.C. Stanfield, 1836. *Stanfield's Coastal Scenery, A Series of Views of the British Channel*, London: Smith, Elder & Co.

Taverner, William (1703–72)

*Sand Pits, Woolwich, c.*1760, body colour on paper, 36.2 × 80.3 cm. British Museum, London.

Turner, Joseph Mallord William (1775–1851)

The reference to Turner's sketches, drawings and watercolours are given below for items not held in The Turner Bequest at Tate Britain, London. Details of those in the Turner Bequest can be found in the catalogue in the website https://www.tate.org.uk/art/research-publications/jmw-turner/

Marford Mill, Wrexham, Denbighshire, 1794/5, pencil and watercolour on paper, 28 × 19.7 cm. National Museum of Wales, Cardiff.

*View of Sheffield from Derbyshire Lane, c.*1797, watercolour on paper, 11.4 × 16.5 cm. TW0841, Collection of Guild of St George, Sheffield Galleries and Museums Trust.

Aberdulais Mill, Glamorganshire, 1797, watercolour on paper, 37.6 × 48.8 cm. TW1575, WlΛbNL, 003381769, National Library of Wales, Aberystwyth.

Limekiln at Coalbrookdale, 1797, watercolour on paper, 29 × 40.3 cm. Yale Center for British Art, Paul Mellon Collection, New Haven, Connecticut.

*Man with Horse and Cart entering a Quarry, c.*1797, graphite and wash on paper, 20.7 × 27.5 cm. Yale Center for British Art, Paul Mellon Collection, New Haven, Connecticut.

*A Canal Tunnel near Leeds, c.*1799–1801, watercolour on paper, 40.6 × 25.1 cm. Private Collection,

*A Limekiln by Moonlight, c.*1799, watercolour on paper, 16.5 × 24 cm. TW 0841, Wilton 262, Herbert Art Gallery and Museum, Coventry.

*Margate, c.*1825, watercolour on paper, 15.4 × 25.5 cm. Ashmolean Museum, Oxford.

*A Canal Tunnel near Leeds, c.*1799, watercolour, pen and brown ink on paper, 24.1 × 40 cm. Collection of Richard Ivor, London.

More Park, near Watford on the River Colne, engraved by Charles Turner mezzotint on steel-faced plate, image 15.7 × 22.1 cm, in W.B. Cooke, 1814, *Rivers of England*, London.

Dover Castle from the Sea, 1822, watercolour and gouache on paper, 40.5 × 60 cm. Museum of Fine Arts, Boston.

Kirkstall Lock on the River Aire, engraved by W. Say, mezzotint on steel-faced plate, image 15.4 × 22.8 cm, in W.B. Cooke, 1827, *Rivers of England*, London.

Brighton from the Sea, 1828, oil on canvas, 71.1 × 136.5 cm. N02064, Tate Gallery, London.

Dudley, Worcestershire, c.1832, watercolour on paper, 28.8 × 43.2 cm. TW0792, Wilton 858, National Museums and Galleries, Merseyside, Lady Lever Art Gallery, Port Sunlight.

Coventry, Warwickshire, c.1832, watercolour on paper, 28.8 × 43.7 cm. 1958,0712.434, British Museum, London.

Snowstorm – Steam-boat off a Harbour's Mouth making Signals in Shallow Water, and going by the Lead, 1842, oil on canvas, 91.4 × 121.9 cm. Tate, London.

Rain, Steam and Speed – The Great Western Railway, 1844, oil on canvas 91 × 121.8 cm. NG538, National Gallery, London.

Webber, John (1752–93)

Peak at Castleton, Derbyshire, 1789, graphite and watercolour on paper, 34 × 47.7 cm. Private Collection.

Odin Mine and Mam Tor, Castleton, Derbyshire, 1789, watercolour on paper, 33.2 × 47.9 cm. Whitworth Art Gallery, Manchester.

Williams, Penry (1802–85)

Crawshay's Cyfarthfa Ironworks, 1817, oil on canvas, 51 × 71 cm. 73.231, National Museum of Wales, Aberystwyth.

Cyfarthfa Ironworks Seen from the from the West, c.1820, oil on canvas, 100 × 172 cm.

Cyfarthfa Ironworks, Aqueduct, c.1820, oil on canvas, 48 × 67 cm.

Cyfarthfa Ironworks, Watkin George's Waterwheel, c.1820, oil on canvas, 48 × 67 cm.

Cyfarthfa Ironworks, c.1820, oil on canvas, 48 × 67 cm.

Ynysfach Works, c.1820, oil on canvas, 48 × 67 cm.

All above in Private Collection, previously of Sir W. Crawshay, Llanfair Court, Abergavenny.

The Aqueduct, Cyfarthfa, c.1820, oil on canvas, 48 × 67 cm. Cyfarthfa Castle Museum and Art Gallery, Merthyr Tydfil.

Cyfarthfa Iron Works, 1825, by Penry Williams, watercolour and body colour on paper, 14.9 × 21 cm. Cyfarthfa Castle Museum and Art Gallery, Merthyr Tydfil.

Industrial Landscape (Rhymney), c.1825, oil on canvas, 56.5 × 100.3 cm. National Library of Wales, Aberystwyth.

A View of Lancaster, 1826, oil on canvas, 137.2 × 155 cm. Exhibited RA, 1826 (336), Private Collection.

Also see https://www.peoplescollection.wales/collections/429934 for holdings of works by Penry Williams at Cyfarthfa Castle Museum and Art Gallery, Merthyr Tydfil.

Williams, William (1727–91)

Morning View of Coalbrookdale, 1777, oil on canvas, 102.5 × 125.6 cm. Ironbridge Gorge Museum Trust, Shropshire.

Afternoon View of Coalbrookdale, 1777, oil on canvas, 102.4 × 125.4 cm. Ironbridge Gorge Museum Trust, Shropshire.

The Cast Iron Bridge near Coalbrookdale, 1780, oil on canvas, 86.3 × 101.6 cm. Ironbridge Gorge Museum Trust, Shropshire.

Wright of Derby, Joseph (1734–97)

A Conversation of Girls, c.1770, oil on canvas, 127 × 101.6 cm. On loan to National Museum of Wales, Aberystwyth from a Private Collection.

A Blacksmith's Shop, 1770, oil on canvas, 128.3 × 104 cm. Yale Center for British Art, Paul Mellon Collection, New Haven, Connecticut.

A Blacksmith's Shop, 1771, oil on canvas, 76.8 × 64.4 cm. Private Collection.

A Blacksmith's Shop, 1772, oil on canvas, 125 × 99 cm. Derby Museum and Art Gallery.

An Iron Forge, 1772, oil on canvas, 121.9 × 132.1 cm. Tate Gallery, London.

An Iron Forge Viewed from Without, 1773, oil on canvas, 105 × 140 cm. Hermitage Museum, St Petersburg.

Matlock Tor, Moonlight, c.1777–80, oil on canvas, 63.5 × 76.2 cm. Yale Centre for British Art, Paul Mellon Collection, New Haven, Connecticut.

Matlock Tor by Daylight, c.1778, oil on canvas, 72.4 × 98.7 cm. Fitzwilliam Museum, University of Cambridge.

Italian landscape – a view near Tivoli, c.1783–6, oil on canvas, 76.2 × 96.5 cm. Derby Museum and Art Gallery.

A View of Cromford Bridge (aka *Willersley Castle, Cromford*), c.1795–6, oil on canvas, 58.8 × 76.2 cm. Derby Museum and Art Gallery.

Portraits of entrepreneurs and engineers mentioned in or related to the text

Artist unknown

William Williams, Chief Engineer, Cyfarthfa Ironworks, c.1810, oil on canvas, 92 × 71 cm. CCM.2996.005, Cyfarthfa Castle Museum and Art Gallery, Merthyr Tydfil.

Samuel Homfray (possibly by William Williams), c.1790, oil on canvas, 100.8 × 88.1 cm. Private Collection.

Beechey, Sir William (1753–1839)

Matthew Boulton, 1798, oil on canvas, 124.7 × 74.9 cm. The Science Museum, London.

Gainsborough, Thomas (1727–88)

John Wilkinson, c.1766, oil on canvas, 234 × 145 cm. Staatliche Museen zu Berlin.

Hobday, William Armfield (1771–1831)

A Portrait of William Reynolds in Early Middle Age, c.1796, oil on canvas, Ironbridge Gorge Museum.

Jackson, John (1778–31)

George Hay Dawkins-Pennant, c.1820, National Trust, Penrhyn Castle, Gwynedd, Wales.

Lane, Samuel (1780–1859)

Thomas Telford, 1820–22, oil on canvas, Institution of Civil Engineers, London.

Lawrence, Sir Thomas (1769–1830)

James Watt, c.1812, oil on canvas, 142.3 × 111.9 cm. Birmingham Museum and Art Gallery.

Opie, John (1761–1807)

The Reverend Richard Polwhele, c.1778, oil on canvas, 53.3 × 43.2 cm, exhibited in Exeter at the Exhibition of Devon and Cornwall Worthies, 1873 (No. 84). Location unknown.

Percy, Samuel (1750–1820)

Richard Reynolds, c.1810, polychrome wax bust fixed to a brown velvet covered board, 18 × 14 × 4 cm. (NPG 4674) National Portrait Gallery, London. Another example of the wax image is (Ref. 18/81) in the Leeds City Art Gallery.

Reynolds, Sir Joshua (1723–92)

Margaret Morris, 1757, oil on canvas, Dulwich Picture Gallery, London.

Romney, George (1734–1802)

John Smeaton, c.1779, oil on canvas 75.5 × 63.5 cm, after Rhodes of Leeds (d. 1790). National Portrait Gallery, London.

Schaak, J.S.C. (fl. 1761–70)

Matthew Boulton, 1770, oil on canvas, 73.7 × 61 cm. Birmingham Museum and Art Gallery.

von Breda, Carl Fredrik (1759–1818)

Matthew Boulton, 1792, oil on canvas, 145 × 130.5 cm. Birmingham Museum and Art Gallery.

James Watt, 1792, oil on canvas, 127 × 102 cm. National Portrait Gallery, London.

Williams, Penry (1798–1885)

William Williams, Cyfarthfa Engineer, c.1825, watercolour on paper, 18.5 × 15 cm. Cyfarthfa Castle Museum and Art Gallery, Merthyr Tydfil.

Wilson of Birmingham, Richard

Richard Crawshay (1739–1810), c.1796, oil on canvas, 135 × 94.5 cm. NMW A519, National Museum of Wales, Cardiff.

Wright of Derby, Joseph (1734–97)

Richard Gildart, 1768, oil on canvas, 125 × 100 cm. Walker Art Gallery and Museums, Liverpool.

Mrs John (Elizabeth) Ashton, c.1769, oil on canvas, 126.1 × 101 cm. The Fitzwilliam Museum, University of Cambridge.

Thomas Staniforth, 1769, oil on canvas, 93 × 77.5 cm. Tate, London.

Thomas Day, c.1770, oil on canvas, 121.9 × 97.8 cm. National Portrait Gallery, London.

Erasmus Darwin, c.1770–76, oil on canvas, 75 × 62 cm. Birmingham Museum Trust.

Rev. D'Ewes Coke, his wife Hannah, and Daniel Parker Coke M.P, c.1782, oil on canvas, 152.4 × 177.8 cm. Derby Museum and Art Gallery.

Francis Hurt, c.1780, oil on canvas, 127 × 101.6 cm. Derby Museum and Art Gallery.

John Whitehurst FRS, c.1782–3, oil on canvas, 92.1 × 71.1 cm. Derby Museum and Art Gallery, on loan from a Private Collection.

Richard Arkwright, c.1783–5, oil on canvas, 126 × 102 cm. National Portrait Gallery, London and the Harris Museum & Art Gallery, Preston.

Jedediah Strutt (1734–1797), c.1790, oil on canvas, 127 × 101.6 cm. Derby Museum and Art Gallery.

Charles Hurt (1758–1834), c.1789/90, oil on canvas, 229.8 × 138.4 cm. Private Collection.

Samuel Oldknow (1756–1828), c.1790–2, oil on canvas, 243.9 × 152.4 cm. Leeds City Art Gallery.

Bibliography

Contemporary sources

Manuscripts

Birmingham Archives and Heritage, Birmingham Reference Library.
Boulton, Matthew, and Watt, James Papers, 1777–1803. MS 3147.
Correspondence B&W Partners [MB: Matthew Boulton; JW: James Watt].
MS 3147/4. 18 September 1780, MB, Redruth to JW, Birmingham.
MS 3147/3/4. 23 Sept 1780, MB, Redruth to JW, Birmingham.
MS 3147/3/4. 1 October 1780, MB, Redruth to JW, Birmingham.
MS 3147/3/4. 7 October 1780, MB, Redruth to JW, Birmingham.
MS 3147/3/4. 11 October 1780, MB, Redruth to JW, Birmingham.
MS 3147/3/5. 25 Sept 1781, MB, Soho to JW, Cornwall.
MS 3147/3/5. 20 September 1781, JW, Cornwall to MB, Soho.
MS 3147/3/5. 13 October 1781, MB, London to JW, Cornwall.
MS 3147/3/5. 5 December 1781, MB, Truro, to JW, Soho, Birmingham.
MS 3147/3/6. 7 December 1782, MB, Cosgarne to JW, Birmingham.
MS 3147/3/8. 15 July 1784, MB, Cosgarne, to JW, Birmingham.
MS 3147/3/8. 25 September 1784, MB, Cosgarne, to JW, Birmingham.
MS 3147/3/9. 22 August 1785, MB, Chasewater to JW, Birmingham.
MS 3147/3/9. 23 September 1785, MB, Chasewater to JW, Birmingham.
MS 3147/3/11. 6 October 1787, MB, Chasewater to JW, Birmingham.
MS 3147/3/13. 26 March 1789, MB, Soho to JW, London.

Birmingham Assay Office, Birmingham
Boulton Papers.
Boulton, M., 26 December 1791, Correspondence: Matthew Boulton to Messrs
     Monolron.

British Library, London
Thornhill, James, 1699, *Sir James Thornhill's sketchbook*, MS 595602.
Boulton & Watt Papers, Series Part 14, MS 3147/3. *Microfilm A.20068, Reel 269.*
10 June 1785, Thomas Daniell, Truro, to Boulton & Watt, Birmingham.
April 1787, Thomas Daniell, Truro, to Boulton & Watt, Birmingham.
16 June 1787, Thomas Daniell, Truro, to Boulton & Watt, Birmingham.
15 July 1788, Thomas Daniell, Truro, to Boulton & Watt, Birmingham.
1 August 1788, Ralph Allen Daniell, Truro to Boulton & Watt, Birmingham.

National Library of Wales, Aberystwyth
Hanmer, Captain Henry and Mrs Sara, *Tours through part of North Wales*, 13 October
     1819, MS 23996C.

Heinz Archive and Library, National Portrait Gallery, London
Wright, Joseph: *Manuscript Account Book, c.1755–97, fols 9-10.*

Royal Academy of Arts Archive
Richmond, William Blake. Correspondence, from 123 via Felice, Rome to George Richmond, 1866, W.B. Richmond papers, Ref. RI/1/30.
Williams, Penry, Correspondence from 39 Via della Mercede to Thomas Lawrence, 28 March 1827, Ref. LAW/5/113.

Royal Institution, Falmouth, Cornwall
Wilson, Thomas, 1790, *Correspondence: James Watt to Thomas Wilson, 15 September 1790.* Wilson Manuscripts.

Victoria & Albert Museum Archives. Archive of Art and Design
Royal Society of British Artists (RSBA), Council Minutes (M1), 1823–27, Ref AAD/1997/8/1.
RSBA, Deed of Establishment, 27 December 1823, Ref AAD/1997/8/47.
RSBA, Minutes of General Meeting, 3 March 1825.
RSBA, *Catalogues including Press cuttings* (Cat 3), 1855–63, Ref. AAD/1997/8/37.

Periodicals and Journals

British Library:
London Evening Standard, Saturday 13 July 1833.
Morning Post, Friday 17 June 1836.
The Art-Union, Monthly Journal, London, 1 May 1847.
The Morning Post, Wednesday 12 July 1848.
British Newspaper Archive, https://www.britishnewspaperarchive.co.uk/
Derby Mercury, 1776–85.
Sherborne Mercury, 1800.
London Courier and Evening Gazette, 1816.
Public Ledger and Daily Advertiser, 1816.
Cambrian Newspaper, 1831.
Observer Newspaper, 1831.

Royal Academy Library and Archives, Press cuttings, vol. I, fol. 35:
The Porcupine, undated 1801.
St James's Chronicle, 7–9 May 1801.
Oracle and Daily Advertiser, 14 May 1801.
London Packet, 29 April–1 May 1801.

Victoria & Albert Museum Archives, Archive of Art and Design:
Spectator, Saturday 27 March 1841, p. 307, *Spectator 1837–46*, Ref. AAD/1997/8/106.
Spectator, 'Fine Art, The Suffolk Street Exhibition', Week ending Saturday 25 March 1845, pp. 306–7.
The Echo, 5 April 1879, Ref. AAD/1997/8/60.
The Era, 6 April 1879, Ref. AAD/1997/8/60.

Anon, 1830, 'The Welsh Iron Trade' in *Cambrian Quarterly Magazine and Celtic Repertory*.

Hoare, Prince, 'To the memory of John Opie', *The Artist, No. VII*, Saturday 25 April 1807.

Books

Angerstein, R.R., 1755, R.R. *Angerstein's illustrated travel diary, 1753–1755: Industry in England and Wales from a Swedish perspective*, trans. Berg, T. & P., 2001, London: Science Museum.

Anon, 1779, *An account of the Wonders of Derbyshire, as introduced in the Pantomime Entertainment at the Theatre-Royal, Drury Lane*. London: G. Bigg.

Anon. [Joseph Pott], 1782, *An essay on landscape painting*, London.

Anon., 'Statements from medical and other gentlemen in Manchester, 1816, 1817, 1818', in *Observations of the State of children in Cotton Mills*, 1825, London: J. Innes.

Anon., 1832, *Lancashire Illustrated*, London: H. Fisher, Son and P. Jackson.

Anon., 1848, *Amlwch and the celebrated Mona and Parys Copper Mines; Isle of Anglesey*, 2nd edn., Beaumaris: Enoch Jones.

Ayton, R. and Daniell, William, 1814–25, *A Voyage round Great Britain undertaken in the summer of the year 1813. With a series of views illustrative of the character and prominent features of the coast, drawn and engraved by William Daniell*, 4 vols, London: Longman.

Baccini G. *et al*, 1820, *La Metropolitana Fiorentina Illustrata*, Florence: G. Molini.

Barber, J.T., 1803, *A Tour through South Wales and Monmouthshire*, London: T. Cadell & W. Davies.

Barrow, John, 1751–4, *New Universal Dictionary* and *Supplement*, London: John Hinton.

Bicknell, John and Day, Thomas, 1775, *The Dying Negro: A Poem*, 3rd edn., London: W. Flexney.

Bowyer, R., 1805, *The romantic and picturesque scenery of England and Wales from drawings made expressly for the undertaking by P.J. de Loutherbourg*, London: Robert Bowyer.

Burke, E., 1757, *A Philosophical Enquiry into the Origin of our Ideas of the Sublime and Beautiful*, London.

Byng, John, 5th Viscount Torrington, *The Torrington Diaries, Tours through England and Wales, 1781–1794*, Andrews, C. Bruyn (ed.), 1934–8, 4 vols, London: Eyre & Spottiswood.

Colt Hoare, Richard, *The Journeys of Sir Richard Colt Hoare through Wales and England 1793–1810*, Thompson, M.W. (ed.), 1983, Gloucester: Sutton.

Combe, W. and Rowlandson, Thomas, 1817, 'The Tour of Doctor Syntax, in search of the picturesque, a poem', 7th edn., in *R. Ackerman's Repository of art*, London: Diggens, printer.

Cooke, W.B., 1827, *Rivers of England*, London.

Crawshay, William, 1831, *The late Riots of Merthyr-Tydfil*, Merthyr: J. Howell.

Croker, Rev. Temple Henry, 1764–6, *The Complete Dictionary of Arts and Sciences*, 3 vols., London. Cunningham, Allan, 1830, *Lives of British Painters, Sculptors and Architects*, London: John Murray.

Daniell, William, 1818, *A Voyage round Great Britain undertaken in the summer of the year 1813. With a series of views illustrative of the character and prominent features of the coast, drawn and engraved by William Daniell*, vol 3., London: Longman.

Dayes, E., Brayley, E.W. (ed.), 1805, *The Works of the late Edward Dayes containing An Excursion through the principal parts of Derbyshire and Yorkshire, with illustrative notes by E.W. Brayley; Essays on painting; Instructions for drawing and colouring landscapes; and Professional sketches of modern artists*, London: Mrs Dayes.

Diderot, Denis, *Essais sur la peinture, 1765*, Gita May (ed.), *et Salons de 1759, 1761, 1763*, Jacques Chouillet (ed.), 1984, Paris: Hermann.

Diderot, Denis and D'Alembert, Jean Le Rond, 1754–2, *Dictionnaire raisonné des sciences, des arts et des métiers*, 17 tom, Geneva.

Englefield, Sir Henry, and Webster, Thomas, 1816, *Description of the principal picturesque beauties, antiquities and geologic phœnomena of the Isle of Wight*: with additional observations on the strata of the island … by Thomas Webster, London: Payne and Foss.

Evans, Rev. J., 1803, *Letters written during a tour through South Wales in the year 1803 and other times; Letter VI*, London.

Foster, Rev., 1805, *On the application of the Epithet Romantic in Essays in a Series of letters to a Friend*, London.

Gilpin, Rev. William, 1782, *Observations on the River Wye and several parts of South Wales, &c, relative chiefly to Picturesque Beauty: made in the summer of the year 1770*, London.

Gilpin, Rev. William, 1792, *Three essays on Picturesque Beauty; on Picturesque Travel; to which is added a poem, on Landscape Painting*, London: R. Blamire.

Goldthwait, John T., *Observations on the Feeling of the Beautiful and Sublime*, Berkeley, Los Angeles: University of California Press, 1960, trans. from Immanuel Kant, 1766, *Beobahtungen über das Gefühl des Schönen und Erhabenen*, Königsberg.

Hatchett, C. and Raistrick, A. (ed.), 1967, *The Hatchett Diary, 1796*, Truro.

Hoare, Richard Colt, 1806, *The itinerary of Archbishop Baldwin through Wales, A.D. MCLXXXVIII / by Giraldus de Barri; translated into English, and illustrated with views, annotations, and a life of Giraldus*, London.

Hobbes, Thomas, 1678, *De Mirabilibus Pecci, being the Wonders of the Peak in Darby-shire, 1636. … in English and Latine [verse]. The Latine … by T. Hobbes … The English by a Person of Quality*, London.

Hutton, James, 1785, *A Theory of the Earth*, London.

Knight, Richard Payne, 1794, *The Landscape, a didactic poem, in three books. Addressed to Uvedale Price, Esq. by R.P. Knight, L.P.*, London: Bulmer and Co., printer.

Knight, Richard Payne, 1805, *An Analytical Inquiry into the principles of taste*, London.

Lloyd, Hannibal Evans, 1838, *Picturesque views of England and Wales; from drawings by J.M.W. Turner*, London: Longman Orme, Brown, Green and Longmans.

Löwy, Michael and Sayre, Robert, trans. Porter, Catherine, 2001, *Romanticism Against the Tide of Modernity*, Durham and London: Duke University Press.

Lyell, Charles, 1830–33, *The Principles of Geology*, 4 vols., London: John Murray.

Opie, John, 1809, *Lectures on Painting delivered at the Royal Academy of Arts. To which is prefixed a memoir by Mrs. Opie [pp. 1-54], and other accounts of Mr Opie's talent and character*, London.

Owen, Robert, 1817, *Observations on the effect of the Manufactory System: with hints for the improvement of those parts of it which are most injurious to health and morals*, London.

Pennant, Thomas, vol. I, 1778, vol. II, 1781, *A Tour in Wales, Illustrations after Moses Griffith (1747–1819)*, London: Henry Hughes.

Pindar, Peter (pseud of Walcot, John), 1783, *More Lyric Odes to the Royal Academicians, Ode III*, London.

Playfair, J., 1802, *Illustrations of the Huttonian Theory of the Earth*, Edinburgh.

Polwhele, Rev. R., 1831, *Biographical sketches in Cornwall*, 3 vols, London: J.B. Nichols & Son.

Polwhele, Rev. R., 1836, *Reminiscences in prose and verse*, 3 vols, London: J.B. Nichols & Son.

Price, Uvedale, 1810, *Essays on the Picturesque, as Compared with the Sublime and the Beautiful: and On the use of studying pictures, for the purpose of improving real landscape*, Mawman.

Pückler-Muskau, Prince Hermann von, 1832, trans. Austin, Sarah, *Tour in England, Ireland and France, in the Years 1828 & 1829*, 4 vols, London: Effingham Wilson.

Pugh, Edward, 1814, *Cambria Depicta: a series of fifty picturesque views in Wales, engraved in aquatinta by J. Havell, T. Cartwright, J, Hassell and T. Bonnor: from designs made on the spot by a native artist*, London.

Reynolds, Sir Joshua, 1819, *The Literary Works of Sir Joshua Reynolds, Kl*, 3 vols, London: T. Cadell and W. Davies.

Skrine, Henry, 1812, *Two Successive Tours through the whole of Wales with several of the English Counties, 1798*, in Pinkerton, John, *A General Collection of the best and most interesting voyages in all parts of the world, 1808*, London.

Smiles, Samuel, 1863, *Industrial Biography; Iron workers and toolmakers*, London.

Smith, William, 1815, *A Delineation of the Strata of England and Wales, with part of Scotland; exhibiting the collieries and mines, the marshes and fen lands originally overflowed by the sea, and the varieties of soil according to the variations in the substrata, illustrated by the most descriptive names*, London: British Geological Survey.

Thomson, James, 1730, *The Seasons*, pp. 1–168, and 1736, *Liberty*, pp. 169–276 in Gilfillan, G. (ed.), 1853, *Thomson's poetical works* with *Life and Notes*, Edinburgh: James Nichol.

Whitehurst, John, 1778, *An inquiry into the original state and formation of the Earth, … to which is added an Appendix containing some general observations on the strata in Derbyshire*, London.

Wigstead, Henry, 1800, *Remarks on A Tour to North and South Wales in the year 1797, with plates by Rowlandson, Pugh and Howitt etc, aquainted by I. Hill*, London: W. Wigstead.

Woods, John G., 1813, *Rivers of Wales illustrated*, London.

Young, Arthur, 1776, *Tours in England and Wales, selected from the Annals of Agriculture*, No. 14 in Series of Reprints of Scarce Tracts in Economic and Political Science (1932), London: The London School of Economics and Political Science (extracted from Young, A. 1776, *Annals of Agriculture and Other Useful Arts*, vol. IV, London).

Catalogues

Perry, George and Smith, Thomas, 1758, *A Description of Coalbrookdale in the County of Salop, with engravings by Francis Vivares*, published according to Act of Parliament, 1758.

Coxe, Peter, 1812, *Catalogue of all the valuable articles, sketches, sea views, and studies, of the celebrated artist James Philip de Loutherbourg, Esq., R.A. deceased*, London.

Secondary sources

Books

Acton, Viv, 1997, *A History of Truro Vol.1, From Coinage Town to Cathedral City*, Truro: Landfall.

Addis, J.P., 1957, *The Crawshay Dynasty; A study in industrial organisation and development, 1765–1867*, Cardiff: University of Wales Press.

Altrocchi, Rudolph, 1931, 'Michelino's Dante', pp. 15–59, *Speculum*, Jan., Vol. 6, No. 1.

Andrews, J., 2009, '*The Soho steam-engine business*', pp. 63–70, in Mason, S. (ed.), *Matthew Boulton – Selling what all the world desires*, Birmingham, Newhaven and London: Birmingham City Council and Yale University Press.

Anon., 1975, *Works exhibited at the Royal Society of British Artists 1824–1893*, 2 vols, Woodbridge, Suffolk: Antique Collectors Club.

Anon. (ed.), 1998, *Art Treasures of England: the regional collections*, London: Royal Academy of Arts.

Anon., 'Geschichte de Teutschen Sippschaft' pp. 69–88, trans. Thomas Carlyle in *Chartism*, 1940, London, James Fraser.

Anon., 2018, *Penrhyn Castle, Gwynedd*, National Trust.

Ashton, T.H., 1948, *The Industrial Revolution 1760–1830*, Oxford: Oxford University Press.

Barker, Elizabeth E. and Kidson, Alex, 2007, *Joseph Wright of Derby in Liverpool*, New Haven and London: Yale University Press.

Barker, Elizabeth E., 2009, 'Documents relating to Joseph Wright "of Derby" (1734–97)', pp. 1–216, in *The seventy-first volume of Walpole Society*, Wakefield: Charlesworth Group.

Barker, T.C. and Harris, J.R., 1959, *St Helens (1750–1900): A Merseyside Town in the Industrial Revolution*, London: Frank Cass & Co Ltd.

Barrell, John, 1980, *The dark side of the landscape; the rural poor in English paintings, 1730–1840*, Cambridge: Cambridge University Press.

Barringer, Tim, 2005, *Men at Work*, New Haven and London: Yale University Press.

Bemrose, W. and Monkhouse, W.M., 1885, *The life and works of Joseph Wright ARA, commonly called Wright of Derby*, London: Bemrose & Sons.

Boase, T.R.S., 1976, *The Oxford History of English Art*, Oxford: Clarendon Press.

Brighton, Trevor, 2004, *The Discovery of the Peak District*, Chichester: Phillimore.

Burke, Joseph, 'The picturesque and the transition to romanticism' in *English Art, 1714–1800*, pp. 374–400, in Boase, T.R.S, 1976, *The Oxford History of English Art*, Oxford: Clarendon Press.

Clay, R.M., 1948, *Julius Caesar Ibbetson (1759–1817)*, London: Country Life.

Cossons, Neil and Trinder, Barrie, 2002, *The Iron Bridge; Symbol of the industrial revolution*, Chichester: Phillimore.

Daniels, Stephen, 1998, *Joseph Wright*, London: Tate.

Dante Alighieri, trans. 1929, *The Paradiso*, London: J.M. Dent & Sons.

Dehours, F., 1985, Léonard Defrance (de Liège) – L'œuvre peint, Liège.

Derry, T.K. and Williams, D.I., 1960, *A Short History of Technology*, Oxford: Oxford University Press.

Drabble, Margaret (ed.), 1985, *The Oxford Companion to English Literature*, Oxford University Press, Oxford.

Earland, Ada, 1911, *Opie and his circle*, London: Hutchinson & Co.

Egerton, Judy, 1990, *Wright of Derby*, London: Tate.

Finberg, A.J., 1909, *A complete inventory of the drawings of the Turner Bequest … Arranged chronologically by A.J. Finberg*, London: Stationery Office.

Finberg, A.J., 1961, *The Life of J.M.W. Turner R.A.*, 2nd edn., revised Finberg, H.F., Oxford: Clarendon Press.

Fitton, Robert S., 1989, *The Arkwrights, Spinners of fortune*, Manchester.

Fox, Celina, 2009, *The Arts of Industry in the Age of Enlightenment*, Newhaven and London: Yale University Press.

Fried, Michael, 1998, *Absorption and Theatricality: Painting and the beholder in the Age of Diderot*, Los Angeles: Berkeley.

Gage, John (ed.), 1980, *Collected Correspondence of J.M.W. Turner*, Oxford.

Gage, John (ed.), 1986, 'Further Correspondence of J.M.W. Turner' in *Turner Studies*, Vol. 6, London: Tate Gallery.

Garlick, Kenneth and MacIntyre, Angus (ed.), 1979, *The Diary of Joseph Farington*, vol. 4, January 1799–July 1801, Newhaven and London: Yale University Press.

Gillespie, Charles Coulston (ed.), 1959, *A Diderot Pictorial Encyclopaedia of Trades and Industry – Manufacturing and the Technical Arts*, 2 vols, New York: Dover Publications Inc.

Grant, Maurice Harold, 1952, *A Dictionary of British Landscape Painters*, Leigh-on-sea: F. Lewis.

Green, A.H.J., 2009, *The history of Chichester's Canal*. 3rd edn., Brighton: Sussex Industrial Archaeological Trust.

Graves, Algernon, *The Royal Academy of Arts, Exhibitors 1709–1904*, 1906, 4 vols, Bath: Kingsmead Reprints, 1970.

Gwyn, Dafydd, 1998, 'Quarries, Mines and the Chapel Culture', in *British Archaeology*, Issue 36, Council for British Archaeology.

Hamilton, H., 1967, *The English Brass and Copper Industries to 1800*, 2nd edn., London: Frank Cass & Co.

Hamilton, James, 1997, *Turner*, New York: Random House.

Hamilton, James, 1998, *Turner and the Scientists*, London: Tate Gallery.

Hardie, Martin, *Water Colour Painting in Britain*; 1966, *The Eighteenth Century*; 1967, *II: The Romantic Period*, London: B.T. Batsford.

Hill, David, c.1996, *Turner in the North: a tour through Derbyshire, Yorkshire, Durham, Northumberland, the Scottish Borders, the Lake District, Lancashire and Lincolnshire in the year 1797*, New Haven and London: Yale University Press.

Herrmann, Luke, 1990, *Turner Prints: The Engraved Work of J.M.W. Turner*, Oxford: Phaidon.

Hobsbawm, Eric, 1968, *Industry and Empire: an economic history of Britain since 1750*, Harmondsworth: Penguin Books.

Hughes, S.R., c.2000, *Copperopolis: landscapes of the early industrial period in Swansea.* Aberystwyth: Royal Commission on the Ancient and Historical Monuments of Wales.

Humphries, Jane, 2010, *Childhood and Child Labour in the British Industrial Revolution*, Cambridge: Cambridge University Press.

Jackson, M.H. and De Beer, C., 1974, *Eighteenth century gunfounding*, City of Washington: Smithsonian Institution Press.

Klingender, Francis D., 1947, *Art and the Industrial Revolution*; and edited and revised by Elton, Arthur, 1968, London: Evelyn, Adams & Mackay.

Kriz, Kay D., 1997, *The idea of the English landscape painter – Genius as alibi in the early nineteenth century*, New Haven and London, Yale University Press.

Laing, Alastair, 1995, *In Trust for the Nation: Paintings from National Trust Houses*, London: The National Trust in association with National Gallery Publications.

Latimer, J., 1893, *The annals of Bristol in the eighteenth century*, Frome.

Lefeuvre, Olivier, 2012, *Philippe-Jacques de Loutherbourg 1740–1812*, Paris: Arthena.

Lindsay, J., 1966, *J.M.W. Turner a critical biography*, London: Cory, Adams and Mackay.

Lord, Peter, 1998, *The Visual Culture of Wales: Industrial Society*, Cardiff: University of Wales.

Marx, Karl and Engels, Friedrich, 1848, *The Manifesto of the Communist Party*, 2004, London: Penguin Books.

Mason, S. (ed.), 2009, *Matthew Boulton – Selling what all the world desires*, Birmingham, Newhaven and London: Birmingham City Council and Yale University Press.

Menuge, A., 2001, 'The cotton mills of the Derbyshire Derwent and its tributaries' in *Industrial Archaeology Review*, 1993, reprinted in *Derwent Valley Textile Mills*, Belper.

Mitchel, John, 1999, *Julius Caesar Ibbetson (1759–1817); The Berchem of England*, London: John Mitchel and Sons.

Morris, L. and Radford, R., 1983, *The story of the Artists International Association 1933–1953*, Oxford: The Museum of Modern Art.

Nicholson, Benedict, 1968, *Joseph Wright of Derby, Painter of light*, Vol. I, text and catalogue, and Vol II, reproductions, London: Paul Mellon Foundation for British Art in association with Routledge & Kegan Paul.

Pooke, G., 2008, *Francis Klingender 1907–1955; A Marxist art historian out of time*, London: Gill Vista Marx Press.

Postle, Martin and Simon, Robin (ed.), 2014, *Richard Wilson and the Transformation of European Landscape Painting*, Newhaven and London: Yale University Press.

Raistrick, A., 1989, *Dynasty of iron founders; The Darbys and Coalbrookdale*, 2nd edn., York: Sessions Book Trust and Ironbridge Gorge Museum Trust.

Rodner, William S., 1997, *J.M.W. Turner: Romantic Painter of the Industrial Revolution*, Berkeley: University of California.

Rogers, John Jope, 1878, *Opie and his works*, London: Paul and Dominic Colnaghi and Co.

Roget, J.L., 1891, *A History of the Old Water-colour Society*, 2 vols, London.

Ruddock, T., 1979, *Arch bridges and their builders, 1735–1835*, Cambridge: Cambridge University Press.

Shanes, Eric, 1990, *Turner's England*, London.

Shanes, Eric, 2004, *Turner: The Life and Masterworks*, New York.

Solkin, David H., 1982, *Richard Wilson: The landscape of reaction*, London: Tate Gallery.

Solkin, David H. (ed.), 2001, *Art on the Line*, New Haven and London: Yale University Press.

Tann, J. (ed.), 1981, *The selected papers of Boulton & Watt, Vol. I, The Engineering partnership, 1775–1820*, London: Diploma Press.

Taylor, Bayard (ed.), 1875, *Picturesque Europe*, New York.

Taylor, Margaret Stewart, 1967, *The Crawshays of Cyfarthfa Castle*, London: Robert Hale.

Thomas, E., 1999, *Coalbrookdale and the Darby Family*, Ironbridge Gorge Museum Trust.

Thompson, E.P., 1968, *The making of the English working class*, London: Pelican Books.

Thorne, R. (ed.), 1986, *The History of Parliament: the House of Common 1790–1820*, London.

Tomos, Dafydd, 1987, *Michael Faraday in Wales*, Gwas Gee.

Trinder, Barrie, 2000, *The Industrial Revolution in Shropshire*, Chichester: Phillimore.

Trinder, Barrie (ed.), 2005, *Ironbridge & Coalbrookdale*, 3rd edn. Chichester: Phillimore.

Uglow, Jenny, 2002, *The Lunar Men*, London: Faber and Faber Ltd.

Vaughan, William, 1978, *Romantic Art*, London: Thames and Hudson.

Vine, P.A.L., 2007, *London's lost route to Portsmouth: an historical account of the Portsmouth and Arundel Canal Navigation including the story of the ill-fated Portsea Ship Canal and the Chichester Ship Canal*, Chichester: Phillimore.

Vivian, John, 1970, *Tales of the Cornish Miners*, Truro: Tor Mark Press.

Webley, Derek Pritchard, 1997, *Cast to the Winds, The life and work of Penry Williams (1802–1885)*, Aberystwyth: National Library of Wales.

Wilton, Andrew, 1979, *The life and work of J.M.W. Turner*, London: Academy Editions.

Wilton, Andrew, 1984, *Turner in Wales*, Llandudno: Mostyn Art Gallery.

Žmolek, M.A., 2013, *Rethinking the Industrial Revolution (Five centuries of transition from Agrarian to Industrial Capitalism in England)*, (Historical Materialism Book Series vol 49), Brill, Leiden, Boston.

Catalogues

Peters, Mary, 1962, *John Opie, 1761–1807*, Arts Council Catalogue, London: The Curwen Press.

Smith, Stuart, 1979, *A View from the Iron Bridge*, Catalogue, Royal Academy, London: Ironbridge Gorge Museum Trust with Thames and Hudson.

Wallis, Jane, 1997, *Joseph Wright of Derby (1734–1797): An introduction to the work of Joseph Wright of Derby with a catalogue of drawings held by Derby Museum and Art Gallery*, Derby: Derby Museum and Art Gallery.

Lyles, Anne and Perkins, Diane, 1989, *Colour into Line: Turner and the Art of Engraving*, exh. cat., London: Tate Gallery.

Journals

Abkund, M., 2010, 'Joseph Wright of Derby in a northern light; Swedish comparisons and connections: Per Hilleström & Elias Martin', pp. 33–40, *The British Art Journal*, XI (1).

Cavendish, Richard, 1 February 1998, 'Plas Newydd, Anglesey', pp. 61–63, *History Today*.

Davies, J.M., 1952, 'The Morris family and Swansea', pp. 26–30, *'Gower' Journal*, Swansea.

Forbes, C., 'Images of Christ in the Nineteenth-Century: British Paintings in the Forbes Magazine Collection', *The Magazine Antiques*, December 2001, vol. clx, no. 6.

Hyde, C.K., 1973, 'The Iron Industry of the West Midlands in 1754; Observations from the Travel Account of Charles Wood', *Journal of the West Midlands Studies*, vol. 6.

Lorigan, Catherine, 2002, 'Thomas Rowlandson and the Delabole Slate Quarry', pp. 30–49, *Journal of the Royal Institution of Cornwall*, Truro.

Lovejoy, A.O., June 1941, 'The meaning of romanticism for the historian of ideas', pp. 257–78, *Journal of the History of Ideas*, vol. 2, No. 3.

MacKenzie, Charlotte, 'The mine merchants of Hayle; Commerce and family in an early industrial port', *Journal of the Royal Institution of Cornwall*, 2007.

Seddon, R. and Peatman, J., November 1990, 'Turner's Tilt Forge' in *Turner Society News, No 56*.

Stacey, David B., 2010, 'Images of industry; Material sources in British art, *c.*1800', pp. 62–8, *British Art Journal*, vol XI (1).

Stacey, David B., 2011, 'A Gentleman and a Miner, by John Opie', pp. 7–14, *Journal of The Royal Institution of Cornwall*, Truro.

Websites

Darwin, Erasmus, 1791, *The Botanic Garden: Part II*, https://quod.lib.umich.edu/e/ecco/004850944.0001.000/1:25?rgn=div1;view=fulltext (accessed 21 May 2020).

University College London, *Legacies of British Slave-ownership* https://www.ucl.ac/lbs (accessed 20 June 2020).

Acknowledgements

This book could not have been written without assistance from curators, archivists and their assistants working in some of the excellent libraries, galleries and museums in Britain, and without the support of others who made valuable comments on drafts of the text.

Archives in The Courtney Library at The Royal Cornwall Museum, Truro provided valuable material on John Opie's painting. The Birmingham Archives and Collections, Birmingham City Council, hold the fascinating manuscripts of the Boulton and Watt Partnership correspondence. The Blythe House Archive and Library of the Victoria and Albert Museum and the Royal Academy Archive provided material on Henry Hawkins's career. The research library of the Ironbridge Gorge Museum Trust, Shropshire, holds a valuable collection of material on the development at Coalbrookdale. The very helpful staff in the reading rooms at Llyfrgell Genedlaethol Cymru, The National Library of Wales, Aberystwyth and their e-mail enquiry service assisted with material associated with the Parys and Mona mines, the Penrhyn Quarry and items relating to industrial development in Wales. Cyfarthfa Castle Museum and Art Gallery, Merthyr Tydfil provided material on works by Penry Williams. Details of sketches and drawings in the Turner Bequest can be found in the continuously updated website https://www.tate.org.uk/art/research-publications/jmw-turner/ but thanks are due to the staff of the Prints and Drawings Room at Tate Britain where the original works can be seen. The staff at the British Library have been unerringly efficient and helpful. The following museums, art galleries and institutions, Amgueddfa Cymru, National Museum, Cardiff; Amgueddfa Abertawe, National Museum, Swansea; the Derby Museums and Art Gallery; the Whitworth Art Gallery, Manchester; and The Institution of Civil Engineers, have all provided instructive visual material.

The principal sites pictured in the paintings discussed in the book can all be visited. The Parys and Mona mines and the sites of Turner's canal paintings are all accessible. The remnants of some of Boulton and Watt steam engine houses can still be found in Cornwall. Penrhyn Quarry is still supplying roofing slate and is now also 'home to Zip World Velocity 2, the fastest zip line in the world and the longest in Europe'. At the other sites, my thanks are due to Cromford

Mills, Derbyshire, administered by The Arkwright Society, now part of a UNESCO World Heritage site; the Ironbridge Gorge Museum Trust, Shropshire, the gorge is a UNESCO World Heritage Site; Cyfarthfa Museum and Art Gallery; and the National Trust at Penrhyn Castle.

I would also like to thank the editorial staff at the Unicorn Publishing Group and in particular Lucy Duckworth and Ramona Lamport. Finally, my thanks go to Dan and Kate Stacey for their support and encouragement while I have been writing this book, and to Anthony Langdon, Helen Langdon, Mary Stacey and Michael Starks for the valuable comments and suggestions they kindly made on draft chapters of the book.

Index